W9-CBC-979

L E V I ' S   C H I L D R E N

LEVI'S
CHILDREN

Coming to Terms with Human
Rights in the Global Marketplace

KARL SCHOENBERGER

 GROVE PRESS | NEW YORK

Copyright © 2000 by Karl Schoenberger

All rights reserved. No part of this book may be reproduced in any form or by any electronic or mechanical means, including information storage and retrieval systems, without permission in writing from the publisher, except by a reviewer, who may quote brief passages in a review. Any members of educational institutions wishing to photocopy part or all of the work for classroom use, or publishers who would like to obtain permission to include the work in an anthology, should send their inquiries to Grove/Atlantic, Inc., 841 Broadway, New York, NY 10003.

Selected text from "Walter A. Haas, Jr.," an interview conducted in 1973 by Harriet Nathan in *Levi Strauss & Co.: Tailors to the World* (1976), was reprinted by permission of the Regional Oral History Office, The Bancroft Library, University of California, Berkeley.

The lines from "as freedom is a breakfast food," copyright © 1940, 1968, 1991, by the Trustees for the E. E. Cummings Trust, from *Complete Poems: 1904–1962* by E. E. Cummings, edited by George J. Firmage. Reprinted by permission of Liveright Publishing Corporation.

The lines from "Levi's," by S. Omar Barker, published in 1997 in special limited edition by the Western Writers of America © 1977 by S. Omar Barker, are reprinted by permission of Marjorie Phillips, Trustee of the Robert and Marjorie Phillips Revocable Living Trust.

Published simultaneously in Canada
Printed in the United States of America

FIRST PAPERBACK EDITION

Library of Congress Cataloging-in-Publication Data
Schoenberger, Karl.
    Levi's children : coming to terms with human rights in the global marketplace / Karl Schoenberger.
      p. cm.
    Includes bibliographical references and index.
    ISBN 0-8021-3812-8 (pbk.)
    1. Levi Strauss and Company—History. 2. Clothing trade—United States—History. 3. Human rights—Case studies. 4. Labor policy—United States—Case studies. I. Title.
HD9940.U6 L457 2000
338.7'687'092—dc21
[B]   99-055104

DESIGN BY LAURA HAMMOND HOUGH

Grove Press
841 Broadway
New York, NY 10003

01 02 03 04   10 9 8 7 6 5 4 3 2 1

Dedicated to

Susan, Sonya, and Hannah

CONTENTS

|||

Preface to the 2001 Edition

| | |

The idea that a multinational corporation would willingly accept accountability for human rights violations and labor abuses in developing countries where it does business is as preposterous today as it was a year ago, when the first edition of this book went to press. The protesters who took center stage at the World Trade Organization meeting in Seattle in late 1999 succeeded in raising public awareness of the extraordinary role large companies play in shaping international affairs. But the antiglobalization rhetoric that has flourished since then has not changed minds in the business community.

Corporations are incapable, almost by design, of exercising moral and ethical judgments on matters such as eliminating sweatshop abuse or protecting the right to free association. They react when coerced into accountability by some external force—a legal constraint or the scandal of a negative advocacy campaign. Even for companies with the most noble of intentions, the unwritten laws of the free market do not provide a mechanism to reconcile the true cost of social responsibility with the fundamental need to be profitable. In other words, as the story of Levi Strauss & Co. illustrates, an organization's instinct to succeed prevails over any lofty principles it might espouse.

I chose to study Levi Strauss as a positive example of how companies can deal with the human rights problem, but the company proved to be a moving target. While I was writing, the fabled jeans maker went through traumatic changes that raised serious questions about its commitment to corporate social responsibility. Suffering from a devastating plunge in sales, the company retrenched with massive layoffs and joined its competitors in moving the bulk of its production overseas to low-wage contractors.

Levi Strauss continues to struggle under the burden of a huge bank debt that former CEO Robert Haas took on in 1996 to finance the concentration of ownership of the private company among selected family members. Ironically, this indebtedness had the net effect of lifting the company's shroud of intense privacy. For the first time in years, Levi had to open its books to the Securities and Exchange Commission and invite close public scrutiny, because it planned to float new corporate bonds to help pay off $2 billion in bank loans. It was in the context of this legal obligation for transparency that I was finally granted interviews with Levi's two top executives—after being denied such access during the entire time I was writing *Levi's Children*.

Those interviews resulted in an article I wrote for *The New York Times* (published June 25, 2000) that attempted to unravel some of the mysteries surrounding Levi's financial—and ethical—future. The article provoked sharp criticism from several former Levi executives, who faulted me for downplaying evidence of management chaos during Robert Haas's reign. It is clear now that Haas, whom I essentially lionized in absentia in the book, is a far more complicated and less effective leader than I had estimated. It also seems safe to conclude that the real steward of Levi Strauss's incredible ethical legacy was his father, Walter Haas Jr. It may not be a coincidence that the company went into a tailspin not long after the patriarch's death in 1995.

This book was never intended to be a screed against the alleged evils of economic globalization, nor a broad denunciation of the powerful multinational corporations that have thrived under its spirit of laissez-faire capitalism. My aim is to identify some of the basic problems that snag the contentious debate over human rights and business wrongs. I try to point to possible solutions. I conclude with questions, not answers.

Karl Schoenberger
Albany, California
December 2000

ACKNOWLEDGMENTS

||||

I'd like to express my appreciation to my colleagues at the Graduate School of Journalism at the University of California, Berkeley, and to the many friends and associates who encouraged me to tackle the writing of this book. Orville Schell, dean of the Journalism School, and Eric Stover, director of UC Berkeley's Human Rights Center, deserve special thanks for providing institutional sponsorship for my research. The project was made possible in part by financial support from the Koret Foundation Teaching Fellowship program at UC Berkeley and a grant from the Japan Foundation Center for Global Partnership's Abe Fellowship Program. My sincere appreciation also goes to the staff of the Social Science Research Council in New York and to the faculty of the Institute of Social Science at the University of Tokyo for their kind assistance.

I'm particularly obliged to my longtime colleague and China mentor, Todd Carrel, for his abiding inspiration and guidance. Jeffrey Bartholet and Spencer Sherman slogged through a dirty rough draft of the book and gave me much appreciated feedback. Many thanks as well to all those who helped me tell this story, from anonymous business sources to human rights zealots to masterful public relations people.

Most of all, I am eternally grateful to my family for indulging me in the isolation of my obsession and for persevering during the two long years it took to bring the project to completion.

||||

Prologue

America's troubled relationship with China was going to change dramatically. This much was clear from an extraordinary encounter over breakfast in Beijing one spring morning in 1994. After years of tense political confrontation over human rights practices and caution over security concerns, Sino-U.S. relations would soon give way to an awkward subservience to the bottom line of economic pragmatism.

There was no grand summitry between leaders of the two nations when it happened. No Kissingeresque secret diplomacy, nor any Ping-Pong ambassadorship paving the way for mending fences. Not even an iconic photograph, like the one capturing Richard Nixon looking cross-eyed at a cashew nut at the end of his chopsticks during a banquet with Chinese Communist leaders. Those events had happened some two decades in the past, allowing Washington and Beijing to forge a cynical cold war alliance against the Soviet Union. This time, following a round of Chinese economic reforms that had transformed the once zealous Marxist state into a capitalist hothouse, what was at stake was not strategic security, but money—lots of money. The new "China card" was untold billions of dollars in potential U.S. corporate revenues.

The venue was a breakfast meeting hosted by the American Chamber of Commerce in Beijing and attended by some 150 members representing an elite roster of U.S. companies. These industrialists and bankers and high-technology merchants embodied the spirit of the $1.6 billion that sanguine U.S. interests would pump into the Chinese economy in 1994 in the form of private investment. That figure would more than triple in three years to $5 billion, and the reason can be found at this breakfast. American investors were buying pieces of newly privatized Chinese companies, snapping up risky stock offerings on the B-share exchanges in Shanghai and Shenzhen, and cobbling together joint-venture partnerships that would take advantage of diligent low-wage Chinese factory labor and at the same time establish beachheads for future sales to what seemed destined to become the world's greatest consumer bazaar. They represented the best of America's internationally minded business community, which was reshaping the global economy and setting national priorities for a new chapter in China relations.

The Chamber's special guest that morning was Secretary of State Warren Christopher, who was visiting Beijing on an urgent mission to persuade Chinese leaders to reform their reprehensible human rights practices or risk losing trade privileges with the United States. What ensued was a humiliating rebuke of America's most senior diplomat by the businesspeople in his audience. Christopher came looking for allies in his mission, but instead he encountered fierce criticism that echoed the views of hard-line Chinese officials. The audience's brazen expression of contempt for the Clinton administration's ostensibly principled stance on human rights constituted a defining moment, a scene that revealed troubling questions about the moral responsibilities of corporations that profit in a marketplace tainted by political repression.

Conspicuously absent from this meeting—and from the rolls of the American Chamber of Commerce in Beijing—was Levi Strauss & Co., the world's largest apparel manufacturer, whose hallowed brand was synonymous with quality blue jeans, rugged individualism—and freedom.

The San Francisco–based company had shocked the business world a year earlier by announcing its intentions to shelve investment plans and begin a phased withdrawal from its contract manufacturing base in China. For God's sake, everyone had to wonder, why? The company cited provisions in its new global code of conduct that forced it to evaluate the ethical dimensions of conducting business in a country tainted by pervasive human rights violations.

In the eyes of the human rights advocacy community, Levi Strauss deserved the utmost respect as a champion of their cause, venturing boldly into a new frontier of corporate policy with a social conscience. If any single company symbolized the hope that international business can manage the challenges of the human rights scourge, it would have to be Levi Strauss.

In pointed contrast, the membership of the American Chamber of Commerce in Beijing spoke for the vast majority of U.S. entrepreneurs whose eyes were fixed on the incalculable rewards that the Chinese market—serving a swelling population of 1.2 billion people—might yield one day to persevering investors who were inured to the furor of the international human rights debate.

In a few short years Levi Strauss's phenomenal success in the blue jeans business would falter, resulting in financial distress that would call into question whether the company could afford to continue its long tradition of progressive social policies. The message of its human rights agenda would become so ambiguous and its traditional paternalism in the workplace so conflicted that the company risked losing credibility as a leader of the corporate social responsibility movement. Levi's viability as a model for corporate accountability would be seriously undermined by an obsession with privacy.

The Levi Strauss that everybody loved and thought they knew is still undergoing a crisis of identity, and how it emerges from its struggle to adapt to new realities will have considerable influence on the way corporations conceive of ethical behavior in the future. This is the story of one of America's greatest brands—Levi's—and its travails in navigating the moral dilemmas of the global marketplace. It's also a rough guide to an emerging environment of intolerance for the injustices that are the unintended side effects of economic globalization. In the simplest of terms, it all boils down to putting a price on the conflicting values of political freedom and wealth accumulation, social responsibility and profit seeking.

The human rights debate on China lends itself to much passion and no small amount of hyperbole, but it is hardly unique. The conflict festers in nearly every developing country, large and small. It is no longer just a question of jailing dissidents and muzzling the press, or perpetrating the horrors of ethnic cleansing and filling mass graves. The issues of economic justice and the responsibilities of multinational corporations are now squarely established on the international human rights agenda, and their importance can only grow in the new millennium.

CHAPTER ONE

| | |

True West

When Moses stood in the gate of the camp, and said, Who is on the Lord's side? let him come unto me. And all the sons of Levi gathered themselves together unto him. And he said unto them, Thus saith the Lord God of Israel, Put every man his sword by his side, and go in and out from gate to gate throughout the camp, and slay every man his brother, and every man his companion, and every man his neighbour. And the children of Levi did according to the word of Moses: and there fell of the people that day about three thousand men.

—Exodus 32:26–28

On the scale of things, the slaughter of some three thousand Israelites by the swords of their brethren—when Moses instructed the sons of Levi to smite the worshipers of the golden calf—was a relatively minor event in the context of the many appalling atrocities described in the Old Testament. Had the scene been captured live on Cable News Network, or depicted in sober tones in the next morning's *New York Times*, the citizenry of a modern wired world would recoil in absolute horror at this brutal party discipline. And in doing so, we would probably miss the allegorical point altogether. Moses had descended from Mt. Sinai with a mandate from heaven inscribed in stone, ten zero-tolerance rules of human behavior dictated by God, only to find his people enraptured in spiritual anarchy, dancing wantonly before a false idol. This was a flagrant violation of the First Commandment. Certainly some form of punishment was called for if Moses was ever going to lead his flock to the Promised Land, even if it did mean casting the Fifth Commandment (*Thou shalt not kill*) to the wind. Perhaps this was why Moses smashed the stone tablets in utter frustration.

Now consider replacing Moses in the passage from the Book of Exodus with the eminent personage of Deng Xiaoping, the late patriarch of contemporary China. Deng was once China's most prominent political prisoner. He had suffered persecutions of biblical proportions during the anarchy of the 1966–1976 Cultural Revolution, only to resurrect himself and seize absolute power. Mighty Deng was determined to lead his people from the ideological bondage of impoverished communism to the Promised Land of free-market capitalism, albeit with guidance from persistent "Chinese characteristics"—which evidently meant brutal authoritarian control. In May 1989, throngs of student protesters gathered at Tiananmen Square, the sprawling ceremonial plaza in central Beijing, across the street from the Forbidden City, where China's emperors once ruled behind the Gate of Heavenly Peace. As tension rose on the square, the demonstrators fell to worshiping the false idol of the "Goddess of Democracy," a giant Styrofoam-and-plaster statue that bore a distinct likeness to the Statue of Liberty. The goddess was assembled by rebellious art students right under the unblinking gaze of Chairman Mao Zedong's billboard-size propaganda portrait on the Forbidden City's Gate of Heavenly Peace, across the street from the square. Mr. Deng did what any righteous old man would do when his own legitimacy and the binding faith of Communist Party is challenged. He called in the troops, the sons of Mao.

The story of what happened next has been told and retold many times, becoming a modern-day parable of innocent idealism and state evil. It may never be known exactly how many unarmed students and citizens were mowed down by China's People's Liberation Army (PLA) on the night of June 3–4, 1989, when peasant soldiers shot their way down a jammed boulevard toward the square. The official count is around two hundred, but informed estimates range far higher. Unlike the grim scribes of Moses' long march, China's chroniclers have yet to devise a credible system of statistical accountability in such matters.

The idea here is not to make light of mass political murder, or to justify the paranoia of Deng Xiaoping and his pathological hard-line supporters. Nor is any disrespect intended for the powerful archetypes and origin myths that are embedded deeply in the psyches of those of us who descend from the Judeo-Christian tradition and who venerate the story of Moses. Western civilization orients itself around these stories and must navigate by them, however imperfectly, through the chaos of life's meaning.

The point, rather, is that when idealistic nongovernmental organization (NGO) activists engage corporations in dialogue about the preachy concepts of human rights theory, it is important to bear in mind what everybody should already know: Moral conflicts cannot be distilled neatly into a choice between right and wrong, good and evil. Sometimes you have to go with the best solution, even if it means violating some cardinal rule. This is *situational ethics,* the amoral, politically expedient, and sometimes astoundingly hypocritical process that has prevailed since the dawn of civilization.

The words *moral* and *ethical* get tossed around so loosely, they are too often used interchangeably, conveniently muddling discussions among people who are responsible for making moral and ethical decisions. Indeed, even the dictionary definitions overlap somewhat. But for the sake of consistency, let us say that morality relates to the capacity to distinguish between right and wrong, and ethics has to do with conforming to a particular set of standards for behavior. Situational ethics might be understood as the practice of using a fluid set of values to justify doing what is necessary to serve one's pragmatic self-interests, collectively or individually. This self-centeredness is mitigated by an intrinsic assumption that it would be against one's own interests to do horrible things to others, lest they be done in return or otherwise invite the wrath of an external wielder of power. Learned theologians and philosophers and academicians no doubt have contrary and more sophisticated views on this. But they seldom have to make business decisions in the real world.

Ethics is a balancing act, whereby behavior is constrained by obligations to the collective interests of one's immediate group or community. The overriding obligation can then extend diffusely in concentric circles to larger societies, political parties, nation states, religious sects, international conspiracies—"stakeholders," as proponents of corporate social responsibility would say.

It doesn't matter if it's the biblical Moses liquidating worshipers of the golden calf, or Soviet leader Joseph Stalin murdering millions of counterrevolutionary peasants, or Harry Truman dropping the atomic bomb on the civilian populations of Hiroshima and Nagasaki. In business it could be Microsoft tycoon Bill Gates snaring unsuspecting consumers into using his Internet browser software at the exclusion of a competitor's product, a practice vigorously contested by the U.S. Justice Department's antitrust division, and if you think about it, you might agree it's simply wrong. But it's also ingenious. With situational ethics, distinguishing between what's wrong and right is something that necessarily depends on your circumstances and your point of view. Notwithstanding all the striving toward piety and global peace, toward the strictures against man's cruelty to his fellow man, history suggests that the puny human's franchise on earth is one of bending the rules, of subjugation, and periodically of calculated carnage.

| | |

Conventional wisdom dictates that the world reached a turning point in collective moral repugnance after bearing witness to the indescribable horrors of the Nazi Holocaust in World War II.

The atrocity has since been conceptualized and encapsulated as an isolated event, perpetrated against European Jewry by a depraved and totalitarian military regime. But at the close of the century, stories continued to emerge about the many civilian accomplices who willfully turned a blind eye to—or secretly supported and profited from—the mechanism of the Holocaust. Swiss banks had laundered the gold that the Germans stole from their Jewish victims, some of it ripped from the teeth of the dead. These prominent and powerful financial institutions were only reluctantly settling claims on the disputed booty after fifty years of denial.

Survivors of the Nazis' slave labor camps filed class action lawsuits claiming billions of dollars in compensation for the work they were forced to perform at factories owned by such German industrial giants as Volkswagen, Daimler-Benz, and Siemens. Investigators examined whether the German subsidiaries of Ford and General

Motors might have collaborated similarly in the Nazi labor scheme—suspicions that American automakers vigorously denied. Volkswagen, the brainchild of Adolf Hitler himself, did not have the option of explaining away its tainted past, and it settled swiftly with lawyers representing former slave laborers. Coincidentally, the company was introducing a newly restyled model of its classic Volkswagen Beetle compact car in 1998, launching a blitzkrieg of nostalgic feel-good television commercials in a gambit to recapture lost market share in the United States. The mere dollars-and-cents cost of settling on alleged corporate liability for past injustices, the VW Bug campaign suggests, pales in comparison with the price of potential fallout from an unresolved human rights scandal. If seeing a cute candy-colored little car on the street evoked lurid visions of Nazi slave labor, emaciated skeletons of Jews and Gypsies and political dissidents working the assembly line, Volkswagen could never repair the damage to its image in the American car-buying public.

In what may prove to be the last act of German war reparation for the crimes of the Nazi era, German government and business leaders agreed in December 1999 to settle the forced-labor law suits with a $5.1 billion payment to surviving victims. Initial reports suggested that the German subsidiaries of GM and Ford were expected to join the accord, but that the settlement may not eliminate the challenges of related class action suits filed in the United States.

If anything can be considered an absolute and unmitigated evil, it would have to be the bureaucratized genocide of the Nazi Holocaust. Civilized people—politicians, jurists, and captains of industry—went insane en masse and kept copious records of the blood-lust. The stories of imperial Japan's gruesome atrocities across Asia also resonated deeply in the aftermath of World War II, adding to the angst. The United Nations in 1948 expressed the world's feelings of outrage, remorse, and shame when it enshrined the principles of a postwar collective conscience in the Universal Declaration of Human Rights.

The moral tone of the document's preamble lays out high hopes for humanity: "Disregard and contempt for human rights have resulted in barbarous acts which have outraged the conscience of mankind, and the advent of a world in which human beings shall enjoy freedom of speech and belief and freedom from fear and want has been proclaimed as the highest aspiration of the common people. . . . It is essential, if man is not to be compelled to have recourse, as a last resort, to rebellion against tyranny and oppression, that human rights should be protected by the rule of law. . . ."

The declaration was a radical document, which, in the words of Henry Steiner, a human rights scholar at Harvard Law School, has had a "subversive effect" on the sovereignty of individual states. "However self-evident it may appear today, the Declaration bore a more radical message than many of its framers perhaps recognized," Steiner wrote on the document's fiftieth anniversary. "It proceeded to work its subversive path through many rooted doctrines of international law, forever changing the discourse of international relations on issues vital to human decency and peace."

Over a period of five decades this document inspired new generations of legal scholars, launched careers in various human rights bureaucracies and NGOs, and generated a canon of literature on theory and practice. Its application in the Helsinki accord contributed to the collapse of the Soviet Union through an open dialogue on human rights. The inspiration it provided in the South Africa divestiture movement helped bring an end to apartheid.

Sadly, however, the aspirations of the declaration appeared woefully unrealized as the document entered its fifty-first year. The 1998 holiday season opened with the United States and Britain raining bombs and cruise missiles on Iraq to enforce a failing United Nations scheme to prevent Iraqi president Saddam Hussein from developing the technology for weapons of mass destruction. At the same time, international relief agencies protested that thousands of Iraqi children were dying each week for lack of adequate food and medical supplies, a tragedy caused by devastating UN economic sanctions, ostensibly aimed at starving out Saddam. In a cynical nod to moral decency in warfare, the Anglo-American bombing strike was halted abruptly on the first day of Ramadan, the Islamic holy month of fasting.

A year later, Serbian strongman Slobodan Milošević took over in the role of America's favorite despot, committing atrocities against ethnic Albanians in Kosovo and greeting air strikes by war planes of the North Atlantic Treaty Organization (NATO) with contemptuous defiance. It was far from clear who had the moral high ground—or how to end the cycle of carnage in the Balkans. Both sides were wrong: American-led NATO extracted an intolerable civilian death toll from the "collateral damage" of its bombing. The Serbian task of ethnic cleansing in Kosovo took on genocidal elements, with hundreds of thousands of civilian refugees fleeing burning villages and mass graves—and dodging NATO bombs. When the smoke cleared and Kosovar refugees returned to their wrecked villages, reports of revenge killings of Serbian neighbors began, making the mission of NATO peacekeeping troops on the ground seem impossible.

Where is the crisp line between the good and evil in these terrifying episodes of international diplomacy? U.S. commander in chief William Jefferson Clinton ordered the attack on Iraq while he was under impeachment by Congress, accused of lying under oath about a sexual peccadillo with a White House intern. The immediate effect of bombing Yugoslavia was to galvanize popular support for Milošević, stoking the fascist fires of Serbian nationalism instead of containing them. In a fluke accident, a U.S. stealth bomber attack on the Chinese embassy in Belgrade had devastating effects on Sino-U.S. relations, cutting off the fragile dialogue on human rights.

Given the fact that not everybody can agree about the existence of a bearded, paternal, and monotheistic Godhead keeping accurate tabs on the human folly below, we are all left to flounder. Perhaps it is a related belief—the illusion that there can be a singular truth in global society—that keeps the international scene from total rudderless drift. A civil religion for the world, if you will, with the United Nations offering the liturgy—and America, the global cop, trying to enforce the peace with minimal collateral damage. Amid this chaos, the Universal Declaration of Human Rights remains a potent reference point—if only by default. It may not be the beacon of bright light that many of its more passionate advocates would hold it to be, but there's nothing else by which to navigate. This set of beliefs and principles is far from perfect, and certainly can be improved, but right now it is the best and only game in town.

It is important to note the extent of sharp disagreement that took place in the United Nations General Assembly when the language of the declaration was drafted, as some nations argued that its lofty goals were simply unattainable. They wanted more latitude, more time to develop their economies and build their political institutions. Had it not been for the stout resolution of Eleanor Roosevelt, the former First Lady who browbeat her fellow UN delegates into a compromise, the declaration might never have won passage. The groundbreaking document was adopted unanimously as a nonbinding resolution, and though it has considerable powers of moral suasion, it does not carry the force of international law.

That lapse was addressed in later attempts to canonize the human rights theory in a set of UN treaties, primarily with the International Covenant on Civil and Political Rights and the Covenant on Economic, Social and Cultural Rights, which nations could sign and ratify should they be so disposed. A dirty little secret is that at the time of this writing, the United States still had not ratified the latter of these two covenants, more than twenty years after becoming a signatory to it. It did not ratify the more important treaty on civil and political rights until 1992, three years after the Tiananmen massacre in Beijing and twenty-six years after its adoption by the UN General Assembly.

Amnesty International (AI), the London-based organization renowned for pressuring dictatorships to release prisoners of conscience, made headlines in October 1998 when it issued a scathing critique on the state of human rights in the United States. The group cited serious violations of international human rights standards in the arbitrary and racially biased application of the death penalty, the widespread abuses of police brutality, and the indefinite detention of political asylum seekers, among other controversial legal practices. Amnesty International accused the U.S. government of maintaining a "double standard" where international law is concerned. "The International system of human rights protection built over the past 50 years is based on the understanding not only that human rights are universal, but that they transcend the sovereignty of individual states," the report said. "Despite the USA's leading role in establishing this system, it has been reluctant to submit itself to international human rights law and to accept the same minimum standards for its own conduct that it demands from other countries."

The AI report had to have caused glee within the ruling circles in Beijing, where officials have long pointed to injustices in the American system in defense of China's own repugnant human rights track record. China, to everyone's surprise, had just committed itself to signing the UN's International Covenant on Civil and Political Rights, making a strategic step toward shoring up its international respectability at the same time it was conducting business as usual, cracking down, for example, on a nascent movement to launch an opposition party. Signing the covenant, of course, was hardly tantamount to a commitment to abide by it in practice, even after ratification by the National People's Congress. China's constitution already granted a host of civil and political rights to its people, rights that for the most part existed only on paper. While the United States has a legal system with serious flaws and inconsistencies, China is a nation where the rule of law exists largely in theory, not in practice.

The subject of human rights provides fertile material for mutual recrimination, particularly when its principles are exploited in the gamesmanship among nations. But what was radically new about the human rights discourse when the Universal Declaration of Human Rights was being feted on its fiftieth birthday—December 10, 1998—was that the scope of its purview had broadened significantly from a historic focus on rogue governments and bloodthirsty armies to an intense interest in international business. In the grips of middle age, the UN document had been rejuvenated and given new meaning by the reckless vitality of the global marketplace. The Dickensian excesses caused by international capitalism in the post–cold war era begged the question of who would take moral responsibility for the injustices—the collateral damage—of economic globalization, and how.

| | |

After the end of the cold war, at the beginning of the 1990s, free-market capitalism reigned triumphant, uncontested by the tired theories of central planning and socialist dogma. Multinational corporations were feeling their oats and, by their sheer size and the amount of capital they controlled, were rapidly expanding their influence in global affairs. A surge in megamergers accelerated this trend. For instance, America's two largest oil companies, Exxon and Mobil, announced a $80 billion merger in late 1998 to resurrect part of the old Standard Oil Trust, which had been broken up at the beginning of the century by antimonopoly regulations. Now the combined annual revenues of these two behemoths, more than $200 billion, would be roughly equivalent to the gross domestic product of Indonesia, one of the world's largest oil-producing nations and the fourth most populous. The new enterprise's CEO went on record boasting about the synergistic efficiencies of slashing nine thousand jobs at one stroke.

In the absence of a coherent international political order, big corporations, more than ever before, were driving government policies with lobbying and fund-raising pressures. Giant hedge funds and foreign-exchange arbitrageurs were moving huge sums of capital in and out of developing countries, causing some devastating effects on local currencies, economies, and societies. Indonesia, where ethnic and religious violence continued to rock the nation long after the collapse of the economy and the fall of the autocratic President Suharto, is a prime example. In this desperate climate the Indonesian military and the local militias under its control ran amok on the disputed island of East Timor in September 1999, terrorizing the local Catholic population after the former Portuguese colony voted overwhelmingly for independence from the Jakarta regime. One likely explanation for the bloodshed was that the thousands of Indonesian troops occupying East Timor were enraged at the prospect of losing their jobs and their stake in the island's economy after independence; there were scant opportunities to make a living elsewhere.

Investing in Indonesia could no longer be considered business as usual. The situation demanded a new approach to setting standards on ethical behavior and accountability for the powerful multinational firms that shaped the destiny of developing nations.

UN secretary general Kofi Annan articulated this growing concern when he spoke to the World Economic Forum in Davos,

Switzerland, in 1999. In calling for a "Global Compact" on human rights with business leaders, Annan lamented the unintended consequences of the new economic order. "Globalization is a fact of life. But I believe we have underestimated its fragility," he said. "The problem is this: The spread of markets far outpaces the ability of societies and their political system to adjust to them, let alone to guide the course they take. History teaches us that such an imbalance between the economic, social, and political realms can never be sustained for very long."

Annan called on his audience to assume greater responsibility for the problems of laissez-faire capitalism, such as the lack of adequate social safety net programs in developing economies. "Specifically, I call upon you—individually through your firms, and collectively through your business associations—to embrace, support, and enact a set of core values in the areas of human rights, labor standards, and environmental practices."

Annan's pronouncement may have greater importance at a symbolic level than in practical terms. But his imprimatur helped legitimize a rising tide of intellectual criticism aimed at economic globalization and the transnational corporations driving it. Literally hundreds of books were published on the topic of globalization in the latter half of the 1990s—the Internet bookseller Amazon.com listed more than four hundred titles containing the word *globalization* in late 1999. Many of these treatments challenged long-held assumptions about the phenomenon's effects on the people it purportedly lifts out of poverty. Dani Rodrik, a professor of international political economy at Harvard, energized the debate on the consequences of the global economy with his 1997 work, *Has Globalization Gone Too Far?* Financial journalist William Greider describes some of the tragic ironies perpetrated on developing societies in his book *One World, Ready or Not.* Thomas Friedman, foreign affairs columnist for *The New York Times,* weighed in with a somewhat more optimistic view of globalization in his popular book, *The Lexus and the Olive Tree.*

The vision of roping corporations into a process taking responsibility for and seeking practical solutions to problems in the global economy is not new to the UN secretary general. But it remains an elusive idea. Despite its prestige, the United Nations is a gigantic international bureaucracy, crippled by all the limitations that beset any bureaucracy, with the additional burdens of linguistic, political, and cultural schisms. It does not appear that the UN's Office of the High Commissioner on Human Rights (UNHCHR), with its plate full of the usual heinous atrocities, was equipped to handle the administrative aspects of a global human rights compact with business, as proposed by the secretary general. A two-man team in the secretary general's office in New York was charged with the task of designing the program, borrowing assistance from the UNHCHR, the International Labor Organization (ILO), and other UN agencies.

Whatever the UN did on business and human rights, it would have to deal with imbedded skepticism among advocacy groups. The San Francisco–based Transnational Resource & Action Center (TRAC), also known by its Internet nom de guerre, Corporate Watch, spewed venom at the world body after learning in March of 1999 that the UN Development Program planned to solicit funds from private corporations to create a "global sustainable development facility." TRAC alleged that the program would seek money from companies with "tarnished records on human rights, labor, and the environment," allowing them to "greenwash" their public images and in doing so undermine the UN's credibility and independence.

It seemed likely that any plan of action for integrating private corporations into operations authorized by the United Nations charter would require a laborious process of consensus building between business groups and NGOs from the advocacy community. It will not be easy to establish the kind of mutual trust necessary to breach a stubborn perception gap and raise awareness among international CEOs about Annan's human rights concerns. This is a challenge explored in the 1998 documentary film *Globalization and Human Rights,* in which prominent political and business leaders—many of them interviewed at the 1998 World Economic Forum in Davos, a year before Annan's proposal—pondered the new responsibilities of international corporations.

Host Charlene Hunter-Gault sets the scene by musing: "Globalization and human rights—how an interdependent global economy affects the rights of people. Can money and morality coexist?" George Soros, the financier and notorious currency trader blamed for worsening the Asian economic crisis by some Third World critics—most notably the firebrand Malaysian leader Mahathir bin Muhammad—concedes the fragility of the capitalist system. "Due to its success, it penetrates into areas of life—of society—where it doesn't really belong," Soros tells the camera. "There are other needs in society which cannot be fulfilled by the market, and those needs are neglected. So there is some market failure, but much greater social failure—in fact, a failure of the political process."

Amnesty International's secretary general, Pierre Sane, describes the limited expectations of the advocacy community. "We do not expect business to become a human rights defender. We know that if business adopts a human rights language and behavior, it will be as a means to the long-term objective of securing greater and greater profits," Sane said in the documentary. "For us, human rights is an end, it's an absolute. So there is a journey that we can go together. There are some tactical alliances we can develop."

| | |

The problem with the discourse on human rights and business is that very few NGOs or agencies can take an honest middle-ground position and build an effective alliance in what has become a highly polarized and emotional debate. The watchdog groups that play a critical role in exposing corporate complicity with human rights violations rarely have the willingness or the resources to work constructively with business on the solutions.

Mainstream human rights NGOs such as Amnesty International and Human Rights Watch have developed business-related programs in recent years, but they don't quite offer a coherent structure to bridge the impasse between corporations and adversarial critics. Any party purporting to take a nonadvocacy, neutral approach is eyed with deep suspicion by both sides. Indeed, gathering objective information for the writing of this book involved an excruciating process of allaying the fears of information sources in both the business and the advocacy communities, nearly all of whom challenged the author in a disarming "identify friend or foe" defense. The level of instinctive mistrust was a tremendous obstacle.

Finding a middle path to navigate this ethical dilemma is not hopeless, however. There have been a few strong efforts to moderate between the extremes. The Minnesota Center for Corporate Responsibility helped the Caux Roundtable—another elite grouping of international industrialists—to adopt a model ethical code, Principles for Business. Britain's Ethical Trading Initiative has brought government officials, human rights activists, and business leaders into dialogue and close collaboration on common problems. The New York–based Council on Economic Priorities uses a positive carrot rather than a negative stick approach to business by ranking corporations on a social responsibility index and offering a certification program for good labor practices. And the Clinton administration prodded the Apparel Industry Partnership (AIP) to build a consensus among companies, unions, and human rights NGOs. That deliberative process failed to keep the unions onboard, but it resulted in the creation of an experimental labor-monitoring organization, the Fair Labor Association (FLA), which may prove to be a step in the right direction.

Most notable among these efforts has been the rapid rise of the San Francisco–based Business for Social Responsibility (BSR), a business-friendly group that conducts training and advises corporations on human rights policies and other social accountability issues. The magazine *Stratos* defined BSR as "an audacious experiment in common sense, research and sharing that aims to prove the obvious but not so obvious fact that what's good for humanity is good for business." To its credit, the organization has had a catalytic effect on getting top executives of some fairly stodgy corporations to think seriously about the ethical framework for doing business. It has established a safe haven for talking about values, short-circuiting the predictable defensiveness one would expect to be provoked by the moralistic concerns of social responsibility.

BSR measures somewhat short in terms of openness to the news media and to legitimate human rights researchers, but it can argue in its defense that this fundamental lack of transparency is necessitated by the skittishness of its press-shy corporate members. Indeed, the motivation for many companies to turn to BSR in the first place is to develop policies that will protect them from having dirty laundry aired in the public domain. To make progress on winning their hearts and minds, a safe environment is essential, even if the process itself eludes public accountability.

Levi Strauss & Co., it just so happens, is a major benefactor and a power behind BSR, providing critical funding and personnel that helped turn the organization from a small operation of gadfly Washington lobbyists and idealistic entrepreneurs—like Ben Cohen of Ben & Jerry's Homemade ice cream—into the influential force it is today.

Robert H. Dunn, the nonprofit group's executive director, was Levi's vice president for corporate affairs and its point man on human rights and social responsibility policies until he left the company after thirteen years to lead BSR in 1994. Dunn, a Connecticut lawyer, had worked in a variety of political positions in the 1970s before joining Levi Strauss, serving as an aide at Jimmy Carter's White House, an assistant to the U.S. ambassador to Mexico, and a cabinet member in Wisconsin state government. His political experience, one might say, equips him well to take on the improbable task of motivating staid corporate executives to rethink some of the fundamental premises of how—and why—they do business.

A pilgrimage to BSR's office on Mission Street in San Francisco is a strange encounter with the "politically correct" business workplace of the future. A brochure displayed in the reception area advises one that the walls are covered with odorless paint that is free of toxic formaldehyde, crystalline silica, and ethylene glycol. The hardwood floors are laid with "certified sustainably harvested pine." The lights that illuminate the airy open loftlike space use low-voltage bulbs connected to energy-saving motion detectors. Partitions, carpets, and furniture are all made of either recycled or recyclable materials. The walls of the office cubicles that ring the space and the conference room in the center are paneled with (recyclable) glass, brightening the sprawling space and giving it—intentionally, said Dunn—an aura of transparency.

This spirit of transparency is something that Dunn's organization cannot claim to embody, at least where the free flow of information is concerned. But it is one of the values that BSR and the businesses it works with hopefully will, in time, learn is to their advantage. The group's 1,400 members are small, large, and very large, including such industrial titans as AT&T, Coca-Cola, General Motors, Johnson & Johnson, Honeywell, and Polaroid. BSR boasts an on-line "Global Business Responsibility Resource Center," a clearinghouse that provides an introductory framework for the major issues of corporate responsibility and lists other organizations with like-minded missions. Cited among the top four sponsors of the resource center are Levi Strauss & Co. and two charitable foundations endowed by the company's proprietary family, the Evelyn and Walter Haas Jr. Fund and the Walter & Elise Haas Fund. BSR's public face and the ethos shaping the organization distinctly bear the fingerprints of the fabled blue jeans company.

Dunn played an instrumental role in developing Levi's trendsetting Global Sourcing Guidelines, a visionary document the company announced in 1992, which sets standards for behavior for the company's outside business partners and addresses the question of doing business in countries where there are pervasive human rights violations. However, Dunn, exuding a rigid, priestly demeanor, declines to talk about his experiences at Levi Strauss. Even his general remarks on the challenges of corporate social responsibility are cautious. Confidential sources explain that Dunn harbors a certain degree of disdain for journalists, based on past experiences of feeling misunderstood or getting "burned" by the press. Indeed, listening to him speak, one can sense an inner conflict between his instincts to guard against intrusion and his intellectual commitment to the principle of transparency. "I read a speech by someone recently who said that a company needs to beware of any fourteen-year-old with a modem and an attitude. It is now possible for people outside the company to proliferate information that's not accurate," said Dunn, surrounded by the recyclable glass walls of BSR's conference room. He adds, however, that a corporation's interests "are better served by providing the public and various stakeholders with broad information about what they represent as a company. And what they contribute, because in the absence of that, they are characterized by others."

Peter Liebhold, one of the curators of a groundbreaking exhibition on the history of sweatshop exploitation at the Smithsonian

Institution's National Museum of American History, said he encountered extraordinary resistance in gathering information from BSR and its members. "For our exhibition we wanted to show codes of conduct to demonstrate how industry is going forward to fight sweatshops. But it was almost impossible to get the codes," he said. "BSR refused to give us the codes of conduct" it had collected, "and it was never clear why."

Is transparency a principle that matters for corporations only in terms of a public relations agenda—preemptive damage control, as Dunn seems to say—and not necessarily in terms of public accountability? What about the importance of the free flow of information in a healthy democracy, which helps businesses make profits every bit as much as it helps museum curators collect knowledge to pass on to an informed citizenry? The cloak of corporate responsibility, without the practice of openness and transparency, is insidious in the extreme.

| | |

The fashion for corporate ethics gathered full force in the late 1970s, about the time orthodox American business leaders started getting their first inkling that laissez-faire capitalism didn't need to be totally craven and mean-spirited. The mainstreaming of corporate social responsibility emerged from a bitter debate over what kinds of obligations companies have to the broader community. It was a time when shocking revelations of environmental degradation caused by business were becoming commonplace. After the hard-won battles of the civil rights movement, allegations of corporate complicity with apartheid in South Africa weighed heavily on the American conscience. An increasingly sophisticated public eyed big business with skepticism unprecedented since the days of the robber barons. President Dwight Eisenhower's parting-shot warning of the dangers of the "military-industrial complex" became palpable as the Vietnam War droned on and defense contractors such as Dow Chemical, purveyors of napalm, became the objects of recrimination.

One critical reference point for the emerging debate on business's role in society was a provocative article written for *The New York*

Times Magazine in 1970 by the dean of conservative economists, Milton Friedman. He posited that the only social responsibility a corporation must abide by is maximizing profits for the benefit of its shareholders. Friedman was not playing devil's advocate. As crass as this might sound, there is an underlying integrity to this view that keeps it alive and powerfully influential today.

Friedman's argument builds on the classic definition of the role of the laissez-faire capitalist in society: to efficiently allocate scarce resources to meet the needs of the community and, in the process, generate wealth that raises standards of living and overall well-being. The idea goes back to Adam Smith, the original free-marketeer. His brilliant writings in the late eighteenth century—when businessmen wore tights, wigs, and three-cornered hats—still set the agenda for the global economy in the twenty-first century. The efficiency of private ownership is not only the name of the game, sayeth Adam Smith and his contemporary disciples like Friedman, it is a fundamental good.

Of course, the purity of this vision does not stand up in the face of the messy social iniquities and injustices that can be caused by impersonal market machinations. That's why there is no true capitalism today, just as true communism could never be achieved. The major industrialized nations subscribing to the ideals of capitalism have all found it imperative to police free markets with regulatory measures and protect citizens with social welfare programs to one degree or another. Within their borders they practice a mixed economy that attempts to balance the interests of market efficiencies with a moral order.

This is the dilemma: What happens outside those boundaries, when multinational corporations yield themselves to the raw capitalist realities of the borderless global economy? Who sets the rules— a toothless United Nations? The World Economic Forum? The U.S.-China Business Council? Classic economic theory does not address what an individual business's responsibility might be in a foreign market where a tyrannical government abuses the fundamental rights of its subjects, scoffs at international standards, enriches elite power holders through systemic corruption, and fails to meet basic social needs.

To Friedman, the proposition that corporations should adopt a broad social responsibility role is subversive—it smacks of socialism and threatens to weaken the free-market system. He wrote in his 1970 article that the responsibility of a corporation is "to conduct business in accordance with [the owner's] desires, which generally will be to make as much money as possible while conforming to the basic rules of society, both those embodied in the law and those embodied in ethical custom."

This is a model for a highly efficient but essentially amoral organization, operating with rectitude in response to situational factors and perhaps local standards, but otherwise acting without the guidance of an internal or external moral rudder. Ethics, therefore, are at best purely situational, executed in a policy of expedience that exists only to serve the company's core social mission of maximizing profits. In this cynical world there is no altruism, no higher grace or purpose. Gross profits are transferred into charitable giving programs solely for purposes of tax abatement and public relations value, not out of a recognition of social obligation to the disadvantaged. In fact, this model is pretty close to the norm. The vast majority of businesses, competing to survive and prosper, follows an ethos that essentially puts rational self-interests first.

To soften this stark picture, business leaders with humanitarian instincts like Walter Haas Jr., then CEO of Levi Strauss & Co., wrestled with the problem of how to define a more compassionate role for business in society. The concept of *stakeholders* was born, a term that is central to the lexicon of the corporate social responsibility movement. It refers to the constituents of a corporate enterprise who have an interest in the organization's activities beyond the traditional concerns of shareholders and senior managers. A moral stake, if you will, instead of an equity stake. The jargon tends to be used loosely, but it generally alludes to a variety of players in society, including rank-and-file employees of the enterprise, business partners, suppliers, the people in the communities where business is conducted, and sometimes—increasingly so in the human rights debate—the NGOs and the muckraking media that act as surrogates for the broader public interest.

In simple terms, the idea is that companies can sustain profitability and compete more effectively in the long term by taking the interests of these stakeholders to heart when making critical decisions about business. The profit motive is still primary, but under the theories of corporate social responsibility, the aim of higher profits—or preventing losses—can be used to rationalize decisions based on a broader set of values. In theory, the raw urge of the profit motive can be channeled into an impulse to do the right thing.

By the late 1970s, with the Vietnam War legacy freshly smoldering and the antiapartheid campaign raging, societal pressures on the business community to face up to its ethical inconsistencies reached critical mass. The Business Roundtable, an influential organization of American chief executives, undertook a major survey of members and conducted case studies of ten companies to explore ethical standards. The results shattered the myth of corporate infallibility. "It was the first time the major corporations of America came out of the closet and admitted they all had problems with ethics, not just the rotten apples," said Charles Sherwood McCoy, professor emeritus of theological ethics at the Pacific School of Religion in Berkeley, California, who prodded the Business Roundtable into making the study. "They all had ethics codes since the 1970s, but now they were preparing to deal with implementation procedures."

The Business Roundtable released a statement on "corporate responsibility principles" in 1981 that would become another key reference in the debate—the antidote to the Friedman formula. The statement, in essence, argues that the interests of shareholders can be best served by taking into account the legitimate claims of stakeholders, making the company both "economically and socially viable."

From this perspective, ethics are animated in a preemptive fashion, evaluating the potential outcome of corporate behavior before a pernicious impact on society is irreversible. In the Friedman model ethics are reactive, responding only to external constraints, such as criminal laws and regulatory sanctions—which is fine when the laws and regulations are in place, but totally deficient when the rules are unclear.

| | |

Consider the perennial problem of graft, as shockingly highlighted in a recent scandal revealing customary bribes paid to members of the International Olympic Committee by cities determined to host the games. Despite its Mormon religious traditions, Salt Lake City, Utah, was one of the principal scoundrels in this story. Unlike these perpetrators, most American corporations would think twice before bribing a foreign official while cutting a business deal and most certainly abstain. Not out of saintliness or a belief that bribery is morally wrong, but because the graft would expose the corporation to the risk of criminal sanctions under the U.S Foreign Corrupt Practices Act of 1977. That's a rational constraint that has nothing to do with the company's internal convictions about social responsibility.

Evidence suggests that this law has been good for business. Levi Strauss, for one, acted on its own 1975 Code of International Business Principles and abandoned its operations in Indonesia because of the pervasive corruption in that market. But the company found it possible to return later and do business ethically because the federal sanctions against bribing foreign officials protected its reputation. Before the act was legislated, investigators for the Securities and Exchange Commission determined that more than four hundred U.S. companies admitted making questionable or illegal payments in excess of $300 million to foreign government officials, politicians, and political parties, according to the U.S. Commerce Department. Today it's safe to conclude that major U.S. multinationals are dead serious about complying with the anticorruption law, calculating that the expedience of graft cannot outweigh the costs of getting caught in a bribery scandal, replete with fines, possible prison sentences, and humiliating bad publicity.

The motivation behind the enactment of the anticorruption law by Congress illustrates the kind of soul-searching the country was undergoing over the role of business in society at the time. The defense contractor Lockheed Corporation had been caught paying bribes to Japanese officials—including a tribute of some $2 million to then Prime Minister Kakuei Tanaka—to promote the sale of its commercial jets to Japanese airline companies. Institutional corruption was deeply entrenched in Japanese society at the time and continued to be for many years. Bribery was largely condoned as customary in the relationships between business and politicians—Lockheed was nominally breaking Japanese law, but following the customary norms of the local business culture. The graft was not detected by local law enforcement but was revealed sensationally in U.S. congressional hearings, a mortifying loss of face for Japan. The public's attitudes started to change radically after the Lockheed scandal shook the foundation of Japan's political establishment and disgraced one of its most powerful prime ministers.

The scandal proved catalytic in reshaping the ethical framework of Japanese society, but perhaps its greatest legacy is to U.S. jurisprudence. The Foreign Corrupt Practices Act became an essential road map for American businesspeople venturing out into the international marketplace for the first time, as globalization got off to a gallop in the 1980s. While some of their competitors from Europe could take tax deductions for the bribes they paid foreign officials until quite recently, Americans were protected from the temptation to cut corners and violate local laws—and more often than not earned the respect of their business partners and host governments as a result. There was an element of dignity and decency to the American practice.

The anticorruption law provides an important conceptual link for understanding today's debate over business and human rights. The law expresses a fundamental moral notion: If a particular act is considered by a society to be wrong within its own borders, members of that society should not be permitted to commit it with impunity overseas—even though the behavior may be condoned as customary in the host country. The criteria for doing the right thing abroad should not fall short of the standards at home.

That's an inflammatory concept, and it has a lot to do with the ideal of "subversion" in the dynamic of universal human rights. It's about transcending state sovereignty with higher aspirations for moral rectitude, as espoused by the 1948 Universal Declaration of Human Rights. It's also about transcending the proprietary rights and the rational commercial self-interests of corporations. To skeptics, the idea is loaded with negative implications, saying that foreign business partners and officials and their societies should subscribe to the same set of values as Americans, on the grounds that these values are universal and not unique to the American experiment in democracy.

Who determines what the "right thing" is, anyway? Propositioning a higher standard or a "superior" set of values in the social and political systems of a faraway land can be written off as "ethical imperialism," replete with blind missionary zeal and all the unfairness perpetrated on less developed societies in our ugly past. The problem is, however, that truly faraway lands no longer exist in today's global gestalt, where jet travel, satellite telecommunications, and interlocking computer networks that form the ubiquitous Internet bind even the remotest of villages into a single mush of the human experience. That's especially true in the eyes of international business, integrating the world into one system of finance and trade and perpetually seeking out new markets to develop.

Having been unleashed in the antiapartheid movement, the moral missionary zeal of human rights advocacy has wormed its way into the ongoing debate on corporate social responsibility. There is no turning back now, even if the polarized views on business's social role can never be truly reconciled. It all boils down to a matter of what is palatable to the public. A corporation abiding by Milton Friedman's profit-maximization model conceives of its social responsibility only in the context of abiding by local laws and ethical customs. That would mean that managers and owners would have considered themselves perfectly justified in abiding by South African laws—and the customs of white supremacy—that mandated abhorrent racial discrimination against the majority population.

Economically speaking, South Africa was the China of the newly developing continent. You had to be there or miss out. It was a huge emerging marketplace literally studded with diamonds and gold mines, promising high yields for foreign investors. Many rational American corporations at first brushed aside concerns about South Africa's egregious human rights practices—that was just local politics—until they confronted the external constraints of a zealous advocacy campaign that targeted their corporate images, threatening to undermine sales and profits and urging universities and public institutions to divest themselves of shareholdings, thereby undermining the company's ability to raise funds in financial markets. There were consumer boycotts, dissident shareholder revolts, campus protests, and state and local "selective purchasing" laws that would pose unacceptable risks to the bottom line and, ultimately, UN resolutions.

Interestingly enough, the effectiveness of the campaign was based on Milton Friedman's classic model of corporate responsibility, whereby external pressures on a corporation define its societal obligations, not the moral instincts arising from within. The solution in South Africa was achieved not by voluntary self-regulation, but by bashing heads.

The current crusade to advance the cause of labor standards and human rights in the global marketplace has a long way to go before it reaches the level of intensity and concentration that marked the antiapartheid movement. The legacy of the civil rights struggle and the moral authority of a politically empowered African American community created a gale-force wind for that cause. But the momentous energy of this righteousness has dissipated as human rights activists applied the tactics of the South African experience to a hodgepodge of situations around the world. The magnitude of the evil in question varies in each case, as does the tangle of laws, politics—and economic opportunities.

Moreover, the web of self-interest is more complicated—nearly all Americans benefit from the cheap goods coming out of Chinese sweatshops, and we're nowhere near prepared to hold ourselves accountable as greedy consumers. Just ask the frustrated human rights protesters manning picket lines in front of Gap and Nike outlets as they watch in despair while people stroll in to buy jeans and sneakers with an oblivious air: *What are those crazy people with the signs talking about?*

Consider what would happen if the full force of the Sullivan Principles—the proscriptive set of moral guidelines for corporations that helped turn the tide in the antiapartheid campaign—were applied to China, demanding that U.S. corporations in that market subvert and violate the misbegotten laws and customs that perpetuate human rights abuses. The Sullivan doctrine maintains that absolute morality must take precedence over situational ethics and local legal standards. But what happens when the moral concerns are downgraded to, say, the right to free association—a cardinal tenet of universal human rights, but not nearly as vital as the rights abused under the monstrosity of apartheid? Does the evil of union busting outweigh the social benefit of job creation? Is the question of what's right and what's wrong something that can be negotiated, depending on the scale and the magnitude and the sticky political complications of a situation?

We need something solid to hang on to here. So why not look once again at Levi Strauss. The company at one point seriously explored the idea of doing business in South Africa as it rapidly expanded its production base globally. The market had favorable infrastructure and a robust domestic consumer market, and it was an obvious choice as a production platform to serve regional markets on the African continent. But the company ruled out the move, preemptively, out of distaste for the racist regime in power. It decided on a policy of waiting for apartheid to end and for internationally certified free and fair elections to be held. It wasn't constrained externally in this choice, but, rather, it was guided internally by its own corporate values.

Levi Strauss, it should be noted, was the first U.S. multinational to invest in South Africa after Nelson Mandela was released from twenty-five years in prison and elected president. The company set up a wholly owned subsidiary in 1995 that would produce one million units of clothing a year for sale in South Africa and the region. In time, however, this paragon of corporate virtue would become as vulnerable to questions of ethical inconsistency as any major multinational company. Transferring the crisp moral equation of the South African experience into a coherent set of ethics for the global marketplace would prove to be a tough challenge, even for the best of companies.

|||

Levi Strauss & Co. occupied a unique position at a time when the champions of universal human rights—legal scholars, NGO activists, zealous Western diplomats, and journalists—began shifting the focus of their interests from the numbing carnage and mayhem of ethnic cleansing in places like the Balkans and sub-Saharan Africa and East Timor to the behavior of powerful multinational corporations.

Few companies had ever gone through the kind of thorough and exhausting evaluation of their core ethical values or agonized to such an extent over how to institutionalize these ethics within the company and then take the next step of implementing them on a universal basis. At the same time, however, Levi Strauss was an irresistible target for criticism. At the end of the 1990s it was struggling to overcome a devastating downturn in sales, and as a consequence it was taking actions that undermined its reputation for corporate benevolence. The proud manufacturer was eliminating its American workforce on a wholesale basis, reversing a long tradition of loyalty to its employees.

Learning from the Levi experience requires bearing in mind the inevitable conflict between aspiring toward absolute principles of moral rectitude and practicing, by necessity, messy situational ethics down here on earth. Shunning the butchers of Beijing and saving blue-collar jobs for American workers may pass the test of right or wrong. But swimming against the tides of global competitiveness and low-wage labor arbitrage can be counterproductive—circumstantially self-defeating.

"Humanity cannot live without a moral yardstick, but we also cannot live up to it," said Charles McCoy, the religious ethicist at Berkeley's Pacific School of Religion. "This isn't contradictory, it's a statement of the human condition."

McCoy was presented with an unusual challenge back in the 1970s when Levi Strauss's then chairman and family patriarch, Walter Haas Jr., approached him and asked for his help. Haas said he wanted to "institutionalize" the ethical principles by which the company did business, McCoy recalls. For decades the family firm had conducted its activities in accordance with a rigorous understanding of ethical principles, Haas told him, but alas, no one had made a point of writing them down. There was no formal policy and no process for instilling these principles among its rapidly growing management team.

When Levi Strauss moved out of the old building it had occupied for decades on Battery Street in downtown San Francisco to occupy spacious new corporate offices at the east foot of Telegraph Hill off the picturesque Embarcadero, the management ranks were imbued with a melancholy sense of loss. It would no longer be the intimate family operation it always was, where company lore and the traditional values of the firm could be transmitted almost by osmosis by constant physical interaction among managers. After going public with its first-ever stock offering in 1971, the family company was growing so fast that it had acquired an impersonal "corporate" feel.

Haas wanted to clarify and formalize the ethics he inherited from his father and grandfather. The principles of ethical business practices at Levi Strauss, McCoy said, were "embodied" by Haas and his brother, company president Peter Haas, both of whom bore a formidable mantle of authority as family heirs to founder Levi Strauss. McCoy had worked on developing a formalized ethics policy for Wells Fargo Bank, another great San Francisco institution, and when Haas learned about this project he came to him. "He said, 'Peter and I are getting older, and before we retire we want to see our ethics institutionalized,'" McCoy recounted in a reverent voice inflected with traces of a southern drawl. Deep respect for the Haas family is a common feature among business ethicists who study the Levi Strauss case.

McCoy's role in advising the Haas brothers on ethics was a curious one. He was a Methodist minister from Scotland County, North Carolina, who had come of age during the civil rights movement and later became a pioneer in the campaign to establish a network of politically active campus ministries, which had a significant role in the protest against apartheid in South Africa. Since his days as a Ph.D. candidate at Yale Divinity School, he had worked extensively with corporations on ethical issues, and he later would found the ecumenical Center for Ethical and Social Policy at UC Berkeley's Graduate Theological Union, which includes the Pacific School of Religion.

Why did Walter Haas Jr., a prominent merchant with a strong Jewish background, seek ethical guidance from a southern Methodist theologian? Apparently it had something to do with the company's own experience in the civil rights movement. Back in the 1950s, as Levi was expanding its manufacturing platform in the southern states, Walter and Peter Haas faced a tough decision on racial integration when they were informed of a serious productivity problem in the all-white workforce at Levi's plant in Blackstone, Virginia.

The senior manager in charge of quality control at the time, Paul Glasgow, proposed opening the plant to workers from the surrounding African American community to improve the caliber of labor, but he knew this would violate local social taboos. With the support of the Haas brothers, Glasgow overcame demands by white civic leaders that Levi's new black employees use separate bathrooms and drinking fountains. When Levi Strauss rejected a demand that a wall be built to segregate the workers, city fathers suggested that a white line be painted on the factory floor, separating the races. The company flatly refused, and within a week of integrated operations, black and white workers were eating at the same tables in the company cafeteria. After this icebreaker, Levi Strauss embarked on a discreet program of desegregating all its factories, helping to reshape the industrial landscape in the American South.

In a 1973 interview reproduced in *Levi Strauss & Co.: Tailors to the World,* an oral history of the company compiled by researchers at the University of California's Bancroft Library, Walter Haas stresses the company's commitment to equal opportunity employment and its responsibility for the welfare of its workers. He recalls how he made a point of stating Levi's dedication to social responsibility in the prospectus for the company's first public stock offering, "in a sense, warning investors to expect this, and that we weren't going to change." The text follows this quote with the parenthetical note "[laughter]."

Haas was not joking, however. Page three of the 1971 prospectus, offering the public 1,390,000 shares of common stock at $47 each, states: "The Company's social responsibilities have for many years been a matter of strong conviction on the part of its management. Well before legal requirements were imposed, the Company was an 'equal opportunity employer.' In 1969, the Company received one of *Business Week* magazine's first 'Business Citizenship' awards in the field of human resources."

Explaining the motivation for integrating factories in the South, Haas told his interviewer: "I get on a soapbox when I say how important it is. We did it because we just thought it was morally correct. It turned out to be very good business. I could say that if this business is going to survive in today's environment, it has to take a look beyond what it used to think its responsibilities were, which was to make a profit for the stockholders."

Indeed, Walter's son Robert, the current chairman, would later cite the anecdote as an example of how the company has flourished by doing the right thing. "Faced with my father's and my uncle's unyielding resolve and economic realities, the city leaders put aside their strongly held views. The plant—and others around the South—accepted workers of all races," Haas said in a 1997 speech to a conference held by the group Business for Social Responsibility. "Our experience has shown—time and time again—that values-based decision making results in 'out of the box,' innovative approaches and remedies to business problems. Our firm's values include a commitment to ethical business conduct; quality in everything we do; respect for people; an openness to new ideas; valuing and embracing diversity; and a dedication to socially responsible conduct. I contend that by following these values and taking into account the interests of multiple stakeholders in our decision making, we are able to make sounder decisions. We're able to promote innovation and, ultimately, enhance sales and earnings."

Clearly, ethical principles embodied by Walter Haas Jr. and his forebears had been successfully implanted in his son, as they had been transmitted to lower-echelon managers like Paul Glasgow across the years. But it's important to think about how such values evolved out of the company's origins in the heyday of aggressive, free-for-all Gold Rush capitalism.

| | |

Levi Strauss the man was not a prospector for gold or otherwise in pursuit of quick riches. He started his career modestly as a peddler, trekking around the wilds of Kentucky with a sack full of incidental goods slung over his shoulder. He was a Bavarian Jew, the son of a peddler. His father's untimely death in the old country moved Levi to immigrate to America with his mother and two sisters in 1847, trailing older brothers who had already set up a dry goods business in New York City. Levi eventually followed his sister Fannie and her husband, David Stern, to San Francisco, where he staked his claim as a merchant in 1853, representing the family's apparel wholesaling business. Strauss was successful and grew wealthy investing in San Francisco real estate, while selling bolts of fabric and ladies' undergarments through a network of salesmen covering the West.

Strauss boosted his fortunes considerably when he went into the manufacturing business in 1873 with Jacob Davis, a tailor from Reno, Nevada, who had innovated the idea of using copper rivets to secure the pockets and seams of heavy work pants. Davis's durable trousers had gained such popularity among miners and workmen that he turned to Strauss—his fabric supplier—for help in getting a patent for his rivet design. The tailor's invention would become "Double-X denim waist overalls," sold with a leather patch depicting two plow horses straining in vain to rip the garment apart. In the new West it became the clothing of choice among miners, stevedores, cattlemen, and farmers. These rustic dungarees—itemized as product # 501 in the Levi Strauss catalog—were the forebears of the classic Levi's 501 button-fly blue jeans that would later become an American icon and define the identity of the company that claimed distinction as the world's largest branded apparel maker more than a century later.

Back in the rough-and-tumble Gold Rush era, proprietor Levi Strauss rose to an elite status in San Francisco's business and civic circles, and later in life he matched his prestige with a practice of philanthropy that would serve as an important precedent to future generations at Levi Strauss & Co. In 1897 Strauss gave money to the University of California to support twenty-eight scholarships; the descendants of his nephews would rank among the school's largest private donors. At his death in 1902 at the age of seventy-three, Strauss, who never married, bequeathed controlling interest in the company to his nephews. He also gave generous sums to Catholic and Protestant orphanages as well as to his favored charities, the Pacific Hebrew Orphan Asylum and the Home for Aged Israelites.

Yet Strauss cannot be singled out as the architect of the ethical business practices that would later distinguish his company. He ran his business more or less in keeping with the ethical standards and the business morality of the time and place, which is to say, fairly laxly in comparison with more modern standards and values. Strauss made it a policy not to hire Chinese workers, for example, after mobs of angry white laborers sacked and burned Chinatown during rioting in 1877. The rationale was that white workmen were his best customers; Strauss and his family partners feared their factory could be the next target of racist rage. Integration would not become a principled policy objective for some time.

The company's earliest factories evidently employed young girls under the age of fourteen in the early part of the century, not an unusual practice in those days. One of them, in an interview with journalist Ed Cray some seven decades later, mentions in passing the typical hazards of the factory floor, the kind that were rampant in early industrial America. Cray's elderly informant, Hortense Thompson, described the dangerous work she did on a metal button machine as a young girl, toiling long hours—a basic six-day, fifty-seven-hour workweek. She recalled vividly how she and the other children at the plant were required to work overtime until as late as ten P.M. on occasions when orders were backlogged.

The machine Thompson operated was dangerous. "You used to have to feed the buttons for the riveted clothes one by one. You had to put the metal buttons in by hand, and you could step on the lever too soon, especially if you were tired," she recalled as an elderly pensioner. "I almost put a button on my finger one time. One girl did—punched a button right in her finger. She just didn't get her finger out. . . . One time a lady's hair got caught in a machine. Her scalp was taken off. She didn't die, but she was in the hospital a long time. People sometimes sewed their fingers. When people were hurt on the job, the company didn't pay medical expenses," she is quoted as saying in Cray's 1978 book, *Levi's,* a generally fawning history of the company.

Thompson's testimony bears striking similarities to the stories of exploited workers collected in more recent years by human rights investigators. Levi's nineteenth-century factory—comparatively clean, large, and well lighted for its time—would no doubt arouse the ire of today's self-appointed sweatshop police.

But Thompson was happy enough with her dangerous and demanding job to work another fifty years at the company. She and the other Levi employees who survived San Francisco's devastating earthquake of 1906 realized they were employed by an unusually generous company when Levi Strauss—now run by Strauss's brother-in-law David Stern and his sons—kept them on the payroll after the quake demolished the factory, as well as the head office and store. Later, company workers continued to receive paychecks even as the Great Depression drove the national economy to the brink. A dropoff in demand for Levi's work clothes put Levi Strauss $426,000 in the red, but the company used its idle employees to install hardwood floors in its "mother factory" on Valencia Street in San Francisco—a private version of the federal Work Projects Administration (WPA) job creation programs of the day.

This ethic of generosity and paternalism to the workforce evolved into standard practice as Levi Strauss's nephews Jacob and Sigmund Stern and his grandnephew Walter Haas Sr. took turns at the helm of the company. Their family's cultural and spiritual background strongly influenced the business ethos. The Judaic tradition calls for charity, moral responsibility, and civic duty, and the importance of workers' rights also is stressed in Jewish religious law. Interviewed in the late 1970s, Robert D. Haas recalled growing up surrounded by strong social values. "When I was young, the dinner table conversation did not revolve around business. After friends and the day's adventures, we'd talk about pride in being able to help somebody," he told author Ed Cray. Under young Haas's command, the extended family—Levi's children on the assembly lines of the company's sewing and finishing factories—ranked among the best treated and most generously compensated workers in the U.S. apparel industry right up to the end of the twentieth century, when the dispassionate forces of globalization caught up with them.

One of Levi Strauss's first ethical codes, completed in 1975 and distributed internally as the Code of International Business Principles, spelled out its obligations as a responsible multinational corporation. The language of the code reflected issues of much public concern at the time—bribery of foreign officials and intervention in banana republic politics. "The company is committed to operating well above the minimum legal standard such that its conduct is and intentions are above question," the document stated. "The company recognizes the influence it possesses by virtue of its size. It also recognizes its responsibility to ensure that this influence is not brought to bear on any partisan political activities within any country."

Providing an important precedent for the Global Sourcing Guidelines, Levi's influential code of conduct that would come seventeen years later, the document declared: "The company subscribes to a single global philosophy of fair treatment of employees that is also consistent with local laws and practices." The new code extends that obligation from the employees of the company's foreign subsidiaries to workers at its contractor plants—whoever and wherever they might be. Getting beyond the rhetoric and taking responsibility for the welfare of these stakeholders—according to the Levi Strauss tradition—is going to be an ethical challenge of tremendous proportions.

CHAPTER TWO

|||

Slaves to Fashion

Injustice anywhere is a threat to justice everywhere.
—Martin Luther King Jr., *Letter from a Birmingham Jail*

She scaled a high stucco wall under cover of darkness and made a desperate escape, leaving behind a nondescript apartment complex that concealed the horrors of an illegal sweatshop. There she had toiled as a seamstress from dawn to as late as midnight for six grueling days a week—and sometimes seven—without fair compensation and, even more intolerably, without her basic right to personal freedom. Her captors verbally abused the young woman and her coworkers. They docked her wages when she failed to meet demanding piecework quotas. Overtime pay was not even a remote possibility. Her home was not merely a sweatshop, but a virtual prison.

"Jena" was the assumed name she chose as she told her story of life in the wretched sewing factory, where she and dozens of other Thai women were forced to work under slavelike conditions. Interviewed in an empty courthouse cafeteria in the summer of 1995, Jena spoke in a quavering voice that betrayed the fear behind her cheerful façade. She was in her early twenties, but her slender body was hunched over, as though the trauma of abuse had returned with the memory and was bearing down on her neck. Jena and her coworkers—all indentured to their employer—could not leave the locked compound without a guard escorting them. "They told me that if I left the house, somebody might rape me," she said. "They said the bosses will go after my family and kill them if I left without permission."

Jena and one of her companions decided they could not tolerate the situation. They determined to flee while they still could after learning about plans to ring the tops of the compound walls with barbed wire. The pair of escapees scrambled through the dark streets that night, looking for safety, until a kindly neighbor offered assistance, helping them find their way to a local Buddhist temple where the monks would offer them sanctuary.

Two years after her desperate break for freedom, Jena's nightmare was not over. Most of her tormentors were under arrest and faced criminal prosecution, but not all of them. One fugitive had already made menacing phone calls to the families of the victimized workers who would serve as witnesses in the trial. Jena had come out of the woodwork cautiously to observe the arraignment of suspects in a courtroom down the marble corridor from the room where she unburdened herself to a local newspaper reporter. She still feared the threats of reprisals against her family in rural Thailand. It had been Jena and her boyfriend who dared to complain to authorities, triggering a government raid on the sweatshop.

Jena had other fears besides violent reprisals. She had to be careful about the threat of deportation. This outrage of cruelty and bondage in the workplace did not occur in the urban squalor of Bangkok or in the fetid slums of some other Asian city. It happened in suburban Los Angeles, where Jena lived in peril as an undocumented economic migrant. She had since married her Thai boyfriend, who possessed legal U.S. residency status, and had recently given birth to a child, making her the mother of an American citizen. But the system still placed her in the purgatory of illegal alien status. "I'm still frightened about my situation," said Jena before screwing up the courage to walk down the hallway of the courthouse and observe the arraignment in progress. "My former bosses, they're still not all in jail."

Jena's case is more than your basic crime blotter item. It is a window on a convoluted and seemingly intractable problem that plagues the international economy at the beginning of the new millennium. The El Monte slave shop was shocking news for the 1990s, but also an ancient tale of poverty and its exploitation. Labor bondage, in this contemporary form, was an integral part of a global phenomenon in which an unlimited supply of young women from miserably poor families in countries like Thailand and in Indonesia and China would jump at the chance to enter the very same trap that preyed upon Jena.

Just as the sordid side of the apparel industry revealed itself in the horrific sweatshops of America's early industrial past, and just as rampant labor exploitation came to light more recently in developing nations around the world, the problem now reared its ugly head amid the palm trees and strip malls of Southern California. Jena and some seventy other indentured servants had been brought from Thailand to the nondescript town of El Monte by a family of garment industry entrepreneurs, Thai nationals with Chinese ethnic roots. These businesspeople saw an opportunity to extract the considerable benefits of dirt-cheap labor, stitching clothes that could carry the "Made in the USA" label for the domestic market.

This new and illicit twist on the game of globalization had been gathering steam throughout the 1990s. Nefarious groups of organized criminals from China, Taiwan, and Hong Kong were shepherding a stream of economic migrants out of Fujian province and other areas of China's impoverished countryside, outfitting them with false travel documents, and then loading them on commercial airliners or cramming them into the holds of rusting old freighters. Typically, the end of the line was a grubby sweatshop in the anonymous sprawl of greater Los Angeles or in the back alleys of New York City's Chinatown. Los Angeles earned the distinction as the nation's sweatshop capital by virtue of its plethora of small-scale sewing and finishing contractors—an estimated 5,100 of them—serving Southern California's $28 billion fashion industry.

To be fair, most of Los Angeles' apparel contractors are legitimate businesses, employing tens of thousands of citizens and legally documented aliens and contributing to the heft of the regional economy. But others, according to law enforcement officials and social agencies, seek competitive efficiencies by illegal means, ranging from casually hiring undocumented workers to routinely violating minimum wage and overtime laws. The U.S. Department of Labor's Wage and Hour Division found in a 1998 study that only half the sewing shops it surveyed in the Los Angeles area were in compliance with the minimum wage requirements of the federal Fair Labor Standards Act.

The Los Angeles Jewish Commission on Sweatshops issued a critical report in January 1999, citing "widespread non-compliance with health and safety laws" in the local apparel industry, which it estimated employs more than 160,000 workers. "Garment sweatshops have returned to the United States and Los Angeles for many reasons, including the rise of competitive low-wage offshore production; the weakening of organized labor . . . and a pyramid-like system of subcontracting in which downward price pressure on contractors result in poverty-level wages for workers," the report stated. "The industry's effort at self-monitoring is laudable, but thus far has met with limited success and by itself is unlikely to solve the problems of sweatshops."

The El Monte "slavery" case brought much-needed attention to this sorry state of affairs. It also revealed that Thai criminal gangs were taking a cue from the more notorious scoundrels in the trade, the "coyotes" of Mexico and the "snakeheads" of China. These wily and slithery smugglers of bonded human cargo extracted a cruel price for unsafe passage to the United States, which typically takes the form of high-interest loans ranging anywhere from $2,000 to $7,000 or more—the equivalent of many, many years of hard-earned salary back home. But the math adds up: earning even the minimum wage in the United States theoretically would allow these bonded workers the opportunity to pay off their debts and, in time, send modest remittances home to help hoist their families out of humiliating poverty. In this version of the American dream, destitute people are seduced with false promises of good jobs that don't quite exist. Human chattel is the collateral of this black market in labor.

The phenomenon is not completely unprecedented in U.S. immigration history. Much of the backbone of the young nation was built by African slaves who tilled the southern soil and by Asian contract laborers who toiled on the transcontinental railroads. In the affluent twilight of the twentieth century, however, the notion of indentured servitude was blasphemous to the American way—it could not be reconciled with the prevailing civic ethos of freedom and justice. Yet so powerful is the international appeal of working in the United States, illicit labor bondage was growing common, and most probably still is and undoubtedly will remain so well into the new century.

At the end of 1998 U.S. and Canadian authorities cracked a Chinese smuggling ring that, during a period of two years, allegedly transported more than 3,600 illegal aliens through a Mohawk reservation on the border, taking them to restaurant and sewing factory jobs in New York City. If estimates by federal investigators are anywhere near accurate, the Mohawk case only hints at the scope of the problem. A federal interagency task force in 1995 suggested that as many as fifty thousand mainland Chinese were being smuggled into the United States each year. The numbers pale in comparison with illegal immigration from Mexico, but few Mexicans are subjected to indentured servitude on arrival.

In Jena's case, recruiters visited her at the grim Bangkok sewing factory where she worked and enticed her with promises of a new life. They persuaded her to borrow the equivalent of about $2,200, a deposit she was assured she could pay off within a year or so with modest deductions from her wages. At first the adventure did seem like a dream: her "guides" outfitted her with a false passport and treated her to a few days in a resort hotel in Hawaii during transit. But on arrival in Los Angeles she was put straight to work on a grueling, unrelenting schedule. After a year of exhausting drudgery, she calculated she had paid off her debt. Yet her employers told her she was still deeply in arrears. She learned that the $200 and $300 remittances she asked her bosses to wire back to Thailand had never reached her family. They were holding her false passport—a common practice in international labor bondage—and they kept her working without respite behind the locked gates and the high walls of a suburban apartment complex, sheltered from the view of her middle-class neighbors on the tree-lined streets of El Monte.

| | |

One might argue that the perpetrators of Jena's peonage were thinking globally and acting locally, in accordance with that hackneyed management mantra. These ambitious entrepreneurs had unfettered themselves from the inconvenience of import quotas and tariff barriers that the United States places on textile and garment imports to protect its declining domestic industry. The Sino-Thai family invested in a production site with excellent transportation links and proximity to their market. Indeed, the El Monte compound, a seventeen-unit apartment complex zoned for residential use, produced clothing that found its way onto the shelves of leading retailers all over America, from dowdy Mervyn's to upscale Nordstrom's. If the prime villains of El Monte—ringleader Suni Manasurangkun (AKA "Auntie") and her three sons—didn't happen to be involved in a criminal conspiracy, the logic of their business plan might be the model of success. It could be compared to the strategy of Japanese automobile makers who built factories in the American South in the 1980s, within the tariff walls, where they could benefit from nonunion wages and compete effectively against Detroit carmakers burdened by costly labor contracts. All this occurred in the legitimate pursuit of market efficiencies in the brave new world of the borderless global economy and to the ultimate benefit of American consumers—who demand the lowest prices for the goods they buy, from cars to clothing.

The comparison isn't all that simple, however. The Japanese legitimately won the affections of American consumers by making great products with perfectionist quality. Jena's employers, by misrepresenting the conditions under which they made clothing, were deceiving their wholesale and retail customers—and the consumers—as much as they were exploiting their workers. All were made party, both as victims and as perpetrators, to the blatant injustice of the El Monte sweatshop.

In 1996 the seven defendants pleaded guilty to violating federal civil rights laws, admitting to conspiracy, harboring illegal aliens, and forcing workers into involuntary servitude. They received prison sentences ranging from two to seven years. Lawyers representing the victimized El Monte workers—and a group of Mexicans who were not bonded like the Thai women but worked the "front factory" in downtown Los Angeles, which the Thai family used to finish products and meet clients—filed civil suits against the downstream users of the garments. In 1997 they reached a $2.5 million settlement with Montgomery Ward, Mervyn's, Bum International, L. F. Sportswear, Miller's Outpost, F-40, Ms. Tops, Topson Downs, Beniko, and Balmara. The companies settled without admitting wrongdoing.

Federal prosecutors also collected back wages for the 150 Thai and Mexican workers, but Jena, the whistle-blower, missed out on that settlement because the statute of limitations had expired between the time she emancipated herself and the day the state and federal task force stormed the compound in the summer of 1995. Jena is now a legal resident, but she remains fiercely protective of her privacy. Her immigration lawyer said she was offered—and refused—a payment of $20,000 from a Hollywood production agent who wanted to buy the rights to her personal story as a virtual slave.

| | |

The El Monte case is certain to live on as a parable for the contradictions of modern America. Already it has been immortalized as the subject of a theatrical production, portraying Jena and her coworkers as protagonists in the struggle against evil. A staged reading of the play *Fabric,* by playwright Henry Ong, premiered at the Mark Taper Auditorium in August of 1998, starring Jennifer Paz (better known for her appearance in the musical *Miss Saigon*) in the role of Wanda—a composite character representing all the El Monte victims.

The Smithsonian Institution enshrined the El Monte story for posterity when, after considerable controversy, it featured the case prominently in a 1998 exhibition at the National Museum of American History, entitled "Between a Rock and a Hard Place: A Dialogue on American Sweatshops 1820 to the Present." Realizing they were dealing with incendiary material, curators Peter Liebhold and Harry Rubenstein took great care to avoid the furor that surrounded an earlier exhibition at the institute's Air and Space Museum celebrating the *Enola Gay*—the plane that dropped the first atomic bomb, incinerating the city of Hiroshima at the close of World War II. Veterans groups got wind of the original plan to accurately depict the impact of the bomb on the civilian population and quashed that with an argument that the Smithsonian shouldn't portray American history in a negative light.

Anticipating similar trouble, the sweatshop curators cultivated political support for their project in the early stages of their research. They took great pains to ensure academic integrity and included the apparel and retail industries as well as labor and advocacy groups in the planning stages. This model of collaboration worked until they encountered stiff opposition to the crucial role of the El Monte case in the show. The California Fashion Association went ballistic, arguing that El Monte was an aberration and distorted the overall picture of garment production; its attack on the exhibition was joined by the National Retailers Federation and the American Apparel Manufacturers Association, the curators say. But with support from key members of Congress sitting on the Smithsonian Institution's board—and some discreet behind-the-scenes help from Levi Strauss & Co.—the exhibition survived intact.

Testimony to the abominations of El Monte lives on as a computer-generated "virtual exhibition" on the museum's Internet Web site. Introductory text describes the sewing factory as "one of the most horrendous U.S. sweatshops in modern times," where workers "had been held in virtual slavery behind fences tipped with razor wire and forced to sew garments in conditions significantly worse than those found in most sweatshops."

Liebhold and Rubenstein consider the El Monte case as "iconic" to the history of labor in the United States. They rank it along with the 1911 Triangle Shirtwaist Company fire in New York's garment district, where 146 employees were killed as a result of overcrowding and locked exits. Both incidents shocked the American public and raised acute awareness of the problems of sweatshop conditions. The Triangle fire galvanized public support for regulatory reform, eventually leading to the enactment of the Fair Labor Standards Act. In the case of El Monte, dismay over the virtual slavery tale sparked an antisweatshop initiative in the Clinton administration's Department of Labor and inspired the creation of the Apparel Industry Partnership, the White House–sponsored task force of industry, labor, and human rights NGOs, whose ambitious task it was to create a workable code of conduct for the industry that could be effectively monitored and enforced. The federal Department of Labor beefed up its force of inspectors but remains inadequately staffed to monitor compliance with laws on wages and overtime.

The Smithsonian curators, meanwhile, are not sanguine about the prospects for eliminating sweatshops anytime soon. "I think we share a general sense that there aren't going to be any quick solutions," said Rubenstein, who observes that there has been a resurgence of sweatshop abuse in the United States since the late 1960s, roughly correlating to the growth of economic globalization. "There are lots of groups that are going to propose solutions that have the least impact on business operations." His collaborator, Liebhold, adds that sweatshops are "inevitable as long as people view labor as a commodity to buy and sell at the most competitive price."

One important lesson to learn from El Monte is not just that such gross injustices can occur within our own shores, but that these abuses of vulnerable low-skilled workers are rampant in poor nations around the world, as if by design. In a global economic system that thrives by seeking out low wages and lax regulation for labor-intensive industrial production—economic rationalists call this the "international division of labor"—sweatshops, like the poor, will always be with us. There will always be a competitive incentive to create them.

But U.S.-based manufacturers and retailers who have integrated their operations into the global economy face a rising challenge. Human rights advocates and labor activists are demanding that the huge multinational corporations that dominate the global marketplace assume ethical accountability, not just for their own acts, but for the behavior of their business partners. This tactic is based on the idea that there is a joint liability in the business relationship when the efficiencies of substandard labor practices directly benefit U.S. companies at the top of the production pyramid.

Jena's story is, tragically, far from unusual, so it must be interpreted in terms of the powerful economic warp that spawns her and her ilk.

The insatiable demand for inexpensive clothing by American consumers—low-budget slaves to fashion, if you will—and the intense competition among branded clothing manufacturers to meet that demand, in essence, drives the pattern of abuse. Yet is anybody talking seriously about the fact that the gluttonous American consumer is a coconspirator in the chain of responsibility for sweatshops? It's much easier to blame a company, but if you stop to think, we're all culpable, caught up in a demimonde of legal and moral ambiguity in which there are few heroes and plenty of villains. Naming the guilty or, more aptly, picking out a few corporate scapegoats as targets for outrage is not difficult to do at all, as strident human rights activists have demonstrated time and time again. Finding viable and sustainable solutions, however, is a daunting task.

| | |

Levi Strauss, private and taciturn in nature, seems an unlikely candidate to take on a leadership role in the cacophonous realm where business collides with the international human rights community. The company, like any other, has flaws, among which is a painful difficulty communicating its intentions to the outside world. Cloistered and fearful of being burned by the news media's rush to judgment, Levi Strauss has been struggling with the task of reconciling its ethical tradition with the unyielding requirements of doing business ethically and successfully in today's global economy.

Arguably, no single U.S. corporation has done more to establish the moral high ground for social responsibility in business. In addition to its progressive employment policies, the company has set benchmarks for philanthropy. Founder Levi Strauss and his heirs in the Haas family have over the years created a number of well-endowed foundations that have spread the wealth lavishly in the San Francisco Bay Area community and beyond, supporting museums and charities. The trusts have given tens of millions of dollars to the University of California in Berkeley, where it is a family tradition to attend as undergraduates and where the graduate business school is named after a Haas family patriarch.

The Levi Strauss Foundation was the tenth largest corporate foundation in the United States in 1996, with assets of $114.9 million, surpassing the General Motors Foundation. It ranked twenty-ninth in terms of total giving for the year, disbursing $12.2 million in grants. The foundation's track record in giving ranged from extending substantial support for community AIDS education groups to modest contributions to such organizations as Human Rights Watch. In an initiative to counter racism launched in 1991, Project Change, the foundation granted some $8.6 million to grassroots social groups combating racial violence and discrimination. In February 1998 President Clinton cited Project Change when he awarded Levi Strauss CEO Robert Haas the first Ron Brown Award for Corporate Leadership, named after the late commerce secretary, and recognizing the company's "sustained and passionate commitment to employee and community relations."

Haas accepted the award with the kind of dignity that reflected Levi's long record of corporate social responsibility, without betraying evidence of his personal struggle to uphold those high standards against the odds. The successful business machine that paid for the corporate largesse was in a tailspin at that very moment.

"Levi Strauss & Co. has always tried to be a source of positive change in communities where we operate, and nowhere is the opportunity for change greater or more urgent than in the need to end discrimination," said Haas. "The people involved with Project Change have made a significant impact in their communities. They have proven that by working together the struggle for social justice can succeed."

Unfortunately for Haas and the many other people at his company for whom social progress is a sincere objective, this high-profile attention to the company's "do-gooder" reputation only raised fears that Levi Strauss would be a sitting duck for criticism. At the presidential awards ceremony, no one dared mention Levi's announcement a few months earlier that it planned to shut eleven factories and cut its U.S. blue-collar workforce by about one-third, on top of the white-collar layoffs—one thousand out of five thousand domestic positions—announced at the beginning of the year. Nor was there any hint of the even more savage job cuts to come. Despite unusually generous severance packages that mollified the company's unions, the plant closings added to the devastation of the local economies of several small southern towns that relied on the Levi's jobs—some of the very communities where Project Change had brought hope for greater racial harmony.

The layoffs gave ammunition to critics who speculated that Levi planned to shift blue jeans production abroad. Labor activists questioned whether good American jobs would now be replaced by cheap contract workers who are denied labor rights by autocratic governments. The company rebuffed these charges, simply saying that any expanded production overseas would be dedicated to producing goods for the regional market. The company worked hard at micro–public relations in the local communities affected by the layoffs, fanning teams of corporate communications people across the country to talk to small-town news organizations. But it failed to articulate a coherent message to its broader community about what portent the layoffs had for the future. Skepticism lingered.

Levi Strauss was still haunted by the debacle of 1990, when it shut down a plant in San Antonio, Texas, and shifted production from that facility to a contractor plant in Costa Rica—where workers earned about $6 a day, roughly equivalent to the hourly wage at the San Antonio plant. Some 1,100 workers were laid off in the closure, mostly Mexican American women. Some of these disgruntled former employees formed a militant labor group named Fuerza Unida ("United Force") and were still fighting back a decade later. The group launched a strident protest campaign with lawsuits, hunger strikes, demonstrations, and appeals for a boycott of Levi's products. Leader Irene Reynes warned that the scorned San Antonio workers would become Levi's "worst nightmare." Reynes and other leaders journeyed from Texas to Levi Plaza, on the scenic waterfront of San Francisco's Embarcadero, and chained themselves to the front doors of corporate headquarters to draw attention to their cause. To gawking tourists on their way to the carnival at Pier 39, it must have seemed like another demonstration of wacky San Francisco street theater. But to Levi executives spying down from the dark-tinted windows of their handsomely brown-paneled office buildings at Levi Plaza, the scene had to have been painful to watch. Proud and aloof, Levi Strauss had very little experience at being publicly vilified.

A federal court in 1993 rejected a class action lawsuit filed by Fuerza Unida's lawyers, which alleged that Levi's closed the plant to deprive workers of their pension funds, but the embarrassment of San Antonio did not disappear easily. "Levi's really tries to promote the corporate responsibility image," said Miriam Ching Louie, a social activist with the Woman of Color Resource Center in Berkeley who works with Fuerza Unida. "They had already closed down a number of plants in the 1980s, and I think they were really surprised by the intense reaction they got to the closure of the San Antonio plant. There's still a lot of anger and a sense of betrayal for what happened. Some of the workers lost their houses or their cars. They were retrained for low-paying jobs, as beauticians, or jobs that really didn't exist."

The task of breaking the bad news to the San Antonio seamstresses fell to Peter Thigpen, then Levi's vice president of corporate affairs, who had played the role of Grim Reaper for many of the company's earlier plant closures in the 1980s. Thigpen told shocked employees that company officials made the decision with "a lot of pain and sorrow in their hearts." Only two years earlier the plant had been awarded a Miracle Worker award for productivity, Fuerza Unida points out. The union's bitter account of the announcement describes a patronizing Thigpen arriving with "boxes of Kleenex, psychologists and nurses at hand."

It was actually a deflating personal experience, broods Thigpen, who retired from Levi Strauss after rising to the position of president of the company's U.S. division. He now runs his own consulting business and teaches ethics as a lecturer at UC Berkeley's Haas School of Business. Thigpen said he feels remorse about the role he played in places like San Antonio. "The guy in the suit from San Francisco comes in and says, 'Sorry, it costs too much to keep this plant open,'" Thigpen muses in an interview at a bagel shop in a Marin County shopping mall. Tall and craggy and still dressed in Levi's blue jeans eight years after leaving the company, Thigpen wears his sunglasses indoors, but he comes across as completely sincere. "I had to shut down a lot of plants at Levi. It was the hardest thing I ever had to do."

Levi Strauss later found itself in another unpleasant situation at its El Paso, Texas, plant, where it instituted a well-intentioned program in 1993 to retrain employees who had taken disability leave. There was resistance, however, and some 110 workers filed a passel of lawsuits against Levi Strauss, claiming the company had discriminated and retaliated against them for making workers' compensation claims—mostly involving cases of carpal tunnel syndrome, a common malady among assembly-line workers performing repetitious tasks. Workers claimed they were harassed, humiliated, and called names in the program, which they asserted was designed to force them to quit or discourage others from filing claims for disability benefits. In September 1997 a sympathetic jury in one trial found in favor of five of the workers, awarding them $600,000 in compensation and $10 million in punitive damages. Levi Strauss won an appeal of the verdict in 1998; the case was sent back to lower court for a retrial. The company agreed to pay about $5 million to settle with twenty other plaintiffs, while other trials were still pending in the case.

Levi Strauss had been gradually reducing domestic production with a series of plant closings in the 1980s, but with the unfortunate tales of these two Texas cities hanging in the air—and threatening to tarnish its brand image—it almost seemed to hesitate at cutting its workforce any further. There was a seven-year hiatus, and when the company could hold out no longer, it went to extraordinary lengths to project its munificence. Before announcing massive retrenchment plans in November 1997, it went through extensive negotiations with labor unions representing its workers in Tennessee, Arkansas, Texas, and New Mexico, and the company agreed to generous terms. It gave blue jeans workers eight months' notice, extended medical benefits, and offered up to three weeks of severance pay for every year of service. Workers who found new jobs right away were paid a $500 bonus; others received a $6,000 allowance for outplacement costs such as retraining and child care expenses. The Levi Strauss Foundation kicked in an $8 million grant for a community transition fund to aid the affected factory towns.

But this generosity could not resolve the broader economic impact of Levi's action, nor could it reverse the inexorable decline in the U.S. apparel industry that had already maimed these communities. In Hickman County, Tennessee, the company had just built an addition to its Centerville factory, giving workers false hopes of security. Levi Strauss was the largest employer in the predominantly white community of twenty thousand, about fifty miles from Nashville. "It was kind of a shock," said Steve Gregory, Hickman County's executive. "It was obviously devastating to lose almost four hundred jobs. Our unemployment rate shot up into double digits. A lot of my friends were out of a job and had to leave the area to find work."

Gregory said the liberal severance packages took the sting out of the plant closure for most workers, and anger against Levi Strauss was minimal and quickly subsided. But if Centerville, the county seat, wasn't exactly a company town, Levi Strauss was the cornerstone of the community. The company served as the major supporter of recreation and sports activities, and it sponsored educational programs in Centerville schools. Gregory's mother-in-law was typical of Levi's loyal workforce. She worked at the plant making blue jeans for thirty-two years, retiring months before the announcement of the shutdown. The area had already been hit hard by a number of other apparel factory closures when manufacturers took their business offshore, leaving Gregory with the task of filling the economic void. It wouldn't be a new apparel company. Sewing jobs were history.

As a parting gift—and no doubt a good tax write-off—Levi Strauss gave its 158,000-square-foot factory to the county, providing it with a strategic resource for economic development. Gregory was hoping to lure an electronics manufacturer to Centerville, thinking maybe a parts supplier to the new Dell Computer facility in Nashville would be a perfect fit for the nimble-fingered tailors and seamstresses on his unemployment rolls. But as luck would have it, a powerful tornado struck Centerville—and the abandoned Levi plant—in May 1999, destroying a third of the facility. "There has never been a sense of 'Woe is us' here," said Gregory. "This is all bad news, but we manage to suck up and keep going."

||||

All along, Levi Strauss officials insisted that the acrimonious San Antonio plant closure in 1990 was an anomaly. These new workforce reductions in 1998, they said, didn't mean jobs were being transplanted overseas. Rather, the plant closures reflected the problem of factory overcapacity at a time of decreasing demand for blue jeans in the North American market, which Levi Strauss in principle and in practice would continue to supply through local production.

That line had changed 180 degrees by February 1999, when the company disclosed a two-step plan to shut down yet another eleven plants—half of its remaining plants in North America—gutting its workforce by an additional 30 percent in eliminating 5,900 more jobs. In the early 1980s Levi Strauss owned and operated some fifty plants in the United States; now it had eleven left standing. The company offered the same generous severance package to newly terminated workers, but Levi Strauss no longer maintained the pretext that its production wasn't going to move offshore. Said John Ermatinger, president of Levi Strauss's American division: "Shifting a significant portion of our manufacturing for the U.S. and Canadian markets to contractors throughout the world will give the company greater flexibility to allocate resources and capital to its brands. These steps are crucial if we are to remain competitive."

Levi Strauss & Co. had at last come out of denial and acknowledged a strategic need to hollow out its high-wage American manufacturing base and complete the shift of production overseas. After resisting on principle for more than a decade, it now would embrace the graven image of globalization whole hog. "Levi Strauss threw in the towel against the global economy last week," piped an editorial in USA Today, which lauded the move and dismissed any criticism as "protectionism."

In disclosing the job cuts, the company conceded defeat in its noble effort to protect American jobs but pointed out with a display of tattered pride that it held out as long as it could. "LS&Co. is one of the last major U.S. clothing companies to maintain a sizeable North American owned-and-operated production base," said a company statement. "Virtually every major apparel company has eliminated, scaled back or never owned manufacturing facilities. This trend includes some of the largest names in the industry." Ermatinger added that efforts to improve productivity at North American factories had failed to "overcome the competitive disadvantage of the substantially higher costs" of operations.

Robert Haas put the matter more succinctly in his selected conversations with the media: "Certain kinds of work are not going to continue to be done in America," he told *The New York Times*. To his hometown newspaper, the *San Francisco Chronicle,* he explained, "We can't swim against the tide." Levi Strauss was to compete for survival as a rump marketing and design firm and leave most of the manufacturing to others.

The union representing most of the company's workers expressed a melancholy resignation to the inevitable. "The fact is, most garment manufacturing is geared toward a race to the bottom. Most of the companies that compete directly against Levi Strauss either haven't manufactured garments here for years or have never manufactured in North America," said Bruce Raynor, secretary-treasurer of the Union of Needletrades, Industrial and Textile Employees (UNITE). He cited the examples of Guess Inc., Ralph Lauren, Calvin Klein, and Tommy Hilfiger, all producing jeans offshore. "Clearly, Levi Strauss & Co. is under enormous competitive pressure, but we are saddened by their decision to join the race to the bottom."

Fuerza Unida's hyperbolic "worst nightmare" prophecy would come true, but not for Levi's inner family of owners and managers, as the union had hoped. It would be visited upon the stragglers of the U.S. apparel industry's blue-collar workforce, which was now written off as obsolete, a species doomed to irrelevance if not extinction in the age of the global marketplace. They would retrain and take new jobs, probably in the service industry and probably with lower wages and reduced medical benefits, like so many others before them. This conclusion might have been stalled off for a time, but the writing was on the wall, and it was in Spanish, Chinese, and Bahasa Indonesian.

It was also written in international trade treaties. The United States was a signatory to the Uruguay Round of the General Agreement on Tariffs and Trade, the treaty negotiations that created the global trade cop, the World Trade Organization (WTO). Under a WTO accord, quotas protecting the domestic apparel industry were to be phased out over a ten-year period and eliminated by the year 2005 for imports from WTO member nations. A separate agreement reduces U.S. tariffs on textiles and apparel imports from 17.2 percent to 15.2 percent over the same period. No big apparel company can afford to be caught entrenched in a high-cost U.S. manufacturing base when the quotas are gone and still expect to compete successfully against imports made by low-wage labor abroad.

Without the welfare of an American workforce to administer, Levi Strauss's noblesse oblige instincts for corporate social responsibility would have to play themselves out in the murky realm of human rights and labor standards at the factories of its foreign contractors.

The job of making Levi's products would fall almost exclusively on young foreign women—as young as fourteen years old—from poverty-stricken homes in Latin America and Asia. They would be Levi's new children, next in line as beneficiaries of a limited version of the company's famed paternalism. The news release on plant closures suggested as much, saying that contractors would be "bound by the company's stringent code of conduct" and reminding us that Levi Strauss was "the first multinational company of any industry to adopt universal guidelines covering issues such as working conditions, child labor and environmental standards."

This statement also revealed one more awkward detail: The humbled corporate giant now described itself as "*one* of the world's largest brand-name apparel *marketers*" (emphasis added)—abdicating its long-standing claim to be the "world's largest brand-name apparel manufacturer." Imagine Muhammad Ali conceding he was just one of the best entertainers in the boxing ring and no longer the champion, "the greatest." If the company still wished to claim distinction, it would have to act decisively as a leader in corporate accountability overseas and heed the admonition of Amnesty International's William Schultz to "prove to your business colleagues that it is possible to match honor to profit."

| | |

Levi Strauss never promised it would go bankrupt before compromising on its lofty principles. In fact, it was no stranger to outsourcing and offshore production when it capitulated in U.S. blue jeans production. Even before the drastic plant closures, about half of its products were being sewn and finished by independent contractors, at home and abroad. Since the 1970s the company's expanding production base had moved steadily overseas to manufacture clothing for sale in regional markets. With the rapid growth of its Dockers line of casual khaki pants and knit shirts, the percentage of Levi products made by independent contractors and sold in the United States surged from 35 percent in 1991 to 54 percent in 1992. In the case of Dockers, the fruits of cheap foreign labor contributed significantly to the competitive strength of that product line—and partially offset the disappointing performance in denim clothing. As blue jeans sales tanked in 1998, the company said Dockers enjoyed robust sales growth, the best year ever.

Levi Strauss found itself involved in a new jungle of ethical dilemmas as it intensified its activities overseas. Its values weren't necessarily shared by all its contractor-partners, and Peter Jacobi, then president for global sourcing, discovered as much when he visited these plants, according to one account. Jacobi noted that many of the contractors were competing fiercely with each other by cutting the costs of production, often at the workers' expense. The situation threatened to blemish the popular Levi's brand name, which had been nurtured so carefully over the years to represent a company with a conscience. Globalization presented a new challenge for management because revenues and profits soared at the same time the company was losing direct supervisory control of its production base and finding itself forced to work with a scattered patchwork of contractors, subcontractors, suppliers, and sourcing agents around the world.

One bad apple in the bunch—and there was certain to be more than one—had the potential of exposing the brand to damaging publicity. An allegation of complicity with child labor or some other human rights violation would be far more catastrophic to Levi Strauss than to most companies because it had raised the expectations so high by making it a company policy to practice virtue. It would imply sheer hypocrisy, not just ignorance or negligence with regard to the business practices of the errant contractor.

Because of the Levi penchant for opacity, it's difficult to say when this sense of foreboding accelerated to a critical point where action was required or whether there was a specific incident that jolted the company, reactively, into adopting a policy of prevention.

Publicly, the first big test case for the company came in 1991, when a labor abuse scandal brewing on the South Pacific island of Saipan begat allegations of "slave labor"—workers being forced to make clothing for major U.S. brands. Revelations about bonded laborers in the burgeoning sewing factories on Saipan would challenge the moral integrity of the globe-trotting U.S. apparel industry and its partnerships with Hong Kong, Taiwanese, and Korean contractors for years to come. Yet Levi Strauss—because it had a brand-new code of conduct to brandish when the scandal erupted into a media blitz in 1992—managed to escape the recriminations of human rights activists, even as it continued to have its clothing made on the island.

The allegations went as follows: Asian workers, mostly young women from poor regions of mainland China, toiled in conditions of "virtual slavery" on Saipan—the principal island of the U.S. Commonwealth of the Northern Mariana Islands (CNMI) in the South Pacific. They were making clothing for American companies, including Levi Strauss, Gap Inc., Ralph Lauren, Liz Claiborne, and other major brands. The scene emerging in Saipan foreshadowed the shock that would come later in California's El Monte "virtual slavery" case. Migrant workers, bonded by the up-front debts of securing labor contracts and air passage to "American soil" on Saipan, were living in squalid dormitories and forced to work marathon hours in factories with locked fire exits and unsanitary toilets. The workers were contained in factory compounds secured by armed guards and razor wire—the barbs pointing inward. Saipan, of course, is U.S. territory, and its sewing factories attach "Made in the USA" labels to their output.

The high-profile Saipan case marked the beginning of a new crusade for international labor and human rights organizations. It wasn't long before advocacy groups, digging up the dirt in the apparel and sports shoe industry's contractors around the world, sparked a feeding frenzy of "gotcha" investigative journalism in the news media. All it took was a tip from a local NGO and a quick visit by a camera crew to turn allegations of corporate irresponsibility into a juicy exposé for a prime-time TV news magazine. It was good for network ratings and helped the human rights advocates get much-needed public attention for their issues.

Violations of workers' rights by famous brand-name manufacturers became the topic of America's dinner conversations by the mid-1990s. Celebrities like Kathy Lee Gifford and Michael Jordan were caught in the embarrassing spotlight and pilloried for putting their names behind products allegedly made in sweatshops. Evidence of abusive child labor haunted Oriental rug retailers and soccer ball manufacturers. Nike was savagely satirized in the popular cartoon Doonesbury for its labor practices in Vietnam. Sordid allegations confronted Wal-Mart, the paragon of discount superretailing, which was wrapping itself sanctimoniously in a star-spangled "Buy America" campaign. The spectacle of American businesses soiling themselves through associations with human rights problems was squarely on the public agenda by the mid-1990s.

Yet Levi Strauss & Co. emerged largely unscathed from this maelstrom. The company enjoyed a considerable residue of goodwill from an ordinarily skeptical media because of its reputation for ethical integrity. The press gave Levi the benefit of the doubt on its social responsibility—even after it began wiping out U.S. production at the end of the decade.

| | |

To understand how the Levi's brand weathered the bad publicity storm of globalization throughout the 1990s, it's important to take a close look at events on Saipan back in 1991.

The leading man in this drama is Willie Tan, Saipan's putative garment king. Tan could also lay claim to being the quintessential Asian comprador of the 1990s. He is the dominant player in Saipan's major industry, garment stitching, which grew from practically nothing to more than $1 billion in revenues in little more than a decade. Tan is originally a Hong Kong businessman of Philippine birth, who acquired U.S. citizenship. His family operates businesses in Hong Kong and the Philippines in addition to Saipan, where it has interests in banks, shopping malls, and sewing factories that his critics describe as sweatshops. It was Tan's problems with the law that first sparked the furor over alleged labor peonage in the idyllic South Pacific island.

The term *comprador* dates back three hundred years to a pre-modern stage of globalization, when the European powers colonized Asia and made good use of savvy Chinese merchants as middlemen and managers in their economic conquests. By the latter half of the twentieth century ethnic Chinese family businesses in Hong Kong, Taiwan, and Southeast Asia had long outgrown the tutelage of their old Western imperialist masters and were engaging in business networks that moved massive amounts of goods and capital across the region and in and out of Communist China. Emulated by aggressive businessmen from South Korea, and their counterparts in Latin America, they served on the front lines of the "outsourcing" phenomenon in the garment, shoemaking, and toy industries. When U.S. manufacturers shut down costly production at their plants at home, they turned to the Asian compradors to take advantage of less costly labor and materials in developing economies.

The compradors assumed the risk by making capital investments and building factories in emerging markets. These countries may have been politically unstable or tainted by human rights violations, but they offered ample supplies of throw-away labor—typically in the form of unmarried young women migrating to the cities from rural poverty. This pattern was pronounced in the apparel and textile industries, where huge profit margins could be made from the differential between the cost of production in the Third World and the retail price of the finished brand-name product in the emporiums of affluent societies.

By 1992 Levi Strauss maintained relations with an estimated seven hundred such contractors and suppliers around the world. Because of its decentralized operations, devolving the responsibility for production decision to regional divisions, the company's global headquarters in San Francisco wasn't certain exactly how many contractors were producing Levi-branded products when they started taking a comprehensive look at the matter. While they paid strict attention to quality control at these plants, such issues as health, safety, and labor standards were generally left up to the partner. In that regard, Levi Strauss was acting much like any other multinational that relied on contract production overseas, apparently no better and no worse.

Top Levi executives, however, anticipated some of the problems to come. They understood intuitively that manufacturers could be held accountable, under a concept of joint moral liability, for the actions of their contractors. But it apparently took a scandal like Willie Tan's case in Saipan to fully dislodge complacency about the potential threat to the brand, and spur action.

Levi Strauss had found good value in having shirts for its Dockers line made in Saipan, using Tan's factories in addition to those of five other local contractors. Tan had not achieved the supertycoon status of many of the more celebrated ethnic Chinese entrepreneurs in Hong Kong's rag trade, but his business on Saipan is a classic study in how to engineer wealth out of scarcity. He and his fellow compradors shrewdly took advantage of the vagaries of global human resources and at the same time exploited a fluke of U.S. sovereignty.

The largest of a chain of fourteen islands located 1,500 miles south of Tokyo and 3,200 miles west of Honolulu, Saipan was occupied by Japan until it was wrested away by island-hopping U.S. Marines in bloody combat toward the end of World War II. Native residents, mostly indigenous Chamorros, chose to establish their government as a commonwealth of the United States in 1978. The new Commonwealth of the Northern Mariana Islands government later negotiated deals to gain U.S. citizenship for its residents, and in 1986 it struck a deal with Congress to control local immigration and set its own minimum wage standards. Ironically, local control of immigration was originally justified as a means of keeping Asian economic migrants out of the Northern Marianas. Much like Guam, its neighbor in the vast open seas of the South Pacific and also U.S. turf, Saipan is known for its idyllic tropical beaches and its resort scene, which is patronized by droves of Japanese and other Asian tour groups.

In the shadows of the tourism industry, sewing factories started sprouting like mushrooms in the late 1980s, made possible by a loophole in the local immigration law that allowed foreign contract workers to be imported en masse from such places as China and the Philippines. In a now familiar pattern, the migrant workers and their families go into hock to labor brokers for exorbitant fees, ostensibly paying for transport to choice factory jobs in America.

Factory owners like Willie Tan offer Saipan's version of the minimum wage—which was $2.12 an hour in 1991, $3.05 in 1999. The wage would outrage any self-respecting American trade unionist accustomed to the federally mandated $5.15 rate, but it is a fabulous windfall to destitute migrants from the Chinese countryside, where there is virtually no cash economy to speak of. The big benefit for factory owners is that they can legitimately sew "Made in the USA" labels in the garments they ship to the U.S. mainland, free of the import duties and quota allocations imposed on goods made by Chinese workers in China. Garment production promised to be the key to future prosperity in the isolated and lackluster economy of the Northern Marianas, where the majority of the labor force in the local Chamorro population is employed in government jobs. Indeed, production in the apparel industry was booming.

The problem started when local church people began hearing complaints about mistreatment of the guest workers and when human rights investigators started poking around they reported some serious abuses at the island's twenty-six factories—half of which were owned and operated by companies belonging to Willie Tan's family flagship, Tan Holdings Corporation. The bonded laborers were living and working in deplorable conditions, the allegations went. Overcrowded dormitories lacked proper sanitation, and factory floors were dirty and dangerous. It was evident that in many cases workers were held against their will, coerced into toiling overtime without fair compensation, and unable to change jobs or return home at their will—the compradors held their passports and return tickets. Reports abounded of workers being penalized or dismissed for attempting to file grievances with local labor authorities or organize union activities.

Responding to a rise in complaints, some dating back to the late 1980s, the U.S. Department of Labor launched an investigation in the summer of 1991 that resulted the following year in charges alleging that Tan owed nearly $10 million in back wages to 350 of his 1,500 workers. The federal Occupational Health and Safety Administration (OSHA) followed suit, finding "appalling living and working conditions" in Saipan sewing factory compounds and leveling nearly $250,000 in fines against Tan's companies for a range of health and safety violations, including five incidences of locked or blocked fire doors in factories and barracks deemed "willful."

By the time the federal charges came to light in early 1992 and ignited a scandal covered widely by the U.S. media, Levi Strauss was already sitting pretty.

The company had begun an exhaustive review of its contracting practices the previous summer, and it had convened a task force of fifteen senior executives in September—the Sourcing Guidelines Working Group—to draft a set of guidelines that would safeguard its reputation from the aspersions of labor activists. By this time, Levi Strauss had already learned about the pending federal investigation of Tan's operations on Saipan. The company's vice president for offshore operations, Iain Lyon, explored the legal allegations in a meeting with comprador Tan in San Francisco and confirmed the seriousness of the problem. The company's timing was incredibly fortuitous. When the sensational story of "slave labor" on Saipan became a red-hot story in the national news agenda in early 1992, Levi Strauss was able to announce that it had just developed an innovative code of conduct that now required its contractors to adhere to the company's own strict ethical standards.

The new instrument, published in March 1992, was the Global Sourcing Guidelines, Levi's much admired and emulated code of conduct. It had two parts: the Business Partner Terms of Engagement and the Guidelines for Country Selection. These guidelines were unprecedented—the first corporate code of conduct that addressed the rules of engagement with outside contractors, committing the company in principle to taking moral responsibility for the activities of its business partners, even where no specific legal responsibility could be claimed. In its first application, the document was used as justification to summarily cut off Levi's contractual relationship with Willie Tan.

Levi's code marked a historic precedent for corporate governance because it established, in plain language, that the company bore a degree of responsibility for the actions of foreign business partners in whom it had no equity interests. This gave meat and bones to the theoretical concept of joint moral liability. Specifically, the Levi code established criteria that its partners must have "ethical standards not incompatible with our own," that they must be "law abiding" and ensure that workers are "present voluntarily, not put at risk of physical harm, fairly compensated, allowed the right to free association and not exploited in any way."

A team of Levi Strauss investigators went to Saipan and detected substandard conditions at the housing Tan provided his workers but found no evidence of coerced labor at his factory operations. The Tan factory making Levi's brand clothing actually passed muster, comparing favorably with some plants in the United States. But company inspectors learned that Tan had "consistently misled" Levi officials about his business practices, which was sufficient grounds to cancel contracts under the new guidelines. A Tan factory in the Philippines was also cut off. To act on its principles, the company had to pay Tan Holdings contract penalties amounting to several hundred thousand dollars.

It hasn't been revealed what conditions were like at the factories of the other five Saipan contractors making Levi products. Credible reports indicate that nearly all the sewing contractors on Saipan were using bonded foreign labor at that time and continue to do so now. Was Tan a convenient scapegoat, whose purge deflected attention from more serious and enduring human rights problems on Saipan? Recruiting indentured workers was and remains perfectly legal under Saipan's local labor laws, but that would not necessarily make it morally palatable to consumers if they were aware of the general conditions under which their "Made in the USA" Dockers tops were produced. But the in-house arbiters of Levi's new code of conduct were apparently confident that they could enforce compliance with its standards, thereby reconciling the extremely high risk of exploitation in the practice of bonded labor with the company's moral obligation to ensure that the workers were present "voluntarily" and "allowed the right of free association."

Miraculously unbloodied by the Saipan scandal, Levi Strauss went on the offensive to safeguard the integrity of its brand—or, at least, the public perception of that integrity. The company quickly announced it would undertake a massive review of its other partners in Asia and Latin America under the new Global Sourcing Guidelines. In an initial round of audits, it found 70 percent of its contractors to be in compliance with its code and another 25 percent to be in tolerable need of improvement. Contracts were severed with the remaining 5 percent. Annual audits of the contractors followed, bolstering the company's image of accountability, though the results of these audits or the names and locations of the factories were not publicly disclosed.

The auditing was part of a calculated business—and a public relations—strategy that the text of the Levi guidelines makes no bones about. "Levi Strauss & Co. has a heritage of conducting business in a manner that reflects its values," intones the preamble to the 1992 code. "As we expand our sourcing base to more diverse cultures and countries, we must take special care in selecting business partners and countries whose practices are not incompatible with our values. Otherwise, our sourcing decisions have the potential of undermining this heritage, damaging the image of our brands and threatening our commercial success."

Levi Strauss & Co. and the rhetoric of its new Global Sourcing Guidelines code clearly emerged triumphant from the tawdry story of labor peonage in tropical paradise. Its groundbreaking country selection code, which prohibited doing business in countries with "pervasive human rights violations," was revolutionary. It would be the reason for pulling out of Burma later that year and cited again, rather ham-handedly, in leaking the decision to begin a phased withdrawal from China the following year. Levi Strauss positioned itself as a righteous gladiator for the defense of human rights—or so it seemed.

As for Willie Tan, he settled with the Labor Department and paid some $9 million in back wages to current and former workers. OSHA's charges against him were dropped after he agreed to make $1.3 million in factory repairs and pay $73,000 in fines. A Tan Holdings subsidiary, American International, pleaded no contest to felony charges of falsifying government documents relating to overtime hours and agreed to pay a $500,000 fine. But Tan is more powerful now than ever before—and so is the Saipan garment industry. Tan and the Saipan's Garment Manufacturers Association have exercised tremendous influence by lobbying the federal government in Washington. Saipan's leaders offered controversial junkets at luxury resort hotels to sympathetic members of Congress, overcoming harsh criticism from irate officials in the Departments of Labor and Interior.

Consider what's at stake: Saipan in 1991 had close to a 14 percent unemployment rate among local residents, but it also had a promising new industry that could lift it out of the economic doldrums. Its sewing factories had imported about 3,000 contract workers and shipped some $270 million worth of goods to the U.S. mainland. By the end of 1998 those shipments had increased to more than $1 billion in value. Estimates of the number of foreign contract workers on the island had increased more than tenfold to as high as 40,000, vastly outnumbering the 27,478 local residents counted in a 1995 census. But they were invisible, tucked away in jungle labor camps out of sight of the local Chamorros, who shun the factory jobs, and the sun-worshiping resort patrons. "When they're here, they learn about free enterprise, democracy—they become goodwill ambassadors of our precepts of democracy," said Robert J. O'Conner, a lawyer for Tan Holdings, in describing the benefits for bonded foreign workers to *The New York Times*.

| | |

Complaints of inhumane living conditions and labor exploitation on Saipan were continuing apace at the time of this writing. The U.S. official with chief responsibility for the Northern Marianas, Alan Stayman, insular affairs director of the U.S. Department of the

Interior, was particularly outspoken in his criticism. "The local immigration and labor departments are essentially organized crime," Stayman said in an interview with *Time* magazine. "It is one big scam."

Stayman's agency was waging virtual war with the Northern Marianas government, issuing annual reports condemning the "indentured alien worker program" and advocating that the U.S. government reassert its authority over immigration and minimum wage laws on the islands. While defenders of Saipan's apparel industry described the labor practices as an exemplary model of successful free-market economics, Stayman's agency was documenting its egregious abuses.

"The CNMI continues to have difficulty protecting the rights and welfare of the indentured alien workers," said the 1998 Office of Insular Affairs report. It cited examples of "hundreds of alien workers [who] have fallen victim to illegal and fraudulent recruitment scams where they pay large sums of money to fraudulent recruiters only to arrive in the CNMI to find there are no jobs." Some of those who have jobs experience "payless paydays" in which "employers fail to pay the correct wages or do not pay their workers at all." Many of the bonded workers are "virtually prisoners, confined to their barracks during non-working hours," the report said. "Young female nightclub workers from the Philippines have been forced to engage in prostitution."

An outraged Representative George Miller, a Democrat from California, and his allies in Congress held hearings and introduced legislation that would mandate labor reform in the Northern Marianas, charging that a "systematic pattern of violations of labor rights and human rights is continuing in the Marianas in disregard to concerns voiced by human rights activists, labor unions, religious organizations, federal enforcement and oversight agencies and the U.S. Congress."

But the commonwealth's efforts to lobby key Republican representatives appeared to bear fruit. Miller reintroduced his legislation on Saipan in 1999, but it was, for all intents and purposes, stillborn—one of those high-minded gestures at lawmaking referred to in Washingtonian parlance as a "talking bill," with little prospect of being taken up for open debate on the floor of the House of Representatives, let alone passage.

Meanwhile, Levi Strauss & Co. continued quietly sourcing its branded clothing products in Saipan, despite occasional replaying of the 1992 scandal as human rights investigators and the news media unearthed new evidence of abuse in the island's sewing factories. Levi Strauss was once again spared notoriety when, in January 1999, a coalition of labor activists, lawyers, and human rights advocates grabbed headlines with a civil racketeering suit claiming more than $1 billion in damages from a group of major U.S. apparel makers and retailers for allegedly conspiring to violate labor rights in Saipan. In twin federal class action lawsuits backed by a companion suit filed in the California Superior Court, the plaintiffs claimed the apparel companies and the sewing factory owners were engaged in a "garment production system on United States of America soil based upon peonage and involuntary servitude, under which tens of thousands of foreign guest workers, primarily young women, work for subsistence wages in unlawful sweatshop conditions."

The legal argument behind these suits tested whether the moral accountability implied by the codes of the companies could be elevated to *joint legal liability* for the alleged transgressions of their compradors. The suits named as defendants some very prominent companies, including Gap Inc., Nordstrom Inc., Tommy Hilfiger USA, Oshkosh B'Gosh, and Wal-Mart stores.

Among the eighteen Saipan contractors named in the litigation was at least one of the factories used by Levi Strauss to make Dockers shirts, owned by the South Korean firm Sako Corp. A report by the Oakland-based advocacy group Sweatshop Watch—one of the NGOs behind the Saipan racketeering litigation—had voiced earlier allegations that Korean managers hurled intimidating insults at the Filipina, Chinese, and Thai workers at the Sako plant, denied them sick leave, occasionally forced them to work more than one hundred hours a week, and penalized or terminated workers for engaging in union-organizing activities.

The U.S. Equal Employment Opportunity Commission investigated these claims and sought a federal court injunction preventing Sako from terminating a whistle-blower, Carmencita Abad, a

Manila seamstress who had worked since 1993 as an assistant supervisor at the plant. The agency filed two civil rights lawsuits against Sako in July 1999, one in connection with the attempt at firing Abad and the other alleging that Sako discriminated against female workers by denying them maternity benefits. Abad claims the management demoted her in 1997 after she helped organize a union vote, which she said failed because of threats against job security, and then fired her after she continued to file labor grievances. "Everybody was working too hard and too long," she said, describing the violations of local labor standards. Following the class action suit, Abad, now thirty-eight, came to the U.S. mainland, where she is an angry voice in the antisweatshop movement.

Abad said bonded Chinese employees were confined within the barbed-wire compound, though she and other Filipina workers were free to live outside the gates. But setting aside the questions of labor peonage, the alleged conditions at Sako would be at odds with the Levi Strauss terms of engagement, which Abad said was not posted in the plant for workers to see. Sako's largest client was Gap, whose code of conduct was prominently displayed, and contained this freedom of association clause: "Gap Inc. believes workers should be free to join organizations of their own choosing. Business partners may neither threaten nor penalize employees for their efforts to organize or bargain collectively." But these lofty principles were written only in English—unintelligible to Chinese, Thai, and Vietnamese workers. Abad thinks that despite her troubles, Sako compares favorably with most of the other plants on Saipan.

Levi Strauss was not named as a defendant in the racketeering litigation along with Gap—which activists say accounts for a quarter of Saipan's apparel production—and the other major brands. The explanation for the Gap's exposure to negative publicity and Levi's Houdini-like escape from notoriety, according to knowledgeable sources, is that Levi's main U.S. union, UNITE, was the lead plaintiff in the companion suit filed in California. The union had entered into a "partnership agreement" with Levi in 1994 in which Levi Strauss agreed voluntarily to recognize UNITE as the bargaining agent at any plant where the union demonstrated majority support. The agreement also contained a provision that could be interpreted to mean that no legal action can be taken against the company without first exhausting a process of collaborative consultation and arbitration.

By midyear four of the retailers named in the lawsuit—Nordstrom, J. Crew, Cutter & Buck, and Gymboree—had agreed to settle out of court, without admitting any wrongdoing. They were to pay bonded workers some $1.25 million to compensate them for the recruitment fees extracted by labor brokers and allow independent monitoring at the Saipan factories where they had supply contracts. Several other companies were negotiating a similar settlement. But Gap, and some of the more prominent defendants, were not involved in the discussions.

Levi Strauss said it wasn't targeted in the litigation because of the strengths of its stringent auditing process. "I don't think we were lucky," said Clarence Grebey, who represented Levi as director of global communications before he left the company in mid-1999. "I think our record speaks for itself." A Levi Strauss internal audit of the Sako factory in April 1999 revealed no irregularities, he said. The company's message is that it should be taken on faith that Sako and the other remaining Levi's contractors on Saipan are in satisfactory compliance with the code's terms of engagement—even if this cannot be verified externally since the results of the audits are proprietary. How can a record speak for itself, as Grebey suggested, when it is under wraps?

The company's reaction to the latest Saipan furor reflected an attitude of confidence bordering on smugness. The continuing and unresolved allegations of rampant labor abuse were—for now, at least—other people's problems. Grebey said the company had already begun tapering down its business on Saipan out of concern for "general conditions" on the island. It had reduced production levels by 47 percent from 1997 to 1999, he said, down to three million units a year. "The long-term risk in Saipan is to our brand, should it be embroiled in this kind of political quagmire," Grebey said. "For us it makes more sense to get out of there."

Aside from the labor ethics quagmire, phasing out of Saipan makes perfect business sense on a traditional cost-benefit basis. When U.S. textile quotas are eliminated in the year 2005, apparel production in the Northern Marianas will lose much of its competitive edge in the global division of labor. It will still enjoy the privilege of attaching the "Made in the USA" label to its products and will remain a tax haven for the purposes of dodging import tariffs. Assuming China becomes a member of the WTO by then and is freed of onerous quotas on apparel exports to the U.S. market, however, there will be little incentive to transport Chinese farm girls to Saipan and pay them five times the wages they'd earn back home to stitch clothing. Contractors like Sako can be expected to pick up and take their sewing machines to a more beneficial labor market—as Abad said managers threatened to do before the failed vote on union representation. Many of the Asian compradors already have facilities up and running in Latin America and the Caribbean, where the shorter delivery cycle will help restore their competitiveness and where Levi is shifting its domestic production.

Meanwhile, the company exuded confidence that intensified training and monitoring of its code would sufficiently safeguard the Levi's brand on Saipan. Inspectors are now conducting monthly audits of contractors' payroll records to ensure wages and hours are in compliance. The company can live with Saipan's practices of importing indentured labor, so long as it is legal under local law and Levi's contractors are not caught violating the rights of workers. Grebey quipped: "They're not shackled in their dormitories."

|||

The situation on Saipan, like the outrage in El Monte, may be an extreme example of mean-spiritedness and cynicism in the workplace, but it is, sadly, not as isolated as one might hope. In the demimonde of overseas industrial outsourcing, which thrives largely out of reach from effective regulatory protections for workers, labor abuse is simply rampant. The systematic violation of fundamental human rights, in far too many places, is customary.

Levi Strauss has escaped the negative publicity that hounded many of its fellow apparel firms, but it has hardly been a stranger to the aspersions of human rights critics. Global Exchange, a San Francisco advocacy group that had emerged battle hardened from high-profile assaults against Nestlé and Nike, was one of the few groups to take the initiative with Levi Strauss. It launched a low-key protest campaign appealing to a network of university campus activists, which for a troubled fashion company struggling with the loss of its youth market threatened to hit Levi's below the belt. Global Exchange did not call specifically for a boycott, and there's no evidence suggesting the campaign had any direct effect on sales. But the broader issue of sweatshop abatement caught on like wildfire on American campuses, with student activists demanding that university administrators adopt codes of conduct on labor standards for the licensees who manufacture for the lucrative market in college brand goods.

Meanwhile, Global Exchange's campaign against Levi Strauss faded into the background as the group shifted its focus to a better target: Gap Inc. A publicly traded company like Gap was far more useful in the campaign against sweatshops because of its fiduciary obligations of disclosure and transparency. Gap was not only an extremely successful brand, it had lots of storefronts across the nation to picket.

Levi Strauss was not entirely off the hook. Other advocacy groups had been monitoring the company's track record on compliance with its code of conduct and issuing damning allegations on labor irregularities at Levi contractor facilities in Asia and Latin America. A Catholic NGO in Canada, Development and Peace, targeted Levi Strauss and Nike in an educational campaign probing the effects of globalization on workers in developing societies. In 1995 the group investigated the operations of a South Korean contractor, Seolim, in the Inhdelva Free Trade Zone in Honduras, uncovering a number of practices violating the Levi code and allegedly inconsistent with local law. Researchers found that seventy-five- to eighty-hour workweeks were typical; the Levi's code sets a limit of sixty hours per week. Wages averaged 43 cents an hour, and workers were not aware of the existence of Levi's code. When Levi Strauss representatives visited the plant, they spoke only to managers, ignoring the operators on the factory floor. Britain's *Sunday Telegraph* also examined conditions at the Seolim plants and claimed to have found evidence of children as young as eleven years old working at the facilities.

The Canadian group's report cites the testimony of Zoila Graciela Gomez, a fifteen-year-old seamstress making Dockers shirts at a Seolim plant, who claims she was physically beaten on three occasions and verbally abused before she was fired, receiving a severance pay of about $50. "Two of my pieces, attaching the neck, came out bad, and the Korean named Miss Woo threw the two shirts in my face, then hit me hard in the back. She had also done the same thing before, locking me in the kitchen and hitting me with a hard blow on my back and slapping me in the face," the girl told Development and Peace investigators. "The third time she did the same thing, locking me in the kitchen, pulling my hair, and saying to me, 'Get out of here, useless shit.'"

The following year, Development and Peace researchers found problems at the Noveca Industries plant in the Philippines, near Manila, which did all of its contract work for Levi Strauss. Men toiling in the laundry department reportedly complained of being required to work interminable shifts, typically as long as sixteen hours a day and sometimes around the clock. The report also cites alleged cases of underpayments on wages and termination for employees refusing to work overtime. "Workers are haunted by the fear of losing their jobs," the report said. "What they fear above all else is being fired for union-organizing-related activities." Prior to scheduled visits by Levi Strauss code compliance inspectors, the report maintains, employees were instructed to clean up the plants, masking underlying problems.

Levi Strauss has acknowledged "allegations that certain of our Guidelines were being violated" at the Philippine plant in 1996 but does not elaborate. The company insists it conducted "a number of surprise visits to the Noveca facility over the period 1996–1998," without prior notice to plant management. The inspections revealed "a number of what we call *Continuous Improvement* items" of code violation—meaning that these minor problems could be fixed. But it did not find more serious violations worthy of immediate action or that crossed the zero-tolerance threshold.

Jacques Bertrand, in charge of Development and Peace's advocacy and research programs at its Montreal office, said he organized a protest campaign that delivered 124,000 signed postcards to chair-

SLAVES TO FASHION | 73

man Robert Haas, advocating a more open accounting of compliance with the company's code. The group advocated what had become a common view in the larger advocacy community, that merely having a good code of conduct was not enough—it had to be monitored independently and transparently with the involvement of local groups to be effective. "Levi Strauss would actually benefit if it were able to count on independent monitoring of its code," concludes the Noveca case study. "These workers quite naturally associate Levi's representatives with their own employer—whom they fear. They are far more likely to trust the representatives of independent local organizations. Independent monitoring would therefore strengthen Levi Strauss's efforts and it would prove to workers that Levi's is doing its best to ensure compliance with its codes."

Gordon Shank, then president of Levi's Canada, stated the company policy in a letter to Bertrand: "Levi Strauss personnel are in a better position than anyone to monitor our guidelines and ensure that they are complied with." Shank would later rise to the position of president of Levi's Americas division. Bertrand felt betrayed by the response he got from Levi's management. "I think 'recalcitrant' is a good way to describe their attitude. I think we were seen as a public relations problem. At no point did they try to show us or convince us they were doing something to address the problems in their factories," he said. "That was disappointing because of their good reputation. We thought that if any company would go along with independent monitoring, it would be Levi's."

The Dutch antisweatshop advocacy group Clean Clothes Campaign (CCC) issued a scathing report on Levi Strauss in May 1998. Again, the accusation was lax enforcement of its code of conduct. The report alleged widespread violations of the code—underpayment, excessive work hours, denial of the right to free association—citing the research its own investigators conducted in cooperation with SOMO, another Dutch NGO, at Levi contractor plants in Indonesia, Bangladesh, and Sri Lanka.

Two years after Levi's code went into effect, workers making Levi's and Dockers brand clothing at the Duta Busana Danastri's factory in Jakarta filed complaints with Indonesia's Human Rights

National Commission, alleging they had been subjected to strip searches by factory security guards, in addition to complaining about substandard wages and poor working conditions, said the CCC report. Only after the grievance about the strip searches was disclosed in the local media did Levi cancel its contracts with the offending company, according to news reports. In fact, the Levi Strauss inspector responsible, Im Choong Hoe, told *The Wall Street Journal* in 1994 he was stunned himself to learn about the abuses so soon after he had visited the plant and given it a clean bill of health. The strip searches, it turns out, were performed by managers to verify whether seamstresses were menstruating when claiming a paid day off, a benefit they are entitled to under Indonesia's Islamic-influenced labor law. "Given the time constraints and the need for diplomacy, [Hoe] is resigned to missing abuses—and to periodic embarrassments," the article said, offering the Singaporean inspector—and Levi Strauss—a generous benefit of the doubt.

The CCC alliance expanded its inquiry into Levi's code compliance, sending its agents to Africa, Eastern Europe, and South Asia. It alleges that it uncovered evidence that personnel at Levi's plant in Poland had never heard of the Global Sourcing Guidelines. Workers making Levi products at the Korea Lanka factory in Sri Lanka toiled seven days a week with no knowledge of the Levi code, it claimed. The controversial report betrayed some slipshod methodology when it claimed investigators found evidence of bonded Chinese labor making Levi products at an unnamed Italian-owned contractor on the island of Mauritius—implying a situation similar to that in the notorious Saipan case.

What followed was a characteristic display of the kind of dysfunctional communication that too often underscores the emotional dialogue between human rights advocates and the corporations they assail.

Levi Strauss reacted by digging in its heels. Patrick Neyts, director of environment, health, and safety for the company's European, Middle East, & Africa division, shot back with a point-by-point rebuttal of many of CCC's allegations. He outlined the rigorous program of mandatory training for employees at the Polish plant and charged that the company had never done business with Korea

Lanka and some of the other contractors cited by CCC. "Your paper contains a series of inaccuracies, unsupported allegations and erroneous statements that convey a misleading portrayal of our company and the actions we have taken over the years," Neyts wrote to the NGO. He said that Levi Strauss had no information about a contractor on Mauritius and asked for details so the company could investigate.

The Dutch NGO answered Neyts's rebuttal with counteraccusations, standing by the integrity of its research. But CCC representatives informed company spokesman Alan Christie they must postpone a proposed meeting with Levi's officials because they were "in solidarity" with striking workers protesting Levi's plans to close factories in Belgium and France. Until the meeting could be rescheduled, they suggested the company consider signing a "Declaration of Intent," agreeing with CCC's terms that it commit to such things as bringing Levi's guidelines into conformity with the International Labor Organization's more stringent code and subject itself to independent monitoring. Tellingly, CCC never got around to posting Neyts's rebuttal or its own glandular response to it in the section of the activist group's Internet Web site devoted to the Levi Strauss campaign, along with the original damning report and other articles critical of the company. CCC's Nina Ascoly, who edited the Levi case study, said the original intent was to post the documents side by side on the site, but that the on-line campaign was "lagging output on paper" because of shortage in staff.

Likewise, Levi Strauss, which cannot blame a lack of resources for the omission, does not post Neyts's rebuttal on its corporate Web site. In fact, it makes no mention at all of Clean Clothes Campaign and its case study or any other critic of its human rights and labor policies—in contrast with the Web sites of other major corporations like Unocal and Nike. Levi Strauss displays its celebrated code of conduct on its electronic forum and talks about its tradition for corporate social responsibility. But the site does not betray a hint of controversy.

A lot of the conflicting assertion of facts in the Levi-CCC dialogue might be explained in one word: counterfeiting. The production of counterfeit Levi's jeans is an industry on its own right in

Asia, and that would explain why investigators uncovered transgressions in plants that the company had never heard of—and cannot be expected to monitor for compliance with its code. A photograph of a pair of Levi's jeans supplied as evidence by CCC revealed the trousers as obvious fakes: the rear belt-line patch depicting the two plow horses bore little resemblance to the genuine trademark.

CCC's methodology was clearly shoddy, undermining the credibility of its indictment. But the group managed to make at least one valid point: A lot of suspicion could be cleared up by greater transparency on the part of Levi Strauss. "A gap remains between what is on paper, what is portrayed in public, and what occurs in practice. By positioning itself as a 'trailblazer' in the pursuit of a higher level of corporate responsibility, Levi Strauss & Co. invites a high level of scrutiny," the CCC report said. "While Levi Strauss & Co. has led the industry by drafting standards for a company with a social conscience to follow, they now have the opportunity to stay ahead of their competition by upgrading, implementing and upholding them to the fullest extent. This would truly distinguish their brand in the most positive of ways."

Chapter Three

| | |

East of the Equator

It is not power that corrupts but fear. Fear of losing power corrupts those who wield it and fear of the scourge of power corrupts those who are subject to it.

—Aung San Suu Kyi, *Freedom from Fear*

A casual visitor to Shwe Dagon Pagoda in the Burmese capital of Rangoon finds it isn't easy to penetrate the meaning of this post-card wonder. After scaling a long flight of pitched stairs to the top of Singuttara Hill, where the nation's most sacred Buddhist shrine presides over the skyline, one encounters a visual challenge of shape and movement. At first exposure, it takes a tremendous amount of energy just to *see* the temple, to comprehend its form.

From a distance, Shwe Dagon offers a glittering navigational land-mark for the city, a golden bell-shaped tower topped by a diamond orb on a jeweled vane. Up close, standing squarely on the marble plaza from which the monolith arises, the scene is both soothing and chaotic, suggesting a fitting metaphor for an impoverished nation at calm and in crisis. The stupa is partly shrouded by scaffolding as arti-sans apply a new layer of precious gold leaf, and it is surrounded by a multicolored riot of *zedi* subtemples and altars and smoky incense burners, all arrayed haphazardly along wavy lines around the platform. Enshrined beneath the pagoda's octagonal pedestal are eight hairs from the scalp of the historic Buddha, Siddhartha Gautama, the story goes. Barefoot worshipers in traditional *longyi* cotton skirts—only soldiers and foreigners wear men's trousers in Burma—shuffle clockwise in hushed reverence, orbiting this most sacred temple.

It is a cooling twilight after a miserably hot, sultry October day. A pair of cheerful young monks in tattered burgundy robes approach an American visitor, one of only a handful of foreign tourists in the turning prayer wheel of the crowd. The more outgoing of the two explains they are pilgrims to Shwe Dagon from a monastery in the countryside, and he wishes to practice his English—which he taught himself by listening clandestinely to Voice of America on the monastery radio. As they chat, strolling clockwise around the giant golden stupa, a small group of giggling young women joins them, describing themselves as students preparing for a rigorous government examination for credentials as tour guides. Thrilled to have found a rare solo foreigner, they describe the Buddhist myths represented in the clusters of statuary arrayed on the base of the pagoda, using determined tour guide English.

As they stroll, a tall young man, a university student, follows along and interjects himself in the group's animated discussion, which turns to the themes of ordinary life in Burma. The American—a journalist who had entered Burma surreptitiously on a tourist visa—ponders how lucky it is to have stumbled into this spontaneous focus group of young Burmese. How sweet these people are, how innocent.

But suddenly, just as the fading light casts a final reddish hue on the pagoda, their strolling stops, and the conversation halts. In an awkward moment, nervous eyes dart about, seeking clues from the attitudes of the others, the monks, the girls, and the tall student. They all see that the stranger has taken out a notebook and asked the student—too bluntly—why he is no longer attending classes at his university. The student steps back, wincing, and says hesitatingly in a low voice: "There are a lot of mosquitoes around here. I must say good-bye." He smiles and walks away, slowly, in step with the circumambulating worshipers. The monks and the girls say polite farewells and scatter. The stranger is left standing alone and perplexed, as darkness descends on Shwe Dagon.

| | |

Burma has two kinds of mosquitoes. There are the pesky little tropical bugs that bite you at dusk, and there are the ubiquitous undercover intelligence agents and police informants who trail foreigners and keep fellow citizens on their toes—especially students. The conversation at Shwe Dagon took on a whiff of danger because the government had once again closed the universities, fearing students might cause unrest on the tenth anniversary of the 1988 bloody crackdown on political dissent. The memory of that grotesque event is a deep wound, left festering beneath the surface of a deceivingly placid society.

Burma, at the turn of the century, was a baffling place. It was populated by beguilingly gentle and intelligent people who were mired in backward preindustrial poverty under the boot of an insufferable military junta, which funded itself partly through illegal drug trafficking. It was, in the words of one Western diplomat in Rangoon, the "human rights poster child." Burma was a storybook land of nostalgic exotica and political terror that evoked intense passions around the world. It had a heroine, Aung San Suu Kyi, who had been awarded the Nobel Peace Prize for her extraordinary courage in the face of tyranny. She was, in effect, a genuine princess—the daughter of the country's most revered independence leader and nationalist, General Aung San. He became modern Burma's father, the first president after liberation from British colonial rule, only to be assassinated in 1948.

Some forty years after the great man's martyrdom, his daughter returned from exile in Britain, electrifying a restless people with her seemingly inherited charismatic traits. In 1990 she defied the odds by leading the upstart National League for Democracy (NLD) to victory in the polls, only to have the results of the parliamentary election abrogated by the military government. She was detained in her family compound for six years and released at last after an international outcry but was still being badgered in public and kept under virtual house arrest. Suu Kyi's efforts to develop a pluralistic society and a viable political opposition were being crushed, mercilessly, by the military. Some two hundred members of her party had been jailed. The streets leading to her compound and to NLD party headquarters were barricaded under heavy police guard.

Human rights advocates liked to call Burma the "South Africa of the 1990s," and although the comparison may be stretched in terms of magnitude, it was clear there were few mitigating factors in the state of political siege. After twenty-six years of isolation under strongman General Ne Win and his ruinous "Burmese way" ideology of socialist autarky, the aging dictator stepped aside in 1988, allowing his stunted nation to open its economy to the outside world. But hope for a restoration of civil society vanished quickly when the army cracked down on prodemocracy demonstrators, shooting the throngs of people it accused of fomenting antigovernment riots. Under international pressure, the twenty-one–man junta in power— the State Law and Order Restoration Council (SLORC)—staged the 1990 elections in a bid for legitimacy but rejected the unanticipated results: a landslide victory for Suu Kyi's opposition party.

In protest, multilateral lending institutions and the leading donor nations, with Japan following the U.S. lead, froze development aid programs for the Rangoon government, which had by now renamed the distressed nation Myanmar.

Suu Kyi took a cue from the strategies of South African opposition leaders Nelson Mandela and Archbishop Desmond Tutu, who had successfully used the tactic of international economic sanctions to help force the apartheid regime to reform. The inspiration came from the Reverend Leon H. Sullivan, the American author of the Sullivan Principles, who preached the idea that the ethical obligations of foreign investors extend far beyond their fiduciary duty to earn profits for investors and owners back home. Sullivan's moral manifesto would evolve into a radical theoretical realm, maintaining that those corporations who capitalize on economic opportunities in developing economies without using their influence actively to reform authoritarian regimes are, in effect, legitimizing and abetting tyranny and helping to perpetuate a social evil. It was a short step from that point to demand economic sanctions and corporate withdrawal.

Human rights NGOs took up Suu Kyi's cause with campaigns targeting private investment and joined her in urging major international firms to pull out of Burma. The rationale was simple: Foreign investment served only to prop up the ruling junta and perpetuate the misery of ordinary people. In a clandestine interview with a *Business Week* reporter in 1998, during a period of severe government restrictions on the international media, Suu Kyi reiterated her message to potential investors: "We want investment to be at the right time—when the benefits will go to the people of Burma, not just a small, select elite connected to the government. We do not think investing at this time really helps the people of Burma. It provides the military regime with a psychological boost. If companies from Western democracies are prepared to invest under these circumstances, then it gives the military regime reason to think that they can continue violating human rights because even Western business companies don't mind."

| | |

Levi Strauss & Co. was one of the first major American companies to act. In 1992 it pulled the plug on its business in Burma, where it contracted production with two local factories—both connected to the Burmese military regime. Unlike the company's action in China the following year, when it stood alone, the retreat from Burma would be followed by the voluntary withdrawal of a succession of major American firms. Advocates would point to Levi Strauss as the model for corporate human rights policy in the rogue nation, and Levi's strategy of protecting its brand from needless exposure to the evils of the Rangoon regime resonated with other multinationals. The decision to withdraw from Burma was the first implementation of the "country selection" clause of Levi's newly revealed code of conduct, which specifically proscribed doing business in countries with pervasive human rights violations. If Burma didn't meet that criteria, no country would.

The company explained it this way: "Under current circumstances, it is not possible to do business in Myanmar without directly supporting the military government and its pervasive violations of human rights." Shielding the brand reputation from problems with labor standards at the factories of local contractors might also have been taken into consideration, as well as the indirect effects that the country's political tyranny might have had on business operations.

Leaving Burma was a decision that could not be refuted easily on a cost-benefit basis. The advantages of sourcing products in Burma's textile and garment industries did not compare favorably with those operating in other regional markets once you take into account the handicaps to the industry inflicted by nearly three decades of Ne Win's lunatic economic policies. At the same time, the political risk and the potential cost to the Levi brand image was tremendous. The growth potential of the consumer market was not particularly bright. Levi's signature blue jeans were not going to sell well in the wretchedly humid climate, where few men wear pants anyway. Other Levi apparel, tropical-weight Dockers shirts and trousers, might have an appeal. But Burmese consumers, struggling for survival without cash to spend, had developed a habit of dressing themselves in Western fashions from bales of cheap used clothing imported in bulk from Asian neighbors.

Ironically, since Levi Strauss unceremoniously extracted itself from Burma, the local apparel industry has picked up steam. Imports of garments made in Burma to the United States more than doubled between 1995 and 1998, topping $110 million for the year, according to the National Labor Committee, a labor rights advocacy group. The volume is still relatively tiny by global trade standards, but perhaps it's only a matter of time before human rights watchdogs start the hunt for "Made in Myanmar" labels in U.S. emporiums and denounce those caught red-handed.

Levi Strauss's simple decision on Burma would contrast sharply with the complex deliberations over withdrawing from China the following year. The Chinese economy was growing by double digits at the time. No one doubted that Chinese consumers had a voracious appetite for Western branded goods. Purely on the basis of a cost-benefit analysis, the argument in favor of walking away from China had to be a tortured one. Burma was a no-brainer.

Does this inconsistency in Levi's policy equate to hypocrisy or pragmatism? The Burmese need apparel industry jobs far more than the Chinese to lift themselves out of preindustrial destitution. Yet observing the taboo on doing business in Burma was a relatively painless way to act "responsibly" on human rights.

One by one, other major U.S. multinationals bowed to public pressure—and the realities of limited business prospects in Burma. Levi Strauss was the only company, however, that stated explicitly that human rights was the reason for leaving.

Firms such as Motorola, Eddie Bauer, and Liz Claiborne put up little fight. Why pay the price of negative publicity for the difficulty of doing business in this backward country and for the paltry returns this market promises? PepsiCo was a bit more reluctant to cave in to criticism by the human rights activists. Pepsi had bested archrival Coca-Cola to set up a joint-venture bottling plant in Burma, gaining a strategic foothold in a thirsty subtropical market with a population of forty-six million. But it finally capitulated to the advocacy furor after unstinting bad publicity and the threat of a boycott campaign. Riding on popular sentiment, Congress passed legislation in 1997 imposing formal economic sanctions that effectively banned any new U.S. investment in Burma.

By the end of 1998 U.S. business in Burma had mostly abandoned ship. There were not enough American business expatriates on the ground anymore to hold the customary gatherings with the commercial attaché at the U.S. embassy in Rangoon. A few U.S. oil companies were still there, grandfathered in under the terms of the economic sanctions. Companies with an established presence in the country were not required to divest and leave, although it was an open question whether or not they would be allowed to expand their business with additional investment. American lawyers and other professionals could still operate freely in Burma, as the law did not forbid the presence of the service sector as long as they did not buy new property. In the energy sector—one of Burma's most significant economic resources along with opium poppy cultivation and heroin trafficking—only one major oil company, Unocal, was persisting under severe adversity.

| | |

Unocal had earned the disapprobation of the human rights advocacy community because of revelations that the military government exploited "slave labor" in infrastructure construction supporting the Yadana gas pipeline. The pipeline was part of a $1.2 billion project undertaken by a consortium led by the French oil giant Total and involving the Myanmar Ministry for Oil and Gas Enterprises as well as Unocal, which holds a 28 percent stake in the project—the largest single source of private foreign investment in Burma. Reliable sources, backed by U.S. State Department officials, give credence to reports that corvée labor—unpaid conscript workers—had been used in infrastructure projects in the area of the pipeline, which connects an offshore drilling platform in the Andaman Sea to a power plant in Thailand across Burma's lower panhandle of rough jungle terrain.

Amid the furor, scant notice has been paid to the fact the Burmese military had the British empire to thank for its practice of "slave labor." Under the legal system inherited from British colonial administration, the objectionable labor practices surrounding the Yadana pipeline were technically lawful. The Burmese military was simply exploiting the "village law," which the British instituted to recruit peasant workers without pay for nation-building projects during their harsh colonial rule. There was no evidence that forced labor had been used in the construction of the pipeline itself. Yet slave labor is a clear violation of international law, and the accusation of corporate complicity was a powerful rebuke. Unocal reacted with indignation and defiance to the attacks on its image.

Under siege by human rights activists, the El Segundo, California–based multinational divested its downstream distribution and retailing businesses in the United States, insulating itself from the prospect of a tarnished brand name causing consumers to boycott Unocal gasoline at the pump. The company obscured its legal residency by establishing a second corporate headquarters in Singapore and announcing it "no longer considers itself a U.S. company." Singapore, it should be noted, is an authoritarian city-state that is Burma's most enthusiastic diplomatic patron and its largest source of inbound investment; Singaporean political leaders, most notably the autocratic Lee Kwan Yew, are notorious for taking a hostile stance against Western human rights advocacy.

In 1997 a judge in California ruled the state had jurisdiction in a controversial lawsuit, *John Doe* v. *Unocal,* which named as defendants Unocal CEO Roger C. Beach and then president John Imle—now vice chairman. In the suit, Burmese villagers alleged that Unocal officials were aware of—and therefore complicit in—crimes against humanity related to the Yadana pipeline infrastructure construction.

The plaintiffs claimed the Burmese government forced them to clear the rain forest and haul supplies for the pipeline—causing them to abandon their children and wives, who were then raped by soldiers back in the villages. In essence the suit claims Unocal has joint legal liability for the actions of its business partners and the Burmese government. The Alien Tort Claims Act, under which the suit was filed, had been used against foreign dictators like Ferdinand Marcos of the Philippines, but never against a U.S. multinational corporation. Gregory J. Wallance, a corporate defense attorney describing the case in a law journal, observed that the suit was unprecedented and that "its implications for American companies doing business overseas are both profound and troubling."

Unocal has vehemently denied the charges and vowed to fight the suit, which may take years to wind its way through the courts. The discovery process was expected to continue though late 1999, with a trial date set for the spring of 2000. Meanwhile, a coalition of human rights and environmental activists has kept up the pressure on the company, petitioning in late 1998 to have Unocal's corporate charter revoked on the grounds that it allegedly violated environmental and labor laws in California and was complicit with violations of international law in its business activities in Burma and Afghanistan.

The $5.5 billion international oil giant finally got around to softening its bristly reaction to criticism by issuing a conciliatory document, "Human Rights and Unocal: A Discussion Paper." The company said: "At Unocal, respect for human rights is fundamental in all of our activities. We strive to convey this respect through our employment, economic development, environmental, security, and community practices." The discussion paper, which does concede that Unocal is a U.S.-based corporation after all, cites the customary "constructive engagement" theory in defense of its international operations. The argument is that democracy flows naturally out of rising living standards. "Unocal, as a U.S. company operating in many different foreign countries, has a legal and ethical obligation to remain politically neutral. Our economic impact, however, is far from neutral. We have seen time and again how our presence has improved the quality of life for people—regardless of politics. And history suggests that economic progress typically promotes increasing respect for human rights."

Unocal's statement of its human rights policy makes the textbook argument for passive constructive engagement, politically neutral and devoid of commitment to do anything beyond business as usual.

| | |

Burma would remain an international pariah state, even after gaining some limited legitimacy by admittance to the Association of Southeast Asian Nations (ASEAN), under the sponsorship of its patron, Singapore, and another autocratic neighbor, Malaysia. It also continued to be an economic basket case, with a slew of fancy new joint-venture hotels in downtown Rangoon standing mostly empty behind their sparkly marble facades. The "Visit Myanmar Year" in 1997 was a bomb, and there were few signs of improvements in the following years. When a group of eighteen young foreigners entered Burma on tourist visas in the summer of 1998 and brazenly handed out leaflets in downtown Rangoon commemorating the tenth anniversary of the slaughter of pro-democracy protesters, they were arrested, summarily tried, and each sentenced to five years of hard labor. Responding to international outrage, the government commuted the harsh sentences and deported the activists. But expatriate hotel managers lamented that the damage had already been done. The incident helped cripple an already pathetic tourist industry

For multinational corporations, a combination of factors had made Burma an unattractive place to do business, even without the scarlet letter of the horrid human rights environment. Unlike Levi Strauss, which cited its human rights policy on withdrawal, Motorola Inc. explained its decision to withdraw in terms of poor business prospects. Burmese businessmen apparently weren't ready to wear Motorola pagers on their beltless *longyi* wrap skirts, and the market was limited for people who could afford to use cell phones once the risk was taken to install costly base station infrastructure. The market didn't seem ripe for a boom in mobile telecommunications, as China was when Motorola established a manufacturing presence in that country, unapologetically, on the heels of the 1989 Tiananmen Square massacre. Motorola was known as an industrial brand, a chip-making technology company, when it leaped into China. But by the time it pulled out of Burma, cell phones were household items in America and the company had a sensitive consumer brand name to protect from the stigma of collaborating with a grotesque military government.

Burma presented more than just an image problem as a violator of human rights. For one, the military regime's bureaucracy, aside from being corrupt and politically draconian, was poorly trained and sorely lacking in competency after decades of economic isolation. Officials were bungling the administration of economic reform policies, creating an unfriendly business environment that did not promise the high rates of return that Western investors experienced in the region's other emerging markets at the first stage of industrialization. To take the political and economic risks of plunging into an emerging marketplace, many infrastructure investors, for example, go by a rule-of-thumb calculation that anticipates at least a 20 percent return on investment. The situation in Burma was far too uncertain and unstable to offer such prospects.

Moreover, a virulent financial contagion had engulfed Burma's neighbors in Asia in the late 1990s, undermining the capacity of its major sources of working capital—neighbors Thailand, Malaysia, Singapore, and China—to propel development. Untold billions of dollars in irredeemable bad loans had crippled the banking systems in Thailand, Indonesia, South Korea, and, more important, Japan, whose import market provided a critical engine for regional prosperity. The immediate result of this financial panic was extraordinarily tight credit and shell shock among investors. The spigot of hard cash that had financed the boom of the neighboring countries was suddenly dry, making investment in Burma far more risky than it would have been just two years before. Burma had expected to be next in line for an economic miracle—to become the next "Asian Dragon" economy—when it joined ASEAN, the regional economic grouping. But it found itself stranded in the preindustrial doldrums, with barely enough inbound capital to line the pockets of the ruling military elite. The foreign exchange rate, still pegged officially at 6.25 kyat to the dollar, was hovering at about 650 to 1 in the black market, a de facto devaluation that made foreign products and commodities prohibitively expensive to local businesses and ordinary people.

Soe Min Aung, a local businessman in Rangoon, complained that the economy is stillborn without financing from multilateral institutions like the World Bank and the Asian Development Bank, which had cut Burma off under international sanctions. But he said his business, Injyn Development Company, has managed to maintain relationships with American partners—despite the federal-level sanctions. "We're feeling a lot of negative effects from the U.S. government policy, but you can always find loopholes to do something," said Soe, a former merchant marine who now trades in seafood, invests in real estate, and runs a private golf course outside Rangoon. "If you want to work with an American company under the sanctions, you can always find a third party to do the business. It just adds a lot of overhead."

Soe, an athletic-looking man in his early forties, was dressed impeccably in native costume—a green plaid *longyi* of fine fabric and a crisp, collarless white linen shirt beneath a traditional Burmese jacket. He paused during an interview at a hotel lounge to answer his mobile phone—a Motorola M-800 handset that gets its signal from a local cellular network operated by the Swedish company Ericsson—which, unlike its American rival, did not have reasons to withdraw from Burma. "I'm still working with an American company," he confided. "With small investments, say, in projects of $10 million or $20 million, you can still find a way. But with bigger projects, there's too great a risk of exposure."

Soe is a well-connected child of privilege. His father, an army general, was educated in Britain and trained in the United States; his wife's father serves as the military government's finance minister. But Soe spent much of his adult life earning a modest living as a seaman. He said he was inspired to go into business to help raise his country out of poverty after seeing the disparity between Burma's crippled economy and the rapid development of its Southeast Asian neighbors. "It made me sad to come home and see that nothing had changed," he said. "We Burmese are raised as Buddhists, and we are very passive, not so concerned about improvement. If you don't like something, you should speak out, but we don't do that because of the Buddhist culture. That has created a lot of setbacks in economic development."

| | |

This was a time when most of the American stragglers in Rangoon were taking their nameplates off their doors and packing up. At the International Business Center, a swank office complex in northern Rangoon overlooking the placid, tree-lined waters of Inya Lake, Atlantic Richfield Company's country representative, Fred A. Avila, waxed philosophical about his fate. Major consolidations were imminent in the industry, and Avila, a veteran of the oil business, was waiting around for a reassignment—or a pink slip. (ARCO would later agree to a $26.8 billion merger with London-based BP Amoco.) ARCO had decided to pull out of Burma and abandon its rights to choice offshore drilling concessions, though it would have been allowed to stay and develop them under the terms of the federal economic sanctions. The prospect of doing business successfully was not good, however. Energy prices had plummeted, and company officials worried that ARCO's offshore gas fields would not yield a commercially viable volume. The concession would make a good project for a smaller, independent firm, Avila said. "It's a shame no U.S. company will be able to step in."

Burma had become a difficult place to hang on for other reasons than the economic sanctions. Board members of the American oil company were being disturbed in the privacy of their homes by late-night phone calls from human rights activists, who demanded that they get out of Burma, according to industry sources. "The anti-Burma people have such a sophisticated network, they've drummed up a fanatical following," said Avila. "The military government has done a poor job defending itself. Somebody has to come in here and take a cold eye to see what's going on."

Avila expressed pain and sadness about the fate of his staff of Burmese employees, who he feared will suffer. His cook earned enough money to pay tuition for English lessons for her daughter, who then landed a coveted job at a hotel. His chauffeur, who has an advanced degree in physics, can't expect to find a comparable opportunity. On a small scale, the spin-off effects of Avila's presence in Burma were not insignificant—a testament to the benefits of constructive engagement on a very personal level. Compound these losses by the number of U.S. firms shunning the market, and Aung San Suu Kyi's argument that only the military benefits from foreign investment seems incomplete. But the tragedy, Avila said, is that the U.S. sanctions appear to have had so little effect on the mind-set of the junta, which in an act of public relations arrogance had tried to soften its image by renaming itself the State Peace and Development Council. "I don't think the people at the high levels really care—they're in it for the power rather than for the money."

| | |

Levi Strauss and Motorola and the other major American companies that had bailed out of Burma, before the Asian financial crisis stopped the country's languorous economic development in its tracks, were looking pretty smart. Above and beyond concerns about the human rights stigma, they had ample short-term business reasons to write off the market. But in the long run, what were they going to miss?

Japanese multinationals will be the ones to watch for the answer to that question. They approached the market with an entirely different attitude. Neither the human rights brouhaha nor the dire economic picture particularly discouraged them from making a commitment to the long-range potential of the Burmese market. Suzuki Motor Corporation typified that optimism by announcing plans in late 1998 to build a $10 million minicar and motorcycle assembly plant in Rangoon in a joint venture with Myanmar Automobile and Diesel Engine Industries. This deal also brought General Motors—where the Reverend Leon Sullivan, the antiapartheid firebrand, had once served on the board of directors—smack dab into the picture. The U.S. auto giant had raised its ownership stake in Suzuki from 3 percent to 10 percent shortly before the Japanese company announced plans to set up in Rangoon, where the streets are already jammed and smoky from battered old secondhand Toyotas.

Suzuki, which had been experiencing problems with labor strife in neighboring Thailand, is the spunky midget of the Japanese auto industry. CEO Osamu Suzuki is renowned for his aggressive high-risk entry into developing markets; the company was on the front lines of the exuberant capitalist advance into Eastern Europe after the fall of the Berlin Wall. Ordinarily Japanese corporate strategies are sober, cautious, and risk-averse. Yet Burma was an enchanting opportunity, even as pessimism prevailed at home. Japan was entering the eighth straight year of recession, and the banking system was reckoning with bad loans now estimated at upward of a trillion U.S. dollars. At the same time that Japanese companies were making hard rational decisions about retrenching and redeploying their vulnerable assets away from trouble spots in Asia, they were gazing, misty-eyed, at Burma.

Akinori Seki, a senior corporate strategist for Marubeni Corporation, acknowledges there is a certain amount of sentimentality involved in Japan's interests in Burma—the one Asian nation that initially welcomed liberation by Imperial Army troops in World War II. But hard logic is involved as well. "From a purely economic perspective, it's a country in Southeast Asia that has been left behind, and it has tremendous potential and untapped resources," he said.

The potential remains remote, however. The trading firm Mitsui & Company was having trouble leasing out its new Mingaladon Industrial Park outside of Rangoon, where Japan's high-tech leader Fujitsu Ltd. was assembling low-tech telephone sets and the diversified food-processing giant Ajinomoto Co. was repackaging bulk containers of MSG seasoning for modest local sales. These weren't major investments, but strategic footholds anticipating the inevitable awakening of a slumbering consumer society. Suzuki's decision to jump on the bandwagon with an auto plant reinforced that vision of a profitable future in Burma. The Japanese weren't alone. Total, the French oil company, was plowing ahead with a new gas pipeline project—in defiance of the international criticism and the uncompetitively high costs of the gas it delivered in its Yadana "slave labor" pipeline. Total led a consortium of Britain's Premier, Japan's Nippon Sekiyu, and controversial U.S. straggler Unocal.

Nearly all the major Japanese *shosha*—the savvy, market-making trading houses—were well established in Rangoon. The capital investment involved was minimal, but the business intelligence network was firmly in place. The directories of office annexes at the otherwise moribund deluxe hotels and at the slick new joint-venture office buildings were plastered with the names of Japanese corporations. Powerful Keidanren, the Japan Federation of Economic Organizations, was continuing to champion trade and investment with Burma through traveling delegations and economic symposiums. The Japanese government offered its support, having recently revised its policy on granting bilateral economic aid to Burma, which it had reluctantly frozen in 1990.

Tokyo broadened its small but uninterrupted program of "humanitarian aid" for Burma with a $20 million fund to upgrade infrastructure and facilities at Rangoon's international airport. Predictably, it was criticized sharply by the U.S. State Department for its haste in easing sanctions. The big civil engineering firm Taisei Corporation was designated the lead contractor at the airport, repeating in miniature the closed-loop pork barrel pattern of Japanese foreign aid disbursement that in recent decades has reshaped the infrastructure throughout developing Asia and turned Japanese construction companies from domestic concerns into international behemoths. "We determined that the airport was in dire need of repair—it's dangerous the way it is now. We were afraid a serious accident might occur," said Akira Chiba, deputy director of the Foreign Ministry's Aid Policy Division. "Our policy is to condition any further aid on the improvement of human rights in Burma. But whether it's going to work or not, we don't know."

The airport assistance package was relatively small potatoes in the scheme of Japan's ostensibly "untied" foreign aid program, which hovered in the $9 billion range in the late 1990s, creating significant commercial opportunities for corporate Japan. But the deal-making *shosha* were smacking their lips at the prospects of a further thaw in the aid policy for Burma. "We in the private sector understand this to be a positive signal to Myanmar from the government of Japan," Iwao Toriumi, CEO of Marubeni and chairman of Keidanren's 150-member Japan-Myanmar Economic Committee, told the junta's economic planning minister, Brigadier General David Abel, at a 1998 conference on economic relations in Rangoon. "As you know, foreign policy is an extremely delicate affair. The government of Japan should refrain from interference in issues that Myanmar needs to resolve on its own, but at the same time must consider multilateral relations."

Despite official government assurances to the international community that restoration of aid would be conditioned on democratic reform, Japanese corporate players disdainfully regarded this policy as a cynical diplomatic dance with Washington. As Marubeni's Toriumi told the Burmese brigadier general: "It is much too large and too complex a world to leave things up to a single country, the United States."

Indeed, many U.S. companies knew how complex the world could be when it came to doing business in Asia. They saw their Japanese rivals not only as fierce competitors, but also as critically important partners for penetrating new markets in Asia—one of the conditions of interdependence is shaping the global economy. Japanese companies like Marubeni offered a strategic window on the forbidden market.

| | |

The business climate in Burma wasn't any better for Japanese trading firms or European oil and telecommunications companies than it was for the Yanks. What made the big difference was the human rights environment back home—or lack thereof in the case of the Japanese. Burma shows how domestic social constraints were as much a critical factor in determining the outcome of risk assessment as business prospects on the ground overseas. Even without the regulatory restrictions of the federal sanctions, it was becoming politically untenable for American firms to stay in Burma because of the heat from human rights activists.

In Japan, effective NGOs devoted to international human rights activism are notably absent from the scene. Influential organizations do exist that advocate the neglected rights of the domestic down-trodden: descendants of Japan's feudal outcast community and the country's large minority population of ethnic Koreans, many of whom remain stateless. The human rights of Japanese women is a powerful new cause célèbre. A coalition of small groups is concerning itself with the legal status of asylum-seeking refugees from places like Burma who complain furiously about shabby treatment at the hands of Japan's xenophobic immigration officials. Japan-based Burma Relief Center has done some important work with Burmese refugees along the Thai border, and a small contingent of Japanese parliamentarians is sympathetic to Aung San Suu Kyi's cause, speaking out occasionally about human rights problems in Burma. A handful of Japanese scholars and journalists openly advocate political reform in Burma, but they are vastly outnumbered by those who support the military regime. A serious debate on Tokyo's Burma policy has been muted for years.

Suffice it to say, human rights activists in Japan are not submitting dissident shareholder resolutions demanding that the country's corporations get out of Burma or face the righteous indignation of consumers. Japanese activists are not talking about organizing boycotts of the ubiquitous Ajinomoto seasoning products or launching campaigns to smear the consumer brand names of Fujitsu or Suzuki because they are supposedly legitimizing the ogres who rule Burma. Unlike their U.S. counterparts, Japanese corporations are not up against the wall, pushed into the defensive mode of public relations damage control or forced to develop strategic policies for human rights. Members of the board of directors of the oil company Nippon Sekiyu were not getting nuisance calls from human rights activists in the middle of the night.

Japanese companies are not bothered by the nuisance of globally minded corporate watchdogs in their own language and society. Confronting a nation without a local culture of human rights advocacy, international NGOs were virtually powerless to engage in dialogue with Japanese companies. Aron Cramer, a level-headed attorney who heads the human rights division at Business for Social

Responsibility, came home from a 1998 trip to Japan scratching his head over the lack of awareness and concern on the issues of conscience he tried to raise with business contacts.

One of the rare precedents for targeting Japanese business is the campaign initiated by international environmentalists—not domestic NGOs—to boycott the Mitsubishi brand. The Mitsubishi Group is one of the old oligarchic *zaibatsu* trusts, which were reduced during the Allied occupation to cross-shareholding *keiretsu* alliances. Its sin was that the group's trading arm and informal flagship company, Mitsubishi Corporation, was participating in the rapacious harvest of endangered tropical rain forest timber in places like Malaysia's Sarawak state on the island of Borneo. The company has responded with a sophisticated public relations counterattack, and there is little evidence that the boycott has had a noticeable effect on sales. The boycott of Mitsubishi products never caught on in Japan, and Mitsubishi Motors still enjoys comfortable sales in the U.S. and European automobile markets.

Human rights activists in the United States, such as the San Francisco-based Transnational Resource & Action Center, are now talking about targeting Mitsubishi on the human rights question as well, reasoning that it is a pervasive brand name and that they can build upon whatever momentum developed in the environmental campaign to draw public attention. To draw participation in Japan, TRAC launched a Japanese-language version of its advocacy information site Corporate Watch on the World Wide Web in October 1999. Mitsubishi's role in Burma does not stand out as particularly prominent, compared with that of Marubeni or Mitsui. But the strategy here is to attack the familiar brand name, as in the selective scapegoating of Nike Inc. for the transgressions of all sneaker makers using contract laborers. There is always the potential that the crusade could induce some American consumers to think, however subliminally, about Mitsubishi's stigmatic presence in Burma before entering an auto showroom. But there is little immediate danger that such negative associations will come to mind for the Japanese consumer.

In the future, however, Japanese corporations may find themselves increasingly susceptible to external pressure, both international and domestic in origin. To a large extent, human rights activism targeting business in the United States and Europe made use of the grassroots political networks established in the environment movement. TRAC, originally an environmental NGO, is a perfect example. Corporate Japan has since the 1960s faced the reality of a strong environmental lobby by irate citizens. In the notorious mercury poisoning case in Minamata, a patently culpable Chisso Corporation fought tooth and nail to avoid responsibility, hiring gangsters to intimidate victims who complained after effluent from the chemical factory contaminated seafood stocks in Minamata Bay with deadly mercury, resulting in crippling nerve disorders, deaths, and horrible birth defects in the local population. The company unconscionably refused to settle compensation lawsuits for decades. But the shameful Minamata case was a turning point in industrial practices and corporate attitudes within Japan. Environmental protection is one of the key elements of corporate social responsibility in Japan today.

What's missing is substantive concern about what Japanese companies are doing overseas. The Japanese public is extremely well educated and has a sophisticated understanding of the patterns of economic globalization. Most people know about the *watari-dori kigyo* phenomenon—the "migratory bird corporations" in pursuit of low wages abroad. They just don't see it in moral context or feel they have reason to care about the implications for human rights.

Tokyo-based Pacific Asia Resource Center (PARC), a left-wing activist group formed in the 1960s to oppose Japan's military alliance with the United States, went to the trouble of publishing in 1998 a Japanese-language report on the international campaign against Nike Inc. under the English title "Just Don't Do It." (Ad slogans in English are as popular in Japan as Nike brand shoes.) But a PARC spokeswoman said the group has no plans for similar research on the overseas labor practices of Japanese companies. Asics Corporation, the leading Japanese brand name in sporting shoes, produces its sneakers at some of the same subcontractor factories in China and under virtually the same conditions as the vilified Nike, but it was not on PARC's radar. Since Asics is not under pressure from Japanese NGOs, it has had no reason to develop a code of conduct that applies to overseas labor standards. Nor has any other Japanese company. In Japan there is nothing approaching Levi's visionary Global Sourcing Guidelines to serve as a benchmark, nor is there any particular need to create one.

"There's very little pressure being mounted on Japanese corporations now as far as labor rights abroad," said Ben Watanabe, a veteran independent union activist who has written critically about Suzuki Motor's labor strife in Thailand. "But that will change in the future. The pressure will come from Asian countries, and Japanese companies and NGOs will be forced to respond."

One Japanese group that may rise to the occasion is a small NGO calling itself People's Action Network to Monitor Japanese Transnational Corporations, or TNC Monitor Japan, which is making efforts to break out of the traditional environmental agenda and focus on human rights and labor issues as well. "The standards within Japanese corporations are too lax," said the group's general secretary, Shinichi Sakuma. "There's a sense they can do whatever they want overseas."

At the end of 1998 TNC Monitor Japan and a dozen or so environmental and labor groups in Japan and Asia issued an ambitious document titled "Asian NGO Charter on Transnational Corporations," which outlines a code of conduct addressing the usual mix of human rights and labor standards. But the terms of engagement described in this detailed document are so demanding and strident in tone that it would seem difficult to sell to even the most progressive international company, let alone a hidebound Japanese firm. Item #17, for example, declares, "The TNC shall not close a plant or factory, or reduce/dismiss employees/workers of low work skills on the grounds that the company is going to transfer its operations overseas or is going to invest overseas. The TNC shall not make foreign investment or transfer business overseas if that leads to destabilized employment conditions at home."

Levi Strauss & Co., America's best hope for corporate social responsibility, would fail that test flat out. So would many a Japanese TNC. The tenet that a company must not shut down production at home in order to seek the competitive advantages of cheap labor abroad is obsolete and inimical to the reality of globalization, which is not going to disappear. The emphasis is on protecting jobs in Japan, not safeguarding against labor abuses caused by Japanese companies overseas, reflecting the entrenched insular mentality of Japanese society, shared by social activists and industrialists alike.

TNC Monitor Japan's manifesto reflects Japan's isolated economic experience. Because of a two-tier employment system at home, the big Japanese corporations did not need to dismiss many regular employees when they moved production offshore in the 1980s to remain internationally competitive with the handicap of a stronger yen currency. They merely cut off business ties with domestic contractors and suppliers doing labor-intensive work, allowing those entities to serve as shock absorbers to the economic dislocation. "Job flight," the issue that has driven U.S. labor activists to agitate about human rights abroad, was never a serious problem in Japan. But that is changing. The mythical lifetime employment system is fraying at the seams, and unemployment is rising rapidly as Japan's marathon recession only recently showed signs of abating. The full shock of globalization hasn't yet hit Japanese society, but it's bound to come sooner or later. In time, TNC Monitor Japan and its allies may mature into more effective advocates for corporate social responsibility and the protection of international human rights. The shrill, Marxist tinge of their message may mellow into something Japanese business leaders will be able to listen to without dismissing it out of hand.

Meanwhile, Japanese companies are not immune to criticism for doing business in Burma. A growing number of local, state, and city governments in the United States are enacting so-called selective purchasing laws, which are aimed at punishing companies—domestic or foreign—that do business in Burma. It is a repeat of the political activism that helped hasten the end of apartheid in South Africa, when activists placed unrelenting pressure on corporations doing business there. Local governments used selective purchasing laws to place conditions on public contracts, imposing sanctions on companies that refused to heed the call to pull out of South Africa. The state of Massachusetts was at the vanguard of that movement, until Nelson Mandela called for an end to economic sanctions.

But the state legislature later resurrected the law and applied the same apparatus to Burma. Japanese companies were prominent on the Massachusetts watch list, including the big international construction firm Obayashi Gumi, which was head of a consortium that won the bidding for a $1.5 billion contract with the Massachusetts Water Authority. Obayashi nearly lost the deal because it had participated in a Japanese government aid project to build a nurses' dormitory in Rangoon. An Obayashi official in Tokyo said the aid project was completed and the company had closed its office in Burma before it bid on the Massachusetts job. The law specifies that companies doing business with the state must pay a penalty of 10 percent of the amount of their contract if they maintain a presence in Burma.

Whether these selective purchasing laws will continue to cast their nets into corporate Japan is uncertain. The European Union, joined by the Japanese government, has filed protests with the World Trade Organization claiming the Massachusetts sanctions law violates the multilateral treaties. The statute is also under challenge in U.S. civil court, alleged to be unconstitutional on the grounds that it would supersede federal law and allow the state to meddle in foreign affairs, a domain reserved exclusively for the federal government. Rather than playing a role in leveling the playing field for U.S. corporations competing against Japanese and European multinationals in human rights hot spots like Burma, the local sanctions laws will serve as symbolic gestures—part of the arsenal of the human rights advocacy strategy that aims to strike at the bottom line through embarrassing bad publicity.

That kind of activism, even if it catches on in Japan, won't necessarily change a fundamental attitude about human rights that is deeply embedded in the cultural and political mind-set. Many Japanese, leaders and followers alike, aren't so sure they can accept the idea that the fundamental precepts of human rights—emphasizing the freedom of expression and the sanctity of the individual—are all that universal.

The views on the Burma question expressed by Kenichi Ohmae, a prominent international business consultant and a conservative political aspirant based in Tokyo, are revealing on that score. "The

West knows about Myanmar [Burma] through one person, Aung San Suu Kyi. The obsession with Suu Kyi is a natural one if you understand that U.S. superficial democracy is golden in the United States; Americans love elections," Ohmae, former head of McKinsey & Co.'s Tokyo office, wrote in a 1997 essay in the regional news-magazine *Asiaweek*. "Just as Myanmar is Buddhist, and Malaysia is Islamic, America has a religion called Democracy. There is merit in promoting democratic reform. But America is a simplistic country. Americans insist that what works for them should work for others at any time and in any stage of economic development."

Ohmae is a best-selling author in Japan who made his name as an internationalist on economic matters. But here he articulates the "ethical imperialism" argument, drawing from emotional strains of Asian nationalism that still lurks among social conservatives in Japan. It is an argument that contests the widespread conviction in Western industrial societies that human rights are universal and not subject to negotiation across sovereign lines. There has long been a view in Asia that these universal concepts are incomplete because they grow exclusively out of a Western, Judeo-Christian tradition of morality and a political philosophy centering on the individual. The argument holds that there are unique cul-tural traits in the Eastern Hemisphere, dominated by Confucian and Buddhist beliefs, and that these "Western" human rights do not necessarily apply to humanity in developing countries of Asia, or even the developed ones like Singapore and Japan. The basis of the argument is that communitarian rights should prevail over individual rights—placing greater priority on collective interests and the goals of the group as opposed to the excessive protection of the individual against the abuse of the state. Asian societies sup-posedly put greater emphasis on personal obligations rather than entitlement.

This line of thinking is sometimes referred to in shorthand as the "Asian way" or "Asian values." Of course it has a certain de-gree of validity—unconstrained individualism has caused its share of social problems in the West, often harming the broader interests of society. America's senseless gun culture is a case in point. But perhaps even more menacing, the precepts of group harmony and social discipline championed in the Asian way can be exploited by totalitarian governments, as they were in prewar Japan, allowing the state to commit egregious crimes against unprotected individuals. This is all subject to an absurdly convoluted and irreconcilable academic debate, typically laid out in terms of a choice between modernism and cultural relativism.

The debate becomes moot, however, when you consider that proponents of so-called Asian values cannot provide a coherent set of principles that could serve as a globally acceptable basis for the rules of behavior. Advocates of the primacy of the individual can point to the Universal Declaration of Human Rights, which most of the nations of the world that existed in 1948 agreed to by consensus, and the established body of international human rights law it inspired. Moreover, it's wrong to view these conflicting values as mutually exclusive—only an anarchist would claim that the freedom of the individual should not be balanced against the collective interests of an enlightened society.

Consequently it seems self-evident that multinational corporations—to the extent they operate in a single international system of trade and finance—have no alternative reference for ethical behavior under the conditions of today's global economy. This would be true whether the individualistic values of universal human rights are valid or whether they are tainted by a Western bias. It's a functioning, working set of guidelines, comparable to the international rules on navigation or to the generally accepted accounting principles (GAAP), which more and more of the world's bean counters are using to communicate with each other in a process of global convergence.

The problem is that when UN secretary general Kofi Annan exhorted international business leaders to join his "Global Compact for shared values and principles" on human rights, his rhetoric had to have gone right past the captains of industry from Japan. Even if they were listening, the UN chief is going to find it very difficult to recruit business partners in Tokyo who share his values. Keidanren, the voice of big business, has published an ethics code to serve as a model for its membership, but the document fails to address the ethical exigencies of globalization. It makes no mention of protecting labor standards or human rights overseas, nor does it address such fundamental issues as freedom of association.

One of the tenets of the Keidanren code offers a glimpse of the reactionary conservatism that runs deeply through Japanese society and its business culture: "Corporations will stand firm against antisocial forces and organizations that threaten the order and security of civil society." Another requires Japanese corporations operating overseas to "respect the cultures and customs of the hosting society," language that can be taken to mean that it's proper to bribe local officials and flout government labor regulations, which is the pervasive culture and custom throughout China and developing Asia.

Canon Inc., which has positioned itself as a leader in corporate social responsibility within Japan, is one of the very few companies that has adopted its own global corporate code of conduct. But it is written only in Japanese and has not been distributed to managers at overseas subsidiaries and subcontractors. Canon's chairman emeritus, Ryuzaburo Kaku, has been a zealous advocate of corporate ethics on the international scene. Along with Dutch industrialist Frederik J. Philips of Philips Electronics, Kaku was cofounder of the Caux Roundtable, a trilateral grouping of business leaders from Europe, Japan, and the United States that has issued the model ethical code Principles for Business. In the drafting of that document, Kaku was a strong advocate of *kyosei,* a vision of social responsibility based on a communitarian philosophy that puts limits on individual rights and is imbued with "Asian way" thinking. The preamble to the Caux Roundtable code offers the *kyosei* ideal as a counterpoint to the more traditional Western principle of human dignity—"the sacredness of each person"—without resolving the question of common universal values.

Since the mid-1980s Japan has been criticized mercilessly by foreign scholars and journalists for being fundamentally different in the way it practices capitalism, trade, and corporate governance, out of sync with U.S. and European models. Japanese business and government leaders have been tenacious in their rebuttal of these views, denouncing the critics as "revisionists" and insisting that Japan follows the rules of the international free-market system. The debate raged around a succession of trade disputes and ultimately went to the question of whether Japan's commercial practices are fair or not, particularly whether the Japanese domestic market was open or closed or provided a "level playing field" for foreign investors and traders.

With Japan's giant corporations conducting business as usual in the global marketplace without the constraints on their behavior that the international human rights movement places on rival European and American firms, there is bound to be further conflict. We will also be hearing complaints about the lack of a "level playing field" in the area of labor standards, because companies from some countries are being coerced into adopting onerous terms of engagement codes and paying high costs to monitor their compliance, while their competitors from Japan are not. At the peak of the hyperbolic U.S.-Japan trade dispute, American officials denounced Japan as an "economic outlier." Japan now runs the risk of being branded a "human rights outlier."

This collision of values is inevitable unless there's an agreement on what multinational corporations need to do about human rights issues, and that can't happen until everybody can come to terms with a common idea of what human rights are.

When Kofi Annan proposed his Global Compact on human rights, he wasn't talking about a range of interpretations based on various beliefs and cultural practices around the world, east, west, north, and south. He was talking about a convergence of shared values on human rights protections, labor standards, and environmental practices. His reference was the canon of international law centering on the UN's Universal Declaration of Human Rights and the International Labor Organization's declaration on fundamental principles and rights at work. "These are universal values. If someone said they're cultural, that's nonsense," said George Kell, an economist in the Office of the UN Secretary General who is the point man for Annan's Global Compact scheme. "Ask the people in these countries who are suffering, and they'll say the values of human rights are universal. It's only the governments who say they are not."

| | |

Levi's blue jeans enjoy a loyal customer base in Japan, but the brand's halo effect has much less to do with the values of personal freedom and rebelliousness than it does with the value of authenticity. Japanese consumers cherish the idea that imported Levi's jeans are the original brand that is merely imitated by their own domestic producers of dungarees. Despite the devastating effects of Japan's prolonged recession on retail consumption, the sales of Levi's products in Japan remained relatively constant from 1994 through 1997 at about $270 million a year. Levi's Japanese subsidiary, which slashed its full-time workforce by 10 percent in 1997, reports that the overall decline in Japan for apparel was offset by a rising popularity of Levi's "Vintage" blue jeans. These U.S.-made special-edition pants, indigo-dyed replicas of models from the 1930s and 1950s, sell for twice as much as regular Levi's 501s imported from the Philippines. Blue jeans maintain a robust demand from Japan's urban youth, for whom denim is a staple uniform for leisure time, not an expendable purchase during times of austerity.

In conservative corporate Japan, of course, wearing a pair of Levi's vintage jeans or even casual Dockers to work would be unthinkable. So would drawing inspiration about freedom and individuality, or corporate social responsibility, from the Levi's brand. There may be a plethora of allegedly irresponsible or unaccountable corporate villains for activists to pursue, should they be so disposed. But what Japan lacks is a conscientious corporate model for progressive human rights and labor policies.

But things are happening in Japan today that may quietly subvert the conservative island mentality of the business culture. The highly respected journalist Mitsuko Shimomura, who broke the gender barrier by becoming the first woman to serve as a foreign correspondent for a major Japanese news organization when she sent dispatches to the Asahi Shinbun from New York in 1980, has now dedicated herself to breaking another taboo. While at her last post with the Asahi, as editor of the weekly *Asahi Journal* magazine, Shimomura launched a research project that ranks Japanese corporations for their policies on social responsibility, adapting the survey method developed by New York–based Council on Economic Priorities to rank American corporations.

Shimomura's researchers have been asking companies pointed questions about such sensitive matters as environmental safeguards and treatment of women in the workplace—the issue of sexual harassment having evolved only recently from locker room humor to a matter as serious as that of corporate governance in Japan. The project had to overcome tremendous resistance and suspicion on the part of cloistered company officials. "At first I was treated like I was doing something scandalous," said an animated Shimomura, coauthor of a popular biography of Sony founder Akio Morita, *Made in Japan*. "Japanese people don't like to be compared to each other. Sony doesn't want to be sized up against Matsushita. I tried to explain at the beginning that we're not going to embarrass you or push you. But let's get together to try to make our society better. They're starting to understand that we're not attacking them."

Shimomura retired early from the Asahi to become chief executive of a nonprofit medical institute but still directs the corporate ranking project at the Asahi Foundation, acting with a sense of mission. Building on the tenuous level of trust she's established with her corporate survey subjects, Shimomura now plans to start asking about ethics codes and eventually hopes to explore the question of human rights policy. "They will always say, 'Our company does not use child labor.' But they don't really know because they are not checking," she said over a sushi dinner at Tokyo's exclusive Ark Hills Club, where she is a member along with many of Japan's corporate elite. She suggests it will be a long time before ordinary Japanese citizens share some of the same values on human rights as their counterparts in the West. "Even the South Africa issue wasn't a big deal here. It was so far away that maybe Japanese people didn't feel it had anything to do with their lives."

History may prove Aung San Suu Kyi's call for international economic sanctions to have been the correct course, leading to a happy result for freedom and democracy, as it did for Nelson Mandela. But then again, maybe not. Challenging the logic of the heroic Nobel Laureate is a taboo for Americans—as pundit Ohmae correctly pointed out. On the other hand, an understanding of the moral relevance of her struggle against despotism is disturbingly missing in Japan. It's difficult to imagine that Japanese consumers would give a hoot whether the blue jeans they buy had been made in Myanmar or in apartheid South Africa, as long as they were of good quality. This fundamental schism isn't going to disappear anytime soon, and it will have some serious implications for the way competing multinationals from the world's two largest economies handle their human rights policies. Kofi Annan and his team at the UN have their work cut out for them in getting international business to truly converge on a common set of values.

CHAPTER FOUR

| | |

Breakfast of Champions

The history of mankind is one of continuous development from the realm of necessity to the realm of freedom. This process is never-ending. In any society in which classes exist, class struggle will never end. In classless society the struggle between the new and the old and between truth and falsehood will never end. . . .

—Quotations from Chairman Mao Tse-tung

The world still remembers that photograph of the lone man in a white shirt, standing defiantly in front of a column of armored personnel carriers on Beijing's Changan Boulevard. It seemed to say everything about the moment, and the spirit of the doomed rebellion, when troops from the People's Liberation Army were restoring order at Tiananmen Square in the spring of 1989. In graphic simplicity the photograph depicts a transcendent idea: the individual asserting his will against the overwhelming power of the state in a heroic act of conscience. Viewing it can send chills down the spine of anyone who cherishes the inalienable right to liberty. In reality, the man's friends quickly whisked him out of grave danger shortly after the shutter clicked, and he disappeared into the crowd. We'll probably never know his name or if he escaped persecution for his act of impudence. But his image is indelible.

Many Americans today find it impossible to think about China without some level of association—conscious or subconscious—to the powerful meaning of this photograph. This is not necessarily a good thing, because it reduces a great civilization and a modern nation of fantastic diversity to a single, emotional impulse, a kind of righteous nervous tic. The same can be said about the larger story of the prodemocracy demonstration at Tiananmen Square, which hard-line leaders of the Chinese Communist Party chose to crush ruthlessly with tanks and guns instead of quieting with dialogue and reason. The military assault caused the deaths of at least several hundred students as well as ordinary Beijing residents who, like the nameless man in the photograph, confronted soldiers advancing on the great public plaza at the symbolic epicenter of the nation.

In the aftermath of this unmitigated tragedy, which was broadcast on live television around the world, the United States imposed various sanctions against China and its military. Primarily it established a requirement for an annual review of China's "most favored nation" (MFN) trade privileges. MFN status offers the lowest possible tariff rates for imported foreign goods and is extended unconditionally to nearly all U.S. trading partners—except those in political hot water. The renewal of China's MFN credentials became an annual rite of spring in Washington, with China bashers on both sides of the aisle in Congress arguing that the administration should revoke the privilege.

Five years after the Tiananmen massacre, Warren Christopher, then secretary of state for the Clinton administration, shuttled to Beijing on a mission to engage in diplomatic brinkmanship with the Chinese leadership over the U.S. government's stance on human rights. The administration's policy had been crafted to make good on Bill Clinton's campaign promises that he'd get tough with the "Butchers of Beijing"—rhetoric aimed at his opponent, incumbent George Bush, who was taking an increasingly conciliatory stance on China relations. Clinton was wooing the vote from the wide swath of the American electorate that still harbored feelings of revulsion over the actions of the Chinese government.

Upon taking office in 1993, however, Clinton had a slight change of heart and decided, under mounting pressure from the business lobby, to take a more moderate approach on the issue. He coopted harsh anti–China legislation in Congress and issued his own executive order that explicitly conditioned MFN renewal in 1994 on "overall significant progress" in improving the country's human rights track record. The president would stand by his principles by subordinating commerce to the higher interests of democracy and human rights. Or so the script out of the White House read.

In that context of righteous ambiguity, Secretary of State Christopher had come to China with an ultimatum, demanding the release of a large number of political dissidents from their wretched prison cells. He called for a more open accounting of Beijing's human rights record before the administration would consider defying critics in Congress and renewing MFN trade privileges. But bellicose Chinese officials already had hammered home their rigid position: Despite international condemnation of China's authoritarian political practices, the matter of human rights standards was strictly off-limits to foreign intervention. To drive that point home, security forces had rounded up and arrested a batch of the usual suspects—some fifteen prodemocracy and labor activists—just before Christopher's arrival, including prominent dissidents Wei Jingsheng and Wang Dan.

The hard-liners in Beijing's ruling circle greeted Christopher's arrival with disdain, vowing that a decision by the American president to revoke trade privileges would trigger retaliatory trade sanctions and cause irrevocable harm to bilateral economic ties, as well as to the regional economy in East Asia. The stage was set for a grim showdown, as Christopher noted in a cable to Clinton from Beijing: "My first day in Beijing mirrored the mood of the week preceding my arrival—rough, somber, sometimes bordering on the insolent."

The next morning, at his breakfast with the American Chamber of Commerce in Beijing, Christopher had to cope with the fact that nearly all of the American executives who filled the room before him in a gallery of finely tailored suits were not his sympathizers. They supported the opinion of Chinese Communist Party leaders in unvarnished opposition to U.S. policy: revoking MFN was against America's own best interests, and the policy of harping on human rights was dead wrong. They were not alone. Some eight hundred major U.S. corporations and trade associations had appealed directly to President Clinton, urging him to back off on his human rights posturing and renew China's MFN privileges unconditionally.

The atmosphere in the elegant banquet hall of the brand-new China World Hotel was sour and tense. Jim Mann, a senior *Los*

Angeles Times Washington correspondent in the State Department press corps, describes the mood of the business executives as that of "righteous irritability." Jim McGregor, a Beijing correspondent who had recently turned business executive for Dow Jones Inc. and would later become president of the Chamber of Commerce, recalls the confrontation as "much to do about nothing."

Depending on how the scene is recalled and interpreted, Christopher had the reckless courage—or the unmitigated gall—to appeal directly to his testy audience that morning for their active support in accomplishing the goals of his human rights mission. Christopher, a dignified senior statesman who rose to distinction as a skilled diplomatic negotiator in the 1980 Iran hostage crisis, is on record making a seemingly modest request for sympathetic allies. But his plea touched a raw nerve among battle-weary executives, many of whom were still struggling to make their operations truly successful in China's mine-laden political environment, where even the best strategic plan can be undermined by the arbitrary currents of a corrupt and complex business culture.

"I encourage each of you to use your influence, which I know can be very considerable," Christopher pleaded to his audience, "to convince the Chinese that it is in their best interests to at least make the limited progress on human rights that is necessary to constitute the overall significant progress in the seven discrete areas called for under the executive order."

On a symbolic level, Christopher was appealing to the very business leaders who profited from China to take some responsibility for the neglected welfare of the Chinese people. The vast majority of ordinary citizens were denied many of the political freedoms outlined in the United Nations' Universal Declaration of Human Rights—and guaranteed by China's own constitution—at the same time the country's economy was steaming ahead but enriching only a select few. Not such an unreasonable concern, it might seem. Why couldn't an influential business executive initiate an informal chat with the Chinese officials with whom he or she deals on a regular basis—officials who are begging for American capital and technology—to exercise some quiet back-channel human rights diplomacy?

American free-market entrepreneurs have a long and proud tradition of rejecting government guidance as unwarranted interference
in the private sector. When they're out in the business trenches of
Yunnan province, they represent their shareholders, not Uncle Sam.
Moreover, many business executives loathe the mere mention of
those two words: *human rights*. Lurking behind Warren Christopher's
appeal was a theory of corporate accountability bordering on the
theological, which not many major corporations were willing to
entertain. Establishing policy guidelines on general business ethics
was one thing; acting out of deep concerns about political repression in host countries was entirely another matter.

| | |

The dialogue between Secretary of State Warren Christopher and
the American business community in Beijing that spring morning
in 1994—just weeks before the fifth anniversary of the Tiananmen
massacre—was what one American television correspondent described as a "verbal pummeling" of the graying presidential envoy
by U.S. executives. They argued vehemently that the administration's policy of linking MFN trade privileges to China's human
rights record was foolhardy. Using MFN as a policy bludgeon could
be ruinous to a robust business environment that would otherwise
reward American investors, create new American jobs, and enhance
corporate America's competitiveness in the global economy.

The head of the Beijing Chamber of Commerce at the time,
Phillip Carmichael, who represented the Massachusetts-based high-
tech defense contractor EG&G Inc. in China, warned of grave
consequences if Chinese goods lost their entitlement to low tariff
rates at U.S. ports. "The bilateral relationship will deteriorate, and
U.S. business will pull back from its investment here in China,"
Carmichael predicted. "China will continue to grow, and they will
continue to export . . . but the U.S. will not be involved."

Negotiating with the threat of punitive economic sanctions,
Christopher's critics continued, was detrimental to the very cause
of improving human rights in China, a goal that would be far better served by opening the door to unrestricted economic engage-

ment. The assumption here was that if U.S. companies helped the Chinese prosper, they naturally would become *more like us* in their political views and practices, as well as in their consumer behavior.

It should be noted that this is the classic argument for "constructive engagement"—a term with origins in the lexicon of geopolitical statecraft, and which has been applied rather loosely in the rhetoric of international business ethics. Over time it has become the stock corporate rebuttal to outside criticism of business involvement in authoritarian regimes. Constructive engagement in this interpretation means that private foreign investment automatically yields a positive trickle-down effect on political consciousness in repressed societies, which in turn emboldens the demand for political reform. In other words, economic growth begets democracy—not the other way around.

This happens on a technical level, the theory goes, by the advent of greater transparency in society through higher standards and "best business practices" in such things as accounting principles and credit analysis. Or perhaps by way of more abstract benefits as, say, the absorption of management practices out of the textbooks of Harvard and Stanford Business Schools. Transferring industrial technology to China creates the possibility of higher value-added production, better-paying jobs, and more personal wealth—therefore seeding nascent middle-class values that foster an irrepressible yearning for freedom and democracy.

By this definition of constructive engagement, it would be absurd for foreign investors to meddle in politics or use their privileged influence in the host country to lobby authorities for greater political tolerance, as they might lobby for preferential tax treatment. Nor would they need to contemplate the subversive measures that the Reverend Sullivan eventually advocated in South Africa: willfully violating local laws and customs that perpetuated injustices.

It's important to make a clear distinction between two kinds of constructive engagement that business can practice—passive and interactive. Critics of the passive form of engagement are quick to point out that China already has the semblance of a fledgling middle class, but that anyone from that class who dares to express inconvenient political views out loud runs the risk of landing in prison for committing crimes against the state. That was the very fate of Chinese intellectuals who found themselves in jail for peacefully registering an ostensibly legal opposition group, the Democratic Party, at the end of 1998. The following year, adherents of a rapidly expanding religious movement, Falun Gong, were likewise persecuted and arrested by skittish authorities, who feared the nonviolent, mystical cult's organizational strength could threaten political stability. The high priests of China's tattered Communist ideology aimed to maintain social order in a one-cult system. State and party were one, and political and religious pluralism was anathema to the authorities.

At the same time, after nearly a decade of phenomenal foreign investment, China's economy was cruising at a respectable growth rate in the neighborhood of 8 percent at the end of the 1990s, despite the Asian financial crisis and a regional economic slump. China was America's fourth largest trading partner and had managed to rack up an irksome bilateral trade surplus of nearly $60 billion. Audacious predictions that China would replace an ailing Japan as the region's engine of economic growth could no longer be taken lightly. By 1999 one Chinese electronics company, Konka Group, had introduced a homegrown and competitively priced high-definition television set, or HDTV, to the U.S. market— belying the notion that Chinese imports were limited to cheap toys and clothing.

Yet by the U.S. State Department's reckoning, China was still jailing thousands of nonviolent prisoners of conscience. "Although the [Chinese] Government denies that it holds political or religious prisoners, and argues that all those in prison are legitimately serving sentences for crimes under the law, an unknown number of persons, estimated at several thousand, are detained in violation of international human rights instruments for peacefully expressing their political, religious, or social views," said the agency's latest human rights report.

There was little evidence to suggest that the bonanza of trade and investment and China's rapid accumulation of wealth have done anything to significantly improve the state's human rights protections. Yet the conventional wisdom persists, an article of faith that presumes that harsh authoritarian control of political freedoms is not necessarily bad for business.

The human rights environment of a host country can, however, have a profound impact on business. It is important to think about how the dynamic of working in China grinds down on the psychology of foreign investors. They are themselves, in a sense, prisoners of conscience. At a fundamental level, foreign executives in China are under pressure from the same limitations on free speech that smother Chinese political dissidents.

The investor doesn't go so far as to fear being dragged off to a dank prison cell after speaking his mind. Rather, the fear is of offending thin-skinned Chinese government officials, who hold extreme powers of arbitrary discretion in making or breaking business deals. It doesn't make sense to invest significant money, time, and energy in cracking China's brutally convoluted marketplace, only to throw it all away by running loose at the mouth about endemic corruption or undemocratic political practices. Articulating constructive criticism of China—publicly and privately—is a chilling taboo for the foreign investor.

| | |

So it was that a uniformity of expression dominated the room that morning in the spring of 1994, when the American Chamber of Commerce in Beijing so brazenly challenged Warren Christopher's principled stance on human rights. Chances are at least a few secret sympathizers of Christopher's agenda were in attendance, chewing quietly on croissants and swallowing lukewarm cups of hotel coffee as they listened to the Chamber's leadership assail their mild-mannered special guest. But there were plenty of reasons why we didn't hear their more textured views.

Two distinct issues hovered in the air at this meeting. One was the question of whether revoking China's MFN status made any sense, and to most objective observers it did not. Everyone knew, including Christopher and his Chinese adversaries, that the threat was a bluff, a measure too drastic to be effective. The other issue was the far more important question of the terms of constructive engagement for American business in China. Did an American business have an obligation to remain true to the democratic ideals of its homeland and encourage the Chinese government to improve its behavior on human rights?

Christopher was not totally isolated in believing this was in the realm of reasonable expectations. Inspired by Levi Strauss's code of conduct, human rights activists had been pressing the Clinton administration to promote a common set of business principles on engagement in China, which companies might be goaded into adopting. Gare Smith, as a legislative aide in the office of Democratic senator Edward Kennedy, had helped draft legislation that would offer persuasive incentives to U.S. investors in China who signed on to such a set of "voluntary" principles. Smith would later promote a watered-down version of this code after joining the State Department's human rights office, but the administration's "Model Business Principles" effort seemed destined to slip into obscurity. Undaunted, the advocacy community would continue its struggle to find a better way of articulating Christopher's message, that business can play a positive role in improving human rights through *interactive* policies of constructive engagement.

In his speech to the World Economic Forum in early 1999, United Nations secretary general Kofi Annan echoed that appeal, beseeching the heads of some of the most powerful multinational corporations to take responsibility for their special influence in countries where they invest. "Many of you are big investors, employers, and producers in dozens of different countries across the world. That power brings with it great opportunities—and great responsibilities," exhorted Annan. "We have to choose between a global marketplace driven only by calculations of short-term profit and one which has a human face." The idea of corporations working to improve human rights protections was an idealistic vision coming from the UN secretary general. Not surprisingly, Annan's proposal was greeted by the business leaders with a dignified clearing of the throat and ignored in the mainstream news media.

Back in 1994, the same argument was not a grand vision at all, but a figment of Warren Christopher's imagination. The American

Chamber represented a group of reputable people who simply wanted to conduct international business rationally, without undue interference by their own government—or the moral aspersions of human rights zealots. After tasting the fury of the business community that morning, the secretary of state made his way to a final and unproductive tête-à-tête with Chinese president Jiang Zemin. Christopher's human rights mission was crushed, and he ended up coming home embarrassingly empty-handed, having been treated with disdain not only by Chinese officials, but by Americans as well.

Jim Mann, the veteran diplomatic affairs correspondent, accompanied Christopher on the trip, and he would later recount the collision with the business leaders in his book, *About Face: A History of America's Curious Relationship with China, from Nixon to Clinton.* Mann contrasted the breakfast meeting with an encounter that Ronald Reagan's secretary of state, George Shultz, had eleven years earlier when U.S. expatriate businessmen complained that government policy was hurting their business prospects in China. Shultz responded angrily, "telling the executives that they weren't responsible for U.S. government policy, and if they didn't like it, they could move to Japan or Europe," Mann writes. "The business community's influence over America's relations with the rest of the world was vastly greater in 1994 than it had been in 1983; commerce was much closer to the heart of the Clinton administration's foreign policy."

Indeed, soon after Christopher's return, Clinton shifted his China policy from assertive confrontation over the issue of human rights to a softer brand of quiet diplomacy favoring enhanced economic relations. That June, on the fifth anniversary of the Tiananmen Square massacre, the president ended his administration's policy of linking MFN renewal to human rights improvement, rejecting options for more limited sanctions that might have demonstrated displeasure over Beijing's recalcitrance. Clinton contained his supposed wrath to a ban on the import of Chinese-made semiautomatic weapons and the vague effort to promote voluntary principles for American business in China. Beijing ended up releasing two prominent political prisoners—but left untold thousands more unaccounted for and languishing behind bars.

Although the U.S. State Department has continued to issue damning reports on the deplorable conditions in China in its annual review of human rights, the demands of the American business community clearly prevailed at a critical juncture in the American foreign affairs agenda. Revoking MFN would have been idiotic, but taking human rights off the table completely was a capitulation to the power of the business lobby. Clinton, who campaigned for his first presidential term as a staunch advocate of human rights, had found he had to cave in—just as the last Democratic president, Jimmy Carter, was forced by the national security establishment to back down after threatening in 1977 to withdraw American troops from South Korea as leverage against the human rights abuses of that country's military dictatorship. It was another decade before "quiet diplomacy"—and the international spotlight of the 1988 Olympic Games—brought the first stages of democratic reform to South Korea. It took another ten years for the first candidate with no ties to the military-backed ruling party, perennial opposition leader Kim Dae Jung, to win the presidency and inaugurate the spirit of true democracy.

The case of democracy flowering along with free-market prosperity in authoritarian South Korea offers hope to many observers that China, too, must eventually see the light on human rights. But the comparison can't be made without considering historical context: during the Cold War, it was taken for granted that internationally accepted ideals of political freedom, as defined by the 1948 Universal Declaration of Human Rights, would be cynically subordinated to America's global strategic interests. Now the argument can be made that after the demise of the Soviet Union, human rights values would be subordinated to crass commercial interests. For decades an Alice in Wonderland logic branded the oppressive regimes of the East bloc as "totalitarian" rogues, off-limits to free trade, while affording the fig leaf of respectability to the repugnant regimes in the Western camp as merely "authoritarian." In the case of South Korea, the thugs were on our side, holding the line against communism. One can claim convincingly that the ruse worked: the Soviet Union collapsed. In China, however, Maoist thought devolved into a new ideological obsession of wealth accumulation.

You have to wonder what the ultimate goals are behind this new commercial diplomacy, where responsibility for U.S. foreign policy is slipping from the hands of veterans at the State Department into the grasp of powerful chief executives at Fortune 500 companies. In the new world order of global capitalism, which emerged triumphantly in the 1990s from the epic ideological battle against Communist expansionism, who is responsible for promoting the principles of self-determination, democracy, and fundamental political freedom? What does it say about moral responsibility in the new world order when the secretary general of the United Nations asks business leaders to step into the breach? How is it that China is essentially condoned in remaining politically repugnant at a fundamental level—simply because it holds the key to vast riches?

On the surface, China was unquestionably a brighter and more prosperous place when the human rights advocacy community observed the tenth anniversary of the Tiananmen massacre in June 1999. But wholly intact at a deeper level were the same instruments of arbitrary power that the ill-fated Tiananmen demonstrators protested in vain: the thought police of the Public Security Bureau with its informants and plain-clothed goons; the All China Federation of Trade Unions (ACFTU), which represents the Machiavellian interests of the Communist Party, not the needs of the proletariat; the corrupt provincial cadres, whom central government officials cannot control; and the venal aristocracy of the reigning party elite and their children. All these elements still function to a large extent outside the purview of China's formal rule of law and the nominal human rights protections of its constitution.

Hollow concessions, such as the carefully scripted release and exile to obscurity of celebrity political prisoners like Wang Dan, the Tiananmen student leader, and Wei Jingsheng, a stalwart "democracy wall" activist from an earlier generation, gave President Clinton the opportunity to remonstrate that China's human rights record was improving when he journeyed with great fanfare to Beijing in June 1998. But it wasn't long before Beijing began cracking down with familiar brutality on the nascent Democratic Party, meting out harsh prison sentences for anyone who dared to participate in a modest first step toward political pluralism. The suppression of the Democratic Party continued even as Beijing agreed to sign the UN's Covenant on Civil and Political Rights, perhaps the single most important treaty in the canon of international human rights law. It was difficult to imagine the treaty having much effect on the exercise of state power in China, even after ratification by the National People's Congress.

China's qualifications for entry into the World Trade Organization would be the next test on the diplomatic agenda, but human rights did not surface as an issue in the negotiations. Despite scandals over the commercial transfer of missile guidance technology to Beijing and a spy case involving the pilfered secrets of miniaturizing nuclear warheads, China would remain, first and foremost, a friend to U.S. commerce.

On one level, this is a rational policy. Interconnected business interests theoretically can be a far more effective deterrent to international conflict than the menace of nuclear weapons, even when they don't do anything for the victims of human rights abuse. The frightening thing, however, is that leaving international relations up to the vagaries of the free market system also means surrendering control of the ultimate objectives. By default, we are operating under the assumption that narrowly focused Wall Street values are suitable for navigating U.S. foreign policy through the fog of the post–cold war era.

Since it seems certain that American leadership will remain dominant for some time to come, U.S.-based multinational corporations will set the ethical tone for the interdependent global economy. Yet it is far from clear whether these corporations are capable of espousing a higher purpose than the cold, amoral logic of the profit motive.

||||

Behold Levi Strauss & Co., the one corporation everyone points to when making the argument that business can be guided by a moral force. The company went totally against the grain in 1993 when it initiated a policy of phased withdrawal from the problematic Chinese market.

Levi Strauss had been one of the very few exceptions to that pattern of benign indifference among U.S. corporations to China's authoritarian political practices. Its response, to pull out of the market, had been extreme. Human rights activists had *not* been calling for corporate withdrawal from China, as they had been for companies doing business in Burma or, in past decades, in South Africa. Levi's announcement of its policy on China left considerable confusion in its wake, which would come back years later to haunt a company struggling with the conflict between fuzzy moral reasoning and hard business logic. Nevertheless, Levi's China policy announcement—or, rather, the widespread perceptions of what that policy represented—would help frame the debate on corporations and human rights in the years to come.

At the time, damning reports were coming from human rights monitors at the U.S. State Department and from reputable human rights organizations such as Human Rights Watch in New York and Amnesty International of London. The overwhelming evidence suggested that China did not meet the standards spelled out in Levi's Guidelines for Country Selection, part of the global code of conduct it had announced the previous year. With the intent of protecting its cherished brand name from scandal, Levi's had been the first major U.S. multinational to translate some of the principles articulated in the antiapartheid campaign into a universal corporate code of conduct that would guide its business activities worldwide.

To date, the gist of the Levi Strauss code remains a model statement of social responsibility that is admired and emulated by corporations in the United States and Europe. Beyond setting standards for the company's own practices, it regulates the terms of engagement with overseas contractors to ensure that Levi products are made according to the company's own standards. The code also contained a provision that established a lofty benchmark: Levi Strauss would not do business where there are pervasive human rights violations.

That was the language of the code in force when Levi Strauss summarily withdrew from Burma in 1992, and again in the spring of 1993, when the company announced its intentions to drop investment plans and retreat from China. Labor conditions at the plants operated by its contractors in China were also a sore point. In

November 1992 a special panel of Levi's senior executives called the China Policy Group was charged with undertaking a copious review of these conditions. They used something known in Levi corporate jargon as the "principled reasoning approach"—a somewhat byzantine method of examining how ethical values intersect with the more orthodox criteria of hard-nosed business decisions. First, the China Policy Group had to identify—and quantify—the interests of the various "high-influence stakeholders" in their decision. Essentially they were bound by the process to weigh the suffering of the victims of political repression in China against the priorities of company owners and managers back in North America and come up with options that did not contradict the company's values and ethical principles.

The panel found some serious problems in the labor conditions at its contractor factories, compounding concerns about the stigma of doing business in an egregious human rights environment. There was a potential danger that allegations of sweatshop exploitation could surface, causing considerable harm to Levi's image-sensitive business. In addition to the usual concerns about low wages, union busting, official graft, and petty bureaucratic red tape that fester in any developing economy, human rights advocates were pointing out disturbing problems unique to China. For instance, the system of enforcing the state's one-child policy at the factory unit level resulted in such abuses as harassment of women at the workplace, coerced abortions, and summary dismissal for the offense of being in the family way. Then there were the stories of prisoners forced into making goods for export, and of child labor—the underage girls who wash up on the sewing factory lines along with the flood of desperate peasant women from the impoverished hinterlands. The girls come seeking relatively lucrative jobs paying in the neighborhood of $40 a week, money they couldn't dream of earning back in their villages. This was all strictly a domestic Chinese matter, at least until U.S. consumers are informed by a blaring television news report that the toys—or blue jeans—they're wrapping for Christmas were made under inhumane conditions.

Predictably, things had gotten messy on the factory floors as the Chinese economy went through the transition from a socialist welfare system of state-owned enterprises toward a Dickensian dynamic of raw capitalism. As the major industrial economies moved their labor-intensive production to low-wage developing nations, investors were legally obligated to comply only with local labor standards—not the burdensome higher standards at home. In China's case, authorities do not allow independent trade unions, a situation that can be a boon to factory owners with an interest in holding down wages and staying competitive in the global food chain.

Put to the test of Levi's stringent code of conduct, the task of sorting out the human rights and labor problems in China might have seemed more trouble than it was worth. At least that appeared to be the company's initial line in 1993. "After analyzing China's human rights situation, we have decided not to pursue any direct investment or sales to China. And we will gradually reduce our subcontracting works in the country," Linda Butler, Levi's manager of communications, told Hong Kong's *South China Morning Post* in early May. "We are hopeful that the conditions of human rights in China will improve, then we can expand our business there."

Butler dismissed speculation that the decision had something to do with the pending debate in Washington over the annual renewal of China's MFN privileges. "The timing was purely coincidental. It was on the board of directors' agenda," Butler would later tell the *San Francisco Chronicle*. "And it was never a public statement. We just told our employees."

Announcing plans to leave China—or leaking an internal decision to do so—was a bold and dramatic gesture, loaded with symbolism that nobody seemed quite able to define at the time, not even Levi's own executives. Not a single major U.S. company followed Levi Strauss in making motions to withdraw from China, which in hindsight clearly put the company in a rather embarrassing position. Levi Strauss had gone out on a limb, and no one else was thinking about following.

It soon became apparent the company was not of one mind on China and did not intend to joust with China over human rights windmills. Butler acknowledged that there were "a variety of perspectives and opinions" voiced during the discussions about whether

Levi's should withdraw from China, but "in the final result, senior management believed that the potential benefits are balanced by the risks associated with doing business in a country that has pervasive human rights violations. Those risks are damage to brand image, corporate reputation, and long-term commercial interests."

In fact, the majority of participants in Levi's China Policy Group had recommended staying in China, albeit under stricter terms of engagement that would include such controversial activities as supporting human rights organizations on the ground. But the minority recommendation—pulling out—was embraced by the company's executive management committee or, more precisely, by the man in charge of Levi Strauss, chief executive Robert Haas. Taking a principled stance on human rights, Haas must have reckoned, would not only protect but also enhance the Levi's brand image.

Haas was no lightweight moralist posturing for public consumption. He derived formidable authority as a descendant of the original Levi Strauss and carried the burden of his family's long tradition of ethical business practices. He was also a tough-minded CEO who took the company semiprivate in 1985, engineering what was at the time the largest leveraged buyout in history, and finished the job of concentrating ownership in family hands eleven years later—ostensibly so he could run the company in accordance with his own values. Haas demonstrated his proclivity to act independently in presiding over the 1993 decision on China.

In a speech some years later Haas reflected on how the company's innovative approach to putting a priority on ethical principles has been challenging—and costly. By enforcing its code of conduct around the world, the company severed ties with a number of contractors and required others to improve their operations to meet its terms of engagement standards. He didn't mention the loss of potential revenues in China. "Going against the grain may add costs to your business or invite publicity and relentless scrutiny. Taking these actions can put your firm at risk," said Haas. "Each action we took added costs to our business . . . costs that our competitors did not bear. Popular wisdom at the time questioned the value and cost associated with such self-imposed regulations. But over the years, we have found that decisions which emphasize cost to the exclusion of all other factors don't serve the company's and its shareholders' long-term interests."

By all accounts, Haas believes sincerely in what he said about ethics and values. But the motivations behind the controversial plan to pull out of China were never fully explained to the public. At the time, no official press releases were issued on the move, only conflicting statements that were tantamount to a show of obfuscation by the company.

Officials in Beijing were quick to dismiss the portent of the action. "There are tens of thousands of foreign companies in China, including thousands of American firms. If one company decides to leave, they are quite at liberty to do so," sniffed Foreign Ministry spokesman Wu Jianmin. Wu told reporters the human rights issue was an "excuse" invented by Levi Strauss to justify leaving China. Contradicting Linda Butler's original statement, Levi officials started spreading the word that the decision was not about human rights at all. One executive was quoted by the *China News Service* as saying: "It is absolutely not because of human rights concerns that makes Levi stop its investment in China." Whether this was a genuine clarification or a message to mollify Chinese officials is impossible to know, but this and other statements would serve to muddle the company's new policy. It left open the interpretation that the move had more to do with labor standards and workplace problems and was not a critical judgment on human rights.

This clumsy spin doctoring may have been a display of incompetence on the part of the company's public affairs team. It also could have reflected factional bickering within the ranks. In any case, it left the human rights advocates, who applauded the bold statement of principle, completely in the dark about the company's real intentions. The net effect was consistent, however, with a logical agenda: to protect Levi's brand equity in the eyes of socially concerned consumers in the short term, while keeping options open to revising business strategies in the future.

Close examinations of Levi Strauss's decision making on China in case study research by business scholars at Harvard and Stanford Universities and St. Mary's College of California support the idea that the decision-making process was indeed equivocal and unresolved. A commitment to leave China was never made. Instead, contractor production was to be phased out over a four-year period, subject to review and revision in a process of "continuing improvement" of its terms of engagement guidelines.

Following the events of 1994—when U.S. business rose up unanimously to denounce the Clinton administration's human rights policy on China—Levi's isolation stood out even more, and the momentum behind its principled stance dissipated. Quietly, out of sight from its admirers in the human rights advocacy community, Levi Strauss froze its plans to withdraw after making initial cuts in its production. Then, in April 1998, five years after its announcement on withdrawal, Levi Strauss let it be known that it was reversing that policy and would now consider expanding production and making direct investments in China.

Company president Peter Jacobi elaborated, in remarks to *The New York Times,* that Levi Strauss had no choice but to engage itself more fully in China or risk losing out in the competitive game of the global apparel business. In other words, the company was balancing its idealism with bottom-line business interests and reaching an entirely different conclusion from the one in 1993. "You're nowhere in Asia without being in China," Jacobi said.

All along, Levi Strauss had maintained its ties to nearly all of its clothing contractors and suppliers in southern China. Its Hong Kong subsidiary had let contracts lapse at several blue jeans plants in accordance with the company's earlier decision. But it still "outsourced" clothing and fabric at about twenty contractor plants in Guandong, the province in southern China adjacent to Hong Kong—the same number cited back in 1993. It was contracting apparel production at some of the same factories that other international brands manufacturers used. Initially, however, the company decreased the volume of its production in China by about 70 percent, from 2.6 million units to 800,000 units.

To explain its about-face, company officials cited improvement in the human rights environment in China, although they did not specify by what measure. In any event, that line of reasoning—that the coast was now clear because Beijing ostensibly was committing fewer human rights violations—did not jibe well with the representations made by the company five years earlier, to the effect that it also was pulling out because of labor standards, not just political repression. To clear up the confusion about the policy reversal, the company issued a peculiar statement on its corporate Internet Web site, titled "Talking Points on Conducting Business in China." This document stated unequivocally that the "self-imposed restrictions on manufacturing in mainland China" would end effective April 8, 1998. The document cites some compelling reasons for the new tack:

- It is not practical for LS&CO to conduct business in Asia without being in Mainland China.
- We would threaten our commercial interests by staying out of Mainland China while others are solidifying footholds in one of the world's fastest-growing economies.
- In a wide variety of industries, other major global companies are showing that it is possible to successfully operate in China in a responsible manner.

The official "talking points" also looked back at the justifications for its initial decision to withdraw, putting a new twist on the human rights factor. Now the company said it believed at the time it "could not do business in China and ensure that its employees, or those working on its behalf, would not be subjected to human rights violations. LS&CO also believed that doing business in China would pose reputational [sic] risk to its brands." The document appears to put to rest the romantic notion that concern about the pervasive pattern of human rights in China influenced the earlier policy—as it clearly had in 1992 when the company withdrew from Burma strictly on human rights grounds. "The decision was never intended to change China's human rights policies or to impose our view on others. The company was simply doing what it felt was right for LS&CO, its employees and its business partners." Jacobi had made the point somewhat more bluntly in his public remarks: "Levi Strauss is not in the human rights business. But to the degree that human rights affects our business, we care about it."

What was left unmentioned by Jacobi and the talking points document and by news media accounts of the policy reversal was that Levi Strauss had revised its code of conduct in the years since it announced, somewhat equivocally, that its withdrawal was influenced by human rights concerns. It changed the terms of the code, rewording its "Guidelines for Country Selection" to "Guidelines for Country Assessment" and in the process softened the standard it set in 1992, allowing a more flexible and nuanced interpretation.

The original code states flatly that the company "should not initiate or renew contractual relationships in countries where there are pervasive violations of basic human rights." The revised code published in 1996 stated that the guidelines were intended to aid in assessing the balance between the "potential risks and opportunities" in a country. In evaluating the risks of damaging the Levi's brand, the company commits itself only to assessing whether the "human rights environment would prevent us from conducting business activities in a manner that is consistent with the Global Sourcing Guidelines and other Company policies." In subsequent editions of the company pamphlet spelling out the code, and on the Levi's corporate Web site, the detailed language under the Guidelines for Country Assessment is omitted altogether. The idea was "to clarify what our position is, to clear up the confusion so we didn't look like we were at odds with our operations," said a company spokesman. Levi Strauss had lowered the bar significantly on the terms of its engagement in repressive societies.

Many would argue that the bar had been set unreasonably high in the first place, that Levi Strauss went overboard with its principled stance on China and left itself no choice but to backpedal. Others in the human rights advocacy community, feeling a sense of betrayal, wondered whether or not Levi Strauss had eliminated the goal post altogether. The scrappy San Francisco–based advocacy group Global Exchange was quick to picket Levi Strauss headquarters and launch a campaign to protest the China policy reversal. "Levi Strauss came out five years ago and said, 'We are a company that cares about human rights. We are going to make a very principled stand and not produce in China,'" the group's director, Medea Benjamin, told reporters at the rally. "But what has changed in those five years to make Levi's change its decision? Nothing." Harry Wu, a strident Chinese dissident émigré and former political prisoner who had been affiliated with Stanford University as a visiting researcher, chimed in with a statement criticizing Levi's decision. "What's improved in China is the business climate," he said. "In fact, human rights violations are getting worse."

The mainstream human rights groups were more guarded in their reaction. Amnesty International takes no position on sanctions against China. But William F. Schultz, director of the group's American operation, used the occasion to admonish Levi Strauss to continue placing principles over profits when it expands operations in China. In a letter to Robert Haas and the Levi board of directors, he wrote: "You are regarded as one of the most conscientious of America's corporations. Indeed, it is exactly because of your reputation that your new presence in China provides you the occasion to do more than turn a few billion fast yuan. You have the chance to model responsible business practices in China and thereby prove to your business colleagues that it is possible to match honor to profit."

| | |

Herein lies the enigma of Levi Strauss & Co. It is an icon of American business mythology, highly respected for having balanced its ethical integrity with commercial success, and at the same time it is a tightly held and surprisingly opaque corporation, castigated by a chorus of outsiders for its arrogance and inconsistency. One set of its detractors ridicules the company for getting carried away with its idealistic beliefs in corporate social responsibility at the expense of the bottom line, pointing smugly to a recent sharp decline in the company's sales. The other group of critics comprises disappointed idealists, who had hoped Levi Strauss would fulfill some sort of quasi-messianic role in shaping the moral universe of big business.

To its credit, the company has more often than not practiced what it preached: it was one of the last major U.S. garment manufacturers to cave in to the seductive lure of globalization, closing domestic factories only reluctantly as it moved production overseas in pursuit of the greater efficiencies of low-wage labor. The company was ahead of its time in a range of innovative social policies, such as desegregation of its factories in the Deep South in the 1950s, supporting AIDS education, promulgating a global code of conduct for the workplace, offering health benefits to unmarried (and same-sex) partners of employees. But the Levi Strauss that was once distinguished as a benevolent employer and a paragon of virtue was now starting to come down to earth.

Even the goodwill of some of its greatest admirers was beginning to wear thin. "It's still a marvelous company with great people, but you can't understand what's happening there. They say one thing and then they do another," said Helen C. Bulwick, a global retailing analyst at Andersen Consulting in Oakland and a lecturer at the University of California's Haas School of Business. "I had assumed, like many other people, that they had completely withdrawn from China, and I'm surprised to hear they never really left. I didn't know that, and that gives you an idea how poorly they communicate with the outside world."

After nearly 150 years in operation, Levi Strauss suddenly found itself on the defensive where its proud business culture was concerned. The company announced massive layoffs in its domestic workforce in the late 1990s, shutting down twenty-two factories and eliminating more than thirteen thousand jobs. These developments and the company's tribulations over its China policy confirmed a self-evident truth that applies to any business enterprise: Values and principles are inextricably linked to the bottom line, with both positive and negative implications. This applies whether you're talking about job security for loyal workers at home or the labor rights of vulnerable contract laborers abroad. Businesses thrive on the integrity of their brand names in the eyes of consumers. But in the intensely competitive environment of the global marketplace, even the most socially responsible corporation does not have the option of crippling itself for the sake of its abstract principles.

At the turn of the century, Levi Strauss & Co. was engulfed in a major shake-up in upper management that reflected a crisis of confidence in its traditions—and perhaps a state of ethical exhaustion. The company was desperately retrenching after enjoying years of a phenomenal trajectory of annual growth in sales and profits. Suddenly it found itself staring at the brink of a downward spiral. Its share of the lucrative blue jeans market it had invented and then dominated for decades had been cut in half. Sales were going into a free fall. One month before Levi Strauss disclosed dismal sales figures for the fiscal year 1998, Peter Jacobi announced his early retirement, after only two years as president, to make way for new blood. Company executives were beginning to muse out loud that Levi Strauss had become too insular and hidebound in its traditions and needed an injection of pragmatism from the outside to restore its financial health.

Will coping with this financial upheaval result in a weakening of the company's commitment to human rights or an abdication of its informal leadership role in the field of corporate social responsibility? The company, in a now familiar pattern, is sending out mixed signals.

On the one hand, it has let it be known that its preoccupation with values will be adapted to conform with more pressing business realities. On the other hand, it hired a heavyweight, diplomat Gare Smith—right out of the State Department's Bureau of Human Rights, Democracy and Labor—to manage its policies on social responsibility as a corporate vice president. "Bob Haas was very clear about it," said Smith. "This is a company based on values." Whatever the future holds for Levi Strauss, one thing is clear: Its actions offer crucial lessons for other multinationals struggling with human rights policy making. The story of Levi Strauss also provides important clues for activists in the human rights advocacy community trying to understand the limits of what businesses can and cannot do to take responsibility for the many gross injustices that surround them in the global marketplace.

| | |

What drives a company to think seriously about human rights? Almost without exception, it's an overarching necessity to protect the integrity of its reputation and safeguard the intangible asset of its brand image. That need is greater than usual for Levi Strauss, because its brand is deeply associated with the emotional values of freedom and individualism in the minds of many of its most loyal customers. Levi's 501 blue jeans, by their very nature, demand protection from the taint of political repression and the exploitation of teenage seamstresses.

Levi Strauss spent decades nurturing and capitalizing on its extraordinary image, and now the company faces a devastating potential that its most important asset—the symbolism of its brand—might be betrayed in the minds of its oldest and best customers. By drawing heat from the watchdogs of the human rights advocacy community, negative impressions of the brand would infect a new generation of young consumers who are already indifferent to the magic of wearing Levi's jeans. The rage in campus protests these days is aimed at sweatshop exploitation, and political attitudes about which brand is culpable and which brand is responsible can be expected to influence purchasing decisions.

Robert Haas and his family were caught in the sticky web of this very dilemma at the end of what apparel marketing analysts might someday describe as "the Levi's century." The company has to survive as a viable and profitable business before it can carry out its ethical mandate to the hilt. In order to retain its position as a leader in corporate social responsibility, Levi Strauss must be taken seriously by its competitors and avoid becoming the butt of jokes for its progressive policies. A $6 billion company cannot afford to be dismissed as another wacky phenomenon from the San Francisco counterculture. To leave a legacy of ethical business principles that can be adopted as the norm by other companies, Haas must reap healthy profits and at the same time manage an extraordinarily vulnerable public image by sticking to his principles.

The idea that corporations would voluntarily regulate themselves in a way that could alleviate the outrages of political abuse and labor exploitation in the developing world is a radical, untested theory. In the midst of its embarrassing downturn in its business, Levi Strauss all but rejected the notion that it is a model for other companies to follow. It steadfastly declined to open itself up for close scrutiny of its human rights policies. As a privately held corporation, it had every right to do so. But the company cannot make itself disappear or expunge from the public record the effects of its behavior on consumers, community neighbors, corporate imitators, human rights advocates, and other stakeholders in the enterprise behind the iconic Levi's brand.

Whether it likes it or not, Levi Strauss is a decisively influential model, the proverbial three hundred-pound gorilla that is bound to pop into conversation whenever the subject of human rights and business is under thoughtful discussion. Not even the tortured ambiguity of the company's policy on engagement in China can change that.

CHAPTER FIVE

|||

Human Rights for Sale

> *as freedom is a breakfastfood*
> *or truth can live with right and wrong*
> *or molehills are from mountains made*
> *—long enough and just so long*
> *will being pay the rent of seem*
> *and genius please the talentgang*
> *and water most encourage flame*
>   —E. E. Cummings, from
> "as freedom is a breakfastfood," 1940

Sialkot was one of those godforsaken corners of the Third World that very few people outside of the Punjab had ever heard of—until it was cast, ephemerally, as center stage for international outrage over the widespread use of child labor. Now Sialkot can boast of being home to Reebok International's "human rights soccer ball." All is quiet again.

The dusty Pakistani city near the border with India, populated by about one million souls, is the source for a significant supply of the world's quality soccer balls. Indeed, stitching leather balls for sporting games has been a traditional local craft here for more than a century, since the days of the British Raj. In recent times the major brands in the sporting goods industry quietly and efficiently contracted with local entrepreneurs to make balls in Sialkot of suitable quality to meet the high standards of international professional soccer leagues.

The method of production was a curious process that combined preindustrial craftsmanship with the machine age. Centralized factories would stamp out leather panels to be stitched into skin sacs at the myriad family workshops in the surrounding villages. Then the balls were returned to the factories to be filled with rubber air bladders and finished for export. The stitching work was a traditional cottage industry for the Punjabi villagers, employing parents and children alike, offering much-needed supplemental income to impoverished villagers. More hands at work meant better income, more food, greater stability in the subsistence economy of the rural household. Stitching balls has always been a family affair, with artisans training their children from an early age in the vocation of precision sewing skills.

Then the whole system—and the fabric of the local culture—came under siege. The glare of the international human rights spotlight revealed that it was common for children well under the age of fourteen to be stitching soccer balls in the Sialkot district. Children, in the social context of this industry, were essential in the production chain, accounting for approximately 20 percent of the labor force. All of a sudden the villagers were told they had to stop doing what they always had done as long as they could remember. International standards dictated that these children must be sent to school and not induced to work as though they were mere chattel. It was now expected that mother and children over the age of fourteen should commute to stitching centers, where production could be monitored to ensure international labor standards were not violated.

Reebok, the Stoughton, Massachusetts–based brand of sneakers and sporting goods, acted quickly in response to the news out of Sialkot, where it had begun laying the groundwork for a small operation making soccer balls. The company has a stellar reputation for progressive human rights policies. It credited Levi Strauss & Co. for inspiration when it started drafting its own code of conduct for offshore production, one of the oldest, back in 1992. Reebok CEO Paul Fireman had already positioned his company as a champion of human rights: it withdrew from South Africa in 1986 and funded Nelson Mandela's tour of the United States after his release from prison four years later. The company started giving out annual human rights awards to young activists in 1988, before the telegenic Tiananmen massacre made human rights a household buzzword, and it distinguished itself by an early response to the allegations of labor abuse at contractors' shoe factories—the same damaging claims that rival Nike had initially shrugged off. Reebok was a founding member of Business for Social Responsibility, and it provided a grant that helped launch BSR's human rights program. The number two sports shoe brand after Nike, it simply tried harder to get things right in the mine-ridden global marketplace.

But how to explain the "human rights soccer ball"—which by its very existence in the marketplace invites charges of crass commercialization of the sacrosanct ideals of human rights?

Reebok's kosher soccer ball was the result of the company's quick footwork in Sialkot. By dint of its activism, the company was tuned in to the indictments of child labor—it honored Iqbal Masih, the Pakistani carpet-making "child slave," with its 1995 human rights award, six months before the boy's martyrdom helped galvanize a global crusade. That year Reebok proposed to the Soccer Industry Council of America that a task force should investigate child labor in the industry. But as the research dragged on, the company made arrangements so that all the steps in producing its soccer ball, including the stitching, would take place under one roof at a new contractor factory devoted exclusively to Reebok. There the company would monitor production to ensure no children under fourteen sewed a stitch on Reebok brand balls.

The label on the new product, which hit the market in 1997, attested to that fact: the words *Reebok, Human Rights* are emblazoned over the company logo depicting the silhouette of an athlete leaping gleefully into the air, below which the ball proclaims: "Guarantee: Manufactured without child labor." In a news release announcing the ball in November 1996, Reebok crowed: "It is believed this represents the first time a guarantee of this kind has been placed on a widely distributed consumer product." Indeed, no other manufacturer had the churlishness to brand its balls with this claim.

Reebok got a jump on its rivals in Sialkot, but the language of its public relations coup did not emphasize the messy problems left largely unresolved back in the villages. Advocates brought into the picture to study the no-child solution to soccer ball stitching were seriously concerned about what would happen to the young children left behind in the villages, unsupervised by parents who now would be commuting long distances to stitching centers. There had been distressing reports that a similar campaign of international outrage over child labor in the carpet-weaving industry in South Asia had resulted in considerable economic dislocation, sending unemployed children into the streets, where in desperation they turned to prostitution or dangerous work like welding to help support their destitute families. The advocates of reform in Sialkot knew something had to be done to provide for the schooling and the general welfare of the young children, now that they had been "saved" from a vocation that consumers in affluent societies might consider inappropriate for a twelve- or thirteen-year-old.

Reebok had a quick fix for the underage children of the workers at its contractor factory. It set aside a percentage of the sales of its soccer balls—up to $1 million—to fund the Reebok Educational Assistance to Pakistan (REAP) program, which supports a new school. Gradually the rest of the international soccer ball industry caught up and agreed at a trade show in Atlanta to work in partnership with advocacy group Save the Children Fund UK, the ILO, and UNICEF in developing a monitoring system for stitching centers as well as remedial educational and vocational-training programs for the bouncing soccer ball children.

It appears that some very sincere people trying to clean up child labor in South Asia may have forgotten that in human rights intervention, as in the Hippocratic oath, the first consideration should be to do no harm. What that situation in Sialkot looks like now is far from clear. A representative of Save the Children Fund UK said nobody there was tracking the issue and referred inquiries to the organization's branch in Pakistan, which did not respond to requests for information on conditions in Sialkot-area villages. The Atlanta Partnership issued a report on the educational and social welfare project in the Sialkot area at the beginning of 1998, a year into the project, disclosing problems with low participation rates and poor compliance among local factories.

Meanwhile, allegations of widespread child labor in the region persisted. The Washington, D.C.–based International Labor Rights Fund, which had exposed child labor practices in the soccer industry in its 1996 "Foul Ball" campaign, issued a scathing report at the beginning of 1999 charging that the Atlanta Partnership program was failing in its goals of keeping underage children out of the industry and providing informal educational opportunities to those who were forced out. Many of the local Pakistani employers participating in the program "are still using children in their stitching centers, and in home-based employment; the ILO is not empowered to apply any sanctions to these employers," read the report, whose information is attributed to independent investigators. The research suggested that soccer ball production was simply moving from Sialkot to nearby regions of Pakistan, where it goes on unregulated, and that some children were moving from soccer ball stitching into jobs in Sialkot's surgical instrument industry. "In short, we are deeply concerned that soccer ball manufacturers and retailers may be using their participation in the program to claim their balls are 'child labor free,' without actually taking sufficient steps to remove children from the production process," the report argues.

These sorts of allegations were vigorously denied by leaders of Sialkot's export-oriented business community, who complained— according to the on-line news service Pakistan Link—that labor activists were "obstructing the country's exports on the pretext of child labor" and insisted that child labor had been eliminated from this city.

Robert A. Senser, a veteran labor activist and former U.S. Foreign Service officer, puts the issue in these terms: "Whatever the labels on soccer balls may say, they are still stained by child labor. And the major lesson is this: Achieving sweatshop reforms in the global economy—even with corporate codes of conduct and the support of the ILO and UNICEF—is difficult, though not impossible."

| | |

Untouched as it was by young fingers, Reebok's soccer ball was not an immediate commercial success, a company representative concedes. Soccer balls were a new product line for Reebok, and the company was having problems with distribution and sales that were unrelated to the human rights issue. The company did not disclose sales figures, but by 1999 nowhere near the $1 million in charitable proceeds had been generated by profits from the ball. Nonetheless, these brazenly branded balls opened a new chapter in the battle for consumer perceptions about corporate social responsibility. Fuzzy good feelings about corporations and products had been induced in consumers for years by advertising techniques that manipulated emotions on a subliminal level. But this message appears to patently hype a moral concept by taking the stigma of repulsive child labor and turning it around into a clever marketing slogan.

Kicking around a regulation human rights soccer ball might not have the fashion statement value of donning a "Save the Rain Forests" T-shirt made out of recycled rags. But the ball tells an evocative story, imbued with a profundity that acts to indemnify the soccer league or the parental shopper from responsibility for the sins of child labor. The consumer is disposed to imagine that the alternative would be paying maybe a little less for a soccer ball stitched by some weepy-eyed eleven-year-old Pakistani girl working slavish hours in a dank mountain hovel. In the universe of twisted moral reasoning that surrounds the debate over corporate responsibility for human rights, freedom is indeed a breakfast food, to borrow the observation of poet e. e. cummings. Human rights, like any other abstraction, can be sold as a commodity.

Doug Cahn, a senior Reebok executive who carries the title "director of human rights," vigorously rejects the perception that the soccer ball, the annual awards, and the company's other high-profile endorsements of human rights activism are motivated by commercial interests. He said the soccer ball has been widely acclaimed and that many of the Reebok Human Rights Awards had been granted despite controversy surrounding recipients that had potential adverse effects on the company's business interests. Cahn cites the 1992 Reebok award to Fernando de Araujo, the East Timorese activist who had been jailed by Indonesia's Suharto government—at the risk of provoking the displeasure of official hosts in a repressive country where Reebok produced some 30 percent of its shoes. Indeed, Cahn said company officials in Indonesia were subject to personal harassment as a result of the award. Authorities raided a Reebok contractor plant to register their displeasure, he said. "The notion that this is some sort of marketing ploy is laughable," Cahn said. "Anybody who tells you we're doing this for public relations is absolutely wrong. If we as a company had used our concerns about human rights for crass marketing purposes, we would have done things very differently."

Levi Strauss & Co., along with Reebok, lays claim to having taken an exemplary position in the battle against child labor. Levi's promotional literature describes an anecdote that has been repeated in numerous news articles about the company's do-good practices. A particular child labor case tops the list of positive outcomes from enforcing the 1992 code of conduct, as advertised on its corporate Internet site. In this incident, the claim is that the company's internal auditors got wind of a problem of child labor, and Levi took action on its own—before the human rights watchdogs could raise a stink:

> In Bangladesh, our initial Terms of Engagement evaluations revealed that several underage girls were working in two contractors' facilities. Rather than dismiss the girls, which would have put them at risk of exploitation and economic hardship, Levi Strauss & Co. teamed up with the contractors to develop an innovative solution. The contractors agreed to stop employing underage workers, and to continue to pay a salary to the girls, provided that they attend school. Levi Strauss & Co. paid for tuition, books, and school uniforms for the girls. The contractors, in turn, pledged jobs for the girls after completion of their schooling.

The Levi's code strictly prohibits contractor-partners from employing children under the age of fourteen or older children below the local minimum age for compulsory education. The company does not disclose data on the results of its internal audits of this particular term of engagement, however, so outsiders cannot know how many underage children have been discovered making Levi's products. The solution applied to the two contractor facilities in Bangladesh was never intended to be instituted as a corporate policy, applying universally to other contractors found employing underage children. The company doesn't know exactly what happened to the Bangladeshi girls cited in the anecdote. Independent sources suggest the Levi's contractor offered the same schooling program to children at two additional factories in Bangladesh and one in Turkey—extending benefits to a total of forty-one underage children. But a company spokesman was not aware of the additional programs in Turkey and did not know what year the case took place. He said he'd heard that a local coalition of apparel contractors in Bangladesh had adopted the program as a model for an ongoing effort to keep young girls in school—and out of the brothels—and he'd heard the Bangladeshi government was interested in studying the program. But Levi Strauss was no longer involved.

The telling and retelling of this anecdote, illustrating Levi Strauss & Co.'s innovative approach to problem solving at the micro-economic level, has become part of the legend and helps to sustain the company's reputation for socially responsible business practices. But as an isolated case, it becomes an absolution for the company, not a solution for the profound and seemingly intractable problems of child labor in South Asia. The depravation of childhood innocence in unhealthy industrial settings is all too common around the world and can have serious implications for developing nations that must rely on literacy and higher education for long-term economic growth.

Levi's Bangladeshi child labor story, like the tale of Reebok's human rights soccer ball, makes for great publicity—whether or not the actions in question were sincerely motivated or more cynically intended to capitalize on the pious aura of human rights. But in the absence of contextual information linking these stories to the big picture—the incorrigibility of child labor—they are no more than diversions from the basic problem at hand; fables, offering a feel-good release from the need to learn about messy truths.

| | |

So much sanctimonious noise has been made about child labor and sweatshops in recent years that human rights has become high fashion. Flipping through the pages of the March 1999 issue of the glamour magazine *Marie Claire,* for instance, one finds a lodestone of human rights content. Admirably, the magazine features a serious story about efforts by the human rights NGO Christian Solidarity International to combat the bondage of women and children in Sudan. Also in this issue—amid the sensual kaleidoscope of perfumed advertisements, sassy mannequins, and vapid articles with such titles as "Men, Sex and You"—one encounters a full-page ad trumpeting Reebok International's human rights program. Here you see a sneaker shoelace bearing the Reebok name and logo, looped in the shape of the AIDS ribbon—the familiar symbol used in the battle against the scourge of acquired immune deficiency syndrome, which Reebok laudably supports with funding. Below the shoelace is written, "Human Rights: Unconditional. Undeniable. Unlimited. Are you feeling it? www.reebok.com."

That's not all. Elsewhere in the same issue is another human rights exploitation "mood pitch," this one a two-page spread depicting dour-faced Tibetans on the left and a pair of haute couture shoes on the right. The phrase *Walk With Us* stretches in red across the fold, mysteriously connecting the emotive image of the Tibetans to a pair of slender legs shod in designer sandals and the brand name Charles David. Once again, an Internet address is cited to ratchet up the *coolness* factor of the message. On the left, the ad invites you to visit the World Wide Web site savetibet.org; on the right, "charlesdavid.com." Charles David's Web page exhorted the fashion-conscious Internet surfer to sign an e-mail petition supporting the "Free Tibet" campaign, without actually saying what that specific cause might be. The site also hosted an on-line auction where sympathizers can bid on "Tibetan white silk Khata" scarves autographed by the likes of Leonardo DiCaprio, Harrison Ford, and Brad Pitt, star of the movie *Seven Years in Tibet.* Minimum bids were set at $500. The Web site doesn't say exactly where the money will go. (A visit to the Tibetan Gift House on Solano Avenue in Berkeley, California, reveals that genuine ceremonial silk Khata scarves, unsigned by movie stars, can be purchased for as little as $15.)

Charles David's marketing director, Rachael Taylor, explains that the company is working with the International Campaign for Tibet in a campaign demanding the release of two political prisoners held by China: Ngawang Choephel, a musicologist from Middlebury College in Vermont, and Gedhun Choekyi Nyima—a ten-year-old boy who had the dubious karma of having been selected by Tibetan religious authorities as the reincarnation of the Panchen Lama. Like so many other acts of human rights outrage in China, this one combines tragedy with absurdity: the authorities seized the holy boy and installed their own choice as a state-approved and presumably atheist Panchen Lama incarnate.

The money raised by the on-line Hollywood Khata auction, meanwhile, goes to support the Tibetan refugee community. "We've had a very positive response," Taylor said. "People need to be made aware of these issues, whether it's through the fashion industry or whatever." The Walk With Us ads ran in the major fashion magazines—*Vogue, Elle, Mirabella,* and *George*—during the spring, and Charles David planned a new version "for the fall line," spending nearly $1 million on the campaign. Charles David's shoe designer, Nathalie Marciano, took on the Tibetan cause as her own and is said to have incorporated what she imagines are Tibetan motifs in her sandal creations. She's the owner's daughter and is married to Maurice Marciano, chief executive of Guess Inc.—the jeans maker with one of the worst track records on sweatshop abuses, according to the apparel industry labor union UNITE. Charles David makes a line of shoes for the Guess brand, but human rights activists have found no reason to investigate its production facilities in Spain and Italy.

Should there be a law, or at least an advertising industry standard, prohibiting ads like this—exploiting the tragedy of cultural genocide in Tibet to sell shoes? Not if you really believe in free speech. But in any case, such regulation—or professional self-restraint—is unlikely to come about because the perpetrators themselves wouldn't comprehend the offensive nature of the message. Indeed, articles in the advertising and fashion trade press fawned over Charles David's bold attempt at "cause marketing."

This kind of huckstering is particularly insidious because it closes the loop of moral culpability for human rights, with astounding hypocrisy. It is one thing for a company to avoid the negative publicity of involvement in a human rights scandal and take policy measures to limit that risk—thus protecting its brand and its financial interests. It is yet another thing to exploit vague and tacitly emotional messages about human rights to tweak the consumer's subliminal desires for material goods they hadn't realized they wanted and probably don't really need—especially for products that in many cases come from the belly of the beast of low-cost production overseas.

This is not to suggest that Reebok sneakers and Charles David pumps are made by abused children in wretched sweatshops, which is not necessarily the case. But if they are not taking advantage of consumer gullibility in promoting the notion that one can buy the feel-good image of human rights in these ads, they are taking a cheap shot at pampered Americans who want desperately to be exonerated of guilt for their considerable role in human suffering in the global economy.

Precisely for this reason—the danger of being perceived as ridiculously hypocritical—Levi Strauss & Co. has been generally reticent about its own conflicted policies on human rights. The much publicized program for child laborers in Bangladesh was a notable exception. One can easily claim that the company's lack of transparency is at odds with the spirit of human rights and corporate social responsibility. But at the same time, it appears to be a matter of choosing between the lesser of two hypocrisies: one would be to flaunt an ideal that by its nature should be kept separate and pure from the corrupting interests of commercialism; the other is to practice a poorly defined human rights agenda by stealth. Perhaps Levi Strauss is, to a degree, guilty of both sins.

| | |

Ever since James Dean's appearance in the classic 1955 films *East of Eden* and *Rebel Without a Cause*—prominently wearing Levi's genuine 501 blue jeans with signature turned-up cuffs—Levi Strauss has capitalized on the amorphous association their blue jeans have with the values of freedom and rebelliousness. James Dean, the sullen-faced antihero, became a cultural icon for a soulful generation of Americans—and so did the denim work trousers he wore on the movie set. Blue jeans became a national sensation, and the company that made them enjoyed considerable mystique. Marlon Brando was actually first to wear Levi's on the big screen when he played the role of a free-spirited motorcycle gang leader in the 1954 movie *The Wild One*. Brando, in his black leather jacket astride a red Moto Guzzi, helped immortalize the turned-up cuffs—a detail that became a fashion statement in and of itself. The insides of the cuffs attested to the authenticity of the brand because they revealed a characteristic "selvage"—the white woven trim left on the indigo denim fabric as it came off the loom, marked with a red thread unique to Levi's jeans. (That detail was lost when the company later switched to denim made more efficiently on larger looms but was recently resurrected when the old looms were put back into service to produce special editions of "vintage" 501s.) Photographs of Lucille Ball and Marilyn Monroe wearing Levi's are treasures in the company's archives.

There's no evidence that Levi Strauss & Co. exerted influence at Hollywood prop departments—it happened serendipitously, before advertisers began taking full advantage of the powerful message of product placement in movies and television. Nor were actors Dean and Brando particularly interested in the subject of human rights at the time, at least not in the way it has become a faddish cause for celebrities in today's Hollywood. But they and their Levi's 501s captured on celluloid the essence of raw American individualism. Their on-screen personae were honest and idealistic, iconoclastic and subversive, rebellious in the face of injustice. This is not so different from the way one might describe the dynamic potential of the ideas of universal human rights.

Even before they became a fashion statement of freedom in the American gestalt, the simplicity of these original denim trousers was identified with the honest virtues of the working class: factory workers, farmers, and ranch hands wore them with dignity. The company played back that idea in its advertising, stressing the sheer durability of the pants. Levi's jeans were the closest thing to a native costume for assimilated Americans, whose ancestors emigrated from far-flung lands and diverse cultures. Native Americans wore them, too, as Levi's promotional material suggests by displaying an evocative photograph from the nineteenth century depicting a member of the Yuma tribe wearing a pair of Levi Strauss denim waist overalls and holding a genuine bow and arrow.

So did the cowboy, that mythical incarnation of bowlegged American knighthood, whose values of independence and rugged individualism fed the nation's fantasies. A real cowboy would not be caught dead without his blue jeans, any more than he'd die in a pair of fluffy bedroom slippers. And you had to assume he was wearing the Levi brand; real-life ranchers and farmers in the West, in fact, have been Levi's most loyal customers since the nineteenth century and continue to wear them lovingly. Consider the 1977 homage to Levi's in this bit of doggerel praising their durability, by New Mexico's venerated cowboy poet laureate, the late S. Omar Barker, which begins: "They asked me 'What are Levi's?' . . . I told 'em they're the pants / That purt near since the year of one have give cowpokes a chance / To ride the roughest ranges in some britches they can wear / Without no need to worry none about a rip or tear." Although the Levi's trademark red tag wasn't explicitly visible on the back pocket of the Marlboro man's blue jeans, one could take it on faith that he was wearing the genuine article.

Indeed, these were not sissy designer jeans, the kind touted in glossy women's magazines. Getting a new pair of Levi's—before the advent of preshrinking and stonewashing—was a tactile experience that involved the buyer in a ritual of claiming personal ownership to a pair of inanimate pants. The stiff indigo denim material had to be shrunk to size, preferably by bathing in the jeans, then beaten to a pulp and lightened by repeated washings. By the time they were optimal in color and suppleness, there was already a true bond to a pair of Levi's that would last for years, long after they had turned whitish blue and been ripped and patched.

I, for one, can remember being ejected from my suburban Chicago high school for wearing a pair of Levi's blue jeans, ostensibly because of draconian school rules that forbade metal rivets on trousers, which purportedly could damage school furniture. The year was 1968, the Vietnam War was raging, and that pair of pants took on an absurd significance as a touchstone for social consciousness— even though it was largely a figment of adolescent posturing. It was this kind of powerful brand identification as the uniform of social rebellion that made the company products irresistible in the minds of baby boomers. Ed Cray, author of the 1978 book *Levi's,* draws a pointed connection between Levi's jeans and the Berkeley free speech movement that erupted on the University of California campus in 1964, one of the seminal events in the wave of student protests that swept the country and the world. It seemed everybody was wearing Levi's 501 blue jeans. "Western work pants had become symbolic of youthful protest," Cray writes. "Levi Strauss's sales of blue denim pants flourished."

The company incorporates into its legend another iconic symbol of the age of Aquarius—Woodstock. A panoramic photograph of the vast sea of jeans-clad bare-chested revelers at the 1969 rock festival rated a two-page spread in *This Is a Pair of Levi's Jeans,* a self-congratulatory coffee table–size book written by Levi Strauss's corporate historian, Lynn Downey, and staff and published by the company at the height of its glory in 1995. The book's dedication cites the wearing of Levi's jeans at the fall of the Berlin Wall and singles out for praise advertising executive Mike Koelker, "creative genius behind many of the advertising campaigns that shaped the Levi's brand." Levi's cultivation of its brand's symbolic portent for freedom was no accident.

Inside PR, a trade magazine covering the public relations industry, recognized the company's skill at delivering its values-laden message by awarding it the second annual Bernays Award for Reputation Management in 1997. The magazine defined the art of public relations as "doing the right thing and getting credit for it" and declaimed: "Levi Strauss is a company that prizes its reputation as a good citizen, and understands how to leverage that reputation for success." Said Paul Holmes, *Inside PR*'s editor, "This is a company that values integrity above all else, and a perfect example of the fact that good public relations is not only about communication, but also—more importantly—about action. Through its actions, Levi Strauss demonstrates that putting values first strengthens relationships, builds credibility, and ultimately guarantees profits."

Where the company's human rights policy is concerned, however, the logic behind the Bernays Award tells the story backward.

It is the amorphous—and potentially fickle—nature of Levi's tremendously valuable brand equity that drove the "action." A product that thrives on its association with freedom and individualism must be protected from the stain of political repression, labor abuse, and the silencing of dissident voices in the countries where it is produced—at least until such precautions are deemed as violating a higher order of business logic and unnecessarily damaging to the bottom line. As a consequence, the perceived betrayal of that image, so carefully constructed and nurtured over the years, now invites the wrath of the human rights advocacy community and, possibly, the indifference of a new generation of consumers who may never feel the Levi's mystique.

| | |

The business of selling human rights is perhaps most prevalent—and annoying—in the entertainment industry. It's one thing to sanctify a material product, like a soccer ball or a pair of Levi's 501 blue jeans, in the warm glow of righteousness, however illusory. But it is far more pernicious to sell a consumer nothing but the cathartic sensation of *caring* about human rights—blurring reality and fantasy and purveying the fleeting emotions that release a potentially conscientious person from the need to otherwise actually do something in real life about real problems. It is the difference between informing an audience and entertaining, ultimately opiating, them.

The problem begins with the occasional purple-prose narrative journalism that reveals shocking tales of egregious human rights violations but neglects to follow up on the factual chain of events or to place the sordid tale into broader context. The consumer of a newspaper article or a TV newsmagazine exposé feels absolved of personal responsibility after experiencing a delicious emotional revulsion to the outrage, without being asked to think about how to prevent it from happening again. For an ephemeral moment, the passive audience for cheesy entertainment journalism can feel good about detesting Nike shoes or virtual slavery on Saipan without any obligation to revisit the intellectual and moral challenges of the issue the next day.

When the human rights narrative abandons the pretext of objectivity and crosses over into the realm of pure entertainment, it can become as preposterous as it is insidious. Hollywood has a tendency to seize serious issues from the human rights agenda and turn them into cartoon morality plays.

The vogue for Tibet's human rights tragedy launched two major motion pictures in the late 1990s, suggesting Hollywood might take a cue from the "teen exploitation" genre and develop a new class of Tibet exploitation films. Fortunately the films were not major box office hits and there was no parallel merchandising of Dalai Lama dolls. *Seven Years in Tibet,* directed by Jean-Jacques Annaud and released in 1997, tells the epic tale—based on supposedly factual autobiographical material—of an arrogant thrill-seeking German mountaineer who turns his back on his wife and child and the Nazi regime to settle in exotic Shangri-la, where he becomes friend and tutor to the boy Dalai Lama just as marauding Chinese Communist troops invade. The cinematography is sumptuous, and the plot is as sappy as it sounds. His Holiness, the Dalai Lama—awarded the 1989 Nobel Peace Prize while leading the Tibetan opposition from exile—is tossed into the script as a comic-relief sideman to the real hero of the film, which parasitically borrows the aura of the Tibetan human rights tragedy to puff up the profundity of an otherwise run-of-the-mill fantasy-adventure narrative.

Martin Scorsese's *Kundun,* released in 1997, gets credit for making a main character out of Dalai Lama, in richly exhausting detail. The film's production and distribution actually became the grist of human rights politics when in 1996 an official in China's Ministry of Radio, Film and Television, declared that *Kundun*'s interpretation of the Dalai Lama's life constituted "an interference in China's internal affairs." Beijing's attitude was widely interpreted as a veiled threat against Walt Disney Co., parent of the movie's co-producer Touchstone Pictures.

Disney was at the time expanding its business interests in China and, like all foreign companies, relied on the goodwill of officialdom to successfully navigate the many pitfalls of the market. A group of forty-one Hollywood Tibet fans—actors, producers, and directors, including Paul Newman and Bernardo Bertolucci—piped up during the controversy by writing Chinese ambassador to Washington Li Daoyu, protesting Beijing's "attempt to impose worldwide censorship on any artistic production that does not meet with official approval." Disney stood its ground, avoiding the risk of appearing to kowtow to the thugs who have mauled Tibetan culture and all but destroyed its politico-religious tradition. Mickey Mouse et alia have been accused by plucky NGOs in Hong Kong of complicity with alleged labor abuse in the production of Disney brand clothing at Chinese contractor factories, but CEO Michael Eisner was resolute in defending freedom of speech and artistic integrity against the seductive logic of keeping relations with Beijing free of hassle.

Bertolucci, one of *Kundun*'s Hollywood lobbyists and auteur of the epic *Last Emperor,* paved the way for the Tibetan exploitation motif with his 1994 fairy tale *Little Buddha,* set in Seattle, where Tibetan monks believe they've found the reincarnation of a venerated lama in the form of a ten-year-old white suburban boy. Verisimilitude is not something you would expect in a plot like this, of course. The master Italian filmmaker would have done better to turn the story into a farce instead of an absurdly straight-faced and shallow drama that offers no more than a muddled comprehension of Buddhist mysticism.

In the short-attention-span theater that is the American mass media, few stories get relegated to such breezy shallowness as the China epic, of which the Tibetan tragedy is a constant companion. Its substance is so complex and its magnitude so profound that it cries out for simplification. Yet the task of interpreting and explaining this critically important subject has been usurped, along with the human rights drama, by the imagineers of Hollywood and the Bernaysian genius of Madison Avenue. In the entertainment and advertising worlds, it doesn't matter what's true or false, as long as the message or the narrative is effective.

If *Seven Years* and *Kundun* leaves anyone confused about who the bad guys are supposed to be, all one needs to do is sit through a screening of the 1997 film *Red Corner.* In this ode to the righteousness of American-style habeas corpus, a visiting businessman, played by activist-actor Richard Gere, gets framed in a murder rap in Beijing and subjected to the Kafkaesque paranoia of the Chinese judicial system. Director Jon Avnet has our hero escaping and prancing like Zorro across the picturesque rooftops of Beijing's back alleys to safety at the U.S. embassy. The story ends happily, on a note of moral rectitude: The leading man does not get the girl, his gorgeous Chinese lawyer, but he does get to go home after a corrupt Chinese general has a fit of sincerity and confesses culpability to the crime.

The plot of *Red Corner* was so over the top and its realism so flawed that the genuine brutality of the Chinese regime—and the fact that businesspeople are in fact routinely subject to arbitrary arrest in that society—got lost in the process of pandering to entertainment value.

Gere, who is undoubtedly quite sincere about the social and political causes he's known to advocate, turned up on television the next year to introduce a segment of CBS's mystical drama series *Touched by an Angel*. In this episode, "Liberty Moon," a Chinese student protester who sought refuge in the United States after the Tiananmen Square incident returns to China to find the daughter she left behind. A fetchingly beautiful angel with a melodic Irish brogue, Monica (Roma Downey), visits the heroine, Jean, in a prison while she's being beaten by Chinese guards. Monica manages to deliver the word of God before Jean dies from a fall down a staircase. All ends well in this melodrama when Jean's American lawyer friend, acting on the angel's instructions, flies a kite on Tiananmen Square, finds the missing daughter, adopts her, and takes her home, rescuing the poor child from heathen totalitarianism.

The evangelical "Liberty Moon" story is a playback of the Christian missionary zeal that runs deep in Sino-U.S. relations. Since the days of early nineteenth-century Yankee clipper ships—many of them engaged in the unconscionable "triangle trade" of Chinese tea, British opium, and African slaves—Americans have never stopped trying to save souls in China. It's a kind of angelic imperialism, if you will, that despite its ulterior religious aims has had some extremely positive secular effects—American missionary schools in Shanghai and Hong Kong introduced the rationalism of the Enlightenment to revolutionaries like Sun Yat-sen, father of modern China. America's fundamental understanding of China was indelibly shaped by children of the missionaries like Pearl Buck, author of the 1931 novel of Chinese peasant life, *The Good Earth,* and Henry Luce, the rabidly anti-Communist patriarch of the Time Inc. media empire.

Proselytism of the universal human rights message in tandem with Christian redemption in the "Liberty Mood" episode went down easy for some of the fans of *Touched by an Angel.* In the TV program's on-line discussion forum on the Internet, several viewers responded to this query: "Can fans who watched the 'Liberty Moon' episode tell me how the show changed their perceptions about China or shaped their impressions about good and evil in the present political system in China?"

A fan identifying herself only as Kathy responded, "What can you expect in a country where God is not allowed except in secrecy and Christians are murdered? The bigger question is what can we do? We as Christians and any other religions must do something to help the human condition in China. We are *all* God's people, and it's appalling that so many are living in unlivable conditions." Melinda Tanng, a second-generation Taiwanese American whose said her parents can't return "because of the government," observed: "Last night's episode was the best I've ever seen. It is [the] closest one to the actual message of the Gospel." Tim Hobbs had this to say: "It is scary to see that a country that possesses nuclear technology has the view it has toward human beings. They seem obsessed with military and political power. To be jailed and killed simply because you voiced opposition to the government is appalling. It is not good for the world as a whole. China wants our trade and Hong Kong for its money but does not want to change its human rights policies or lack of. All business around the world should not go to China. Their products would be made with slave labor. Thanks. I pray for China to be totally *free!*"

The responses go on in this vein, articulating views about Chinese politics that reflected the conventional wisdom among China's critics but also blurred the line between the fact and fiction. It was as though Jean's murder and Monica's efforts at divine intervention had occurred in reality, not on television. Attitudes had been informed by way of a suspension of disbelief, not necessarily through thinking.

| | |

Not all of Hollywood's efforts at portraying human rights tales have taken the form of artistic propaganda, shallow and devoid of critical substance. Steven Spielberg's *Schindler's List,* which swept the 1993 Academy Awards after leaving audiences around the world in tears with the gripping realization of the enormity of the Nazi Holocaust, is the most notable exception. In this morality play, Oskar Schindler is a despicable Catholic war profiteer who has a change of heart—an epiphany of corporate social responsibility, if you will—and takes action to save the lives of more than one thousand Polish Jews, his employees. The motion picture is based on a true story, which along with Spielberg's genius as a director undoubtedly gave the work the persuasive force of verisimilitude. The message of this black-and-white film had no shades of gray; it was universal, timeless, and subversive, drawn from the truth of a single primordial swamp of humanity. Oskar Schindler risked his life and tossed profit maximization to the wind because saving innocent people was simply the right thing to do.

Fortunately, the moral decisions in today's global marketplace are nowhere near as clear-cut as the one that confronted Oskar Schindler during the Holocaust, unless perhaps you were in the business of selling materiel to Serbian troops deployed in Kosovo. History judges people and institutions in moral hindsight, however, as Volkswagen and the Swiss banks learned in recent years when tales of their allegedly willful collaboration with the Nazi regime came back to haunt them. Bad judgment calls in the situational ethics of half a century ago became indefensibly immoral acts generating class action lawsuits today. Even in matters of greater ambiguity, such as the alleged complicity of Royal Dutch Shell in the execution of dissident environmental activists in Nigeria, scandalous stories can take on a life of their own, as facts get lost to the power of the narrative. The distortions of the telephone game, where facts are unwittingly mutilated on repetition, goes into high gear in the new electronic media—particularly in the hyperbolic Web sites of advocacy campaigns.

Levi Strauss is now banking on something called "viral communication"—a mixture of mood advertising, Internet marketing, and urban networking—to reassociate its brand name with the attributes of coolness among young consumers. Yet this process is in fact a double-edged sword, out of control once the germs start to spread. In the cacophony of rich information we live in, stories are telegraphed instantaneously and irresponsibly through all varieties of media, through electronic mail, through shock-jock radio talk shows, through word of mouth, through the facile treatments of Hollywood. For example, unless you check the footnotes of some obscure academic journal, you might be influenced by the vague impression that Nestlé Inc. once marketed unhealthy or tainted infant formula in the Third World, which is a gross distortion of the facts. Nestlé's blunder, which prompted an international boycott campaign, was in marketing its products in places where sanitary water supplies were not readily available to mix with the formula and where baby formula wasn't really needed to replace mother's milk in the first place. But the stigma long outlasts clarification of the facts.

It is not a solution to try to stop the story from spreading like a virus, or control its distortions, or kill the messenger. A finely written code of conduct, if used irresponsibly for purely public relations value, can be as injurious as the problems it purports to resolve—damage control can be tantamount to outright deception and clearly perceived as such. Joshua Karliner, director of the guerrilla-style corporate watchdog Transnational Resource Action Center, coined the term *greenwashing* for companies he accuses of cynically adopting environmental policies to mask rather than resolve problems. The term is working its way into the lexicon of human rights advocacy as more advocacy groups like his broaden their examination of corporate operations.

It may seem counterintuitive, but transparency—openness to an honest and accountable discussion of the facts—is the best remedy to half-truths and avoidable misunderstandings about corporate behavior in society. Nowhere is the need for transparency greater than in the dialogue on the topic of human rights between multinational corporations and their stakeholders and critics in the community at large. Given that economic advancement created by entrepreneurial activity is inextricably linked to the evolution of political rights in the minds of many, if not most, international business leaders, it follows that corporate ethical integrity and economic justice are inseparable.

Human rights policies should not be bought or sold or traded into meaningless rhetoric in the free marketplace of information and entertainment. The facts should be on the table in plain view, warts and all. Otherwise the lines between reality and fantasy, truth and mendacity, blur into a pathetic haze in a world that is frighteningly out of touch with its moral rudder.

CHAPTER SIX

|||

Putting a Price on Social Responsibility

A company's values—what it stands for, what its people believe in—are crucial to its competitive success. Indeed, values drive the business.
> —Robert D. Haas, "Values Make the Company,"
> *Harvard Business Review,* 1990

In the heart of San Francisco's inner Mission district, not far from Mission Dolores, the old Spanish church that marks the beginning of European settlement in the city in the late 1700s, stands another historical landmark of more recent vintage. This one spawned a twentieth-century fashion revolution: denim blue jeans. Erected hastily after the great earthquake of 1906 and lacking architectural distinction, it is a large three-story clapboard building painted canary yellow and crowned with a modest wooden sign reading, in letters reminiscent of the Old West, "Levi Strauss & Co." Twice a week in the mornings, Levi's "Mother Factory" opens its doors to gawking tour groups. The visitors sit down for a viewing of vintage Levi's TV commercials—one ad stars a talking dog whose punch line is "A legend doesn't come apart at the seams." They plod around a museum gallery of memorabilia, including a replica of the denim tuxedo the company made for Bing Crosby after the crooner was ejected from a tavern for wearing blue jeans. Then the pilgrims shuffle across a cavernous factory floor where young Asian and Latina women are on the job, busily sewing Levi's clothing in a human diorama.

Levi Strauss & Co. is such an important piece of San Francisco lore that tourists from around the world arrive by the busload at the old 250 Valencia Street plant, booking well in advance for the limited-capacity shows. The site captures the imagination of foreign blue jeans aficionados from Europe to Japan, who pay homage to this authentic Levi's shrine. Company legends haunt the place—this is the facility where workers were kept on the payroll during the Great Depression, installing hardwood floors instead of standing in breadlines when demand for blue jeans dried up. Groups of California elementary-school children descend on the plant for educational field trips, children who have no idea what the Levi's brand meant to their parents and may never experience the mystique themselves. Kindly tour guide Joe Casaletto, a retired Levi's plant manager, looks as though he'd been born in the pair of faded 501 jeans he's wearing. He rewards a group of children—fourth-graders straining to sit still in their seats at the end of a question-and-answer session—with souvenirs of bluish pencils made from recycled scraps of denim.

"They're too young to understand anything about brands," a gray mustachioed Casaletto says as the children romp quickly in and out of the Levi's store on the first floor of the old plant. Maybe not now, but soon enough it will be clear whether they become Levi's children or GapKids. Or perhaps Levi's orphans. They are the very people who someday will make or break the fortunes of the proud old apparel company. Their powerful judgment as free-spending teenage consumers is not necessarily going to be impressed by the rhetoric of social responsibility or by evocative nostalgia for the Levi brand. Creatures of the fickle, short-attention-span tastes in today's fashion bazaar, they will lust for what their peers are wearing and buy what they are convinced is in vogue, anything that evokes or defines the evanescent value of "coolness" when the needs of belonging prevail.

The items on sale at the Valencia plant store, which opens only briefly after tour hours, suggest how the company is trapped in tradition. Classic five-pocket button-fly riveted 501 Levi's blue jeans line an entire wall of the store. They sell for $42 a pop—about the same price consumers pay at department stores, where the company still sells most of its jeans. The real sticker shock comes from the store's selection of "vintage" Levi's 501 Double-X denim trousers, replicated at the Valencia Street plant by the costly hands of the 150 or so American workers on site in special editions to look and wear just like the humble indigo work trousers the company produced in the 1930s—long before Levi's jeans became an international fashion sensation. A single pair of vintage Levi's, with an outmoded cinch belt in the back and authentic selvage-edge inseam, costs $225. There's a strong demand for them among loyal customers, especially in Japan, where they outsell regular 501s. Genuine vintage Levi's—the tattered old pants actually made in the early part of the century, can fetch tens of thousands of dollars from collectors when they show up at estate sales and auctions. Yet it's difficult to imagine anyone younger than forty gripped by nostalgia and bidding on those pants.

There's a kind of pathos here at the Levi's Valencia Street plant, where history, tradition, and fatalism mix like invisible gasses. Foreshadowing the very predicament that the company faces today, the facility came close to being shut down in the 1970s because San Francisco's unionized labor was too costly compared with low-wage workers in the American South. Walter A. Haas Jr., the current chairman's father, explained the dilemma in the Bancroft Library's Oral History. "San Francisco is a very high cost town. The factory is inefficient, relatively, in view of the fact that it's on several floors and it's an old building," Haas said. "With the inducements that other communities offer us, this production could be more efficiently developed in some other area. So for a long time we considered moving out of San Francisco, and I have to confess that part of our reason for staying is that this is where the business started, and there's some nostalgic desire to stay here. But most of all, the people working at that plant are minorities; they're disadvantaged."

Haas adds in this 1973 interview: "I don't want to sound too self-serving, but in the long run, we should not be operating in San Francisco, particularly since even though we provide steady work and working conditions are good, it's a low-pay industry. We are someday going to get some very bad publicity when some militant organization accuses us of operating a sweatshop in the middle of San Francisco, which we could avoid by going out."

But Levi decided to stay put, investing nearly $1 million to renovate the Valencia Street plant, making it in Haas's words "attractive and bright and comfortable"—and presumably bringing the structure up to contemporary workplace safety codes. "That was a cost we wouldn't have if we didn't have this sincere feeling that we have a responsibility to our employees and to society in general."

Walter Abraham Haas Jr., Levi's modern patriarch and the embodiment of its ethical tradition, died of prostate cancer at the age of 79 in 1995. He was a giant in the community, as a lavish philanthropist and astute business leader who lived to see his family company rise to unprecedented success. "He was charitable for the right reasons and had no personal agenda," eulogized Uri Herscher, executive vice president of Hebrew Union College, in remarks to the *San Francisco Chronicle*. "He was the living, breathing example of business ethics." Haas was spared the indignity of witnessing Levi's recent sharp decline in fortune, and he did not have to hear the callous derision of the values he embraced—as his son and successor would later. The bright yellow factory on Valencia Street is a monument to Levi Strauss & Co.'s commitment to corporate social responsibility at the same time it is an anachronism, an awkward reminder of how much things have changed under the inflexible mandate of economic globalization.

|||

The defining question for Levi Strauss & Co. as it advances toward its 150th anniversary in the year 2003 is whether it will have emerged from the confusion of radical restructuring and a traumatic crisis in confidence with its high ethical traditions intact. It has already reconfigured its paternalistic identity by reneging on a tacit understanding that it would safeguard jobs for American garment workers. The Valencia Plant workers were among the few exceptions, having been saved by nostalgia and an extravagant market niche. But when the company fully surrenders to the cold efficiencies of hollowing out its U.S. production base, even these vestigial jobs are likely to be at risk. Levi Strauss, after all, sees itself now as a design and marketing firm, not a manufacturer.

Following this painful transmogrification, will Levi Strauss's leadership role in the corporate social responsibility movement fade along with the memories of its old-fashioned loyalty to workers? Fortunately, the company had laid the groundwork for transferring its ethical aspirations overseas with an innovative code of conduct that became a benchmark for American industry. Yet the company will not be able to execute its good intentions toward the workforce of its overseas contractors and remain true to its tradition of ethical integrity, if it finds itself losing the struggle for survival. The principles of the moral high ground have got to intersect at some point with the lowly realities of the bottom line.

Levi Strauss, lamentably, made some serious mistakes in the way it merchandized its cash cow product, the iconic blue jeans it had innovated back in the Gold Rush era. Under the aura of the Levi's jeans trademark, consolidated sales soared to a lofty $7.1 billion peak in 1996, yielding a profit greater than $1 billion. Then something went terribly wrong. Sales plummeted by a devastating 15 percent over a two-year period. Profits, no longer publicly disclosed, might be assumed to have slipped commensurately. *Fortune* magazine claims to have gotten a sneak peek at the balance sheet and revealed that "cash flow"—which generally refers to gross earnings—was still as high as $1.1 billion in fiscal 1998. Another unofficial source placed profits at $800 million for the year. The company wouldn't say which is correct.

Whatever the exact numbers may be, Levi Strauss gave every indication that it was descending into deep financial trouble. The cause of this catastrophe was, evidently, hubris. Levi Strauss had become too confident, resting on its considerable laurels as an apparel industry colossus. In the past, the company never had to try very hard to nurture the hip quality of its brand, but now it had lost touch with its core market, the soul of youth. Levi had become hidebound, stuck in the past, suggested its president, Peter Jacobi, in January 1999, when he announced plans to retire early. "I believe the time is right to bring in new leadership that can challenge past practices, long-held views, and historic ways of thinking and working," he said in a prepared statement. Jacobi, who had joined the company as a low-level production assistant, left the company in June before a successor could be named.

Levi's problems obviously ran much deeper than the fact that high-priced American-made jeans could not compete against cheaper imported brands or that dullards in the marketing department were asleep at the wheel while competitors purveying baggy-style jeans nibbled away at the market for fifteen- to 24-year-olds. Within the company there is a painful recognition that systemic management problems contributed to the decline. One popular view seized upon by outside pundits—and given some credence by Levi chairman Robert Haas's own remarks—is that the company was crippling itself with a touchy-feely management style that empowered low-echelon managers and bogged down decisions with the constant delibera- tions mandated by its internal values-oriented mission statement. In other words, Levi Strauss had become exhausted by its ethics, choked into laggard inefficiency by political correctness.

Certainly the company's tradition of ethical integrity cannot take all the blame for its lack of agility in responding to the vagaries of the constantly changing market for mass consumer fashion. But the question remains: Will the urgent task of rectifying the operational mistakes at the root of Levi's financial decline come at the expense of compromising the company's core values? Or will it allow a re- commitment to the kinds of socially progressive beliefs that have guided Levi Strauss over the decades? "We're faced with business decisions that require us to be more nimble in our decision mak- ing," said former corporate spokesman Clarence Grebey. "But we're not abandoning the spirit of our values." Grebey did not stay with the company long enough to confirm that sanguine view.

As the company expands its contractor production in Latin America and the Caribbean to replace domestic output, the task of implementing and monitoring and then stringently enforcing its terms of engagement code is not going to be easy or inexpensive. Proponents of corporate social responsibility, most notably Robert Haas himself, have argued that doing the right thing—acting on a moral basis above and beyond the conventional sanctions of law— can contribute to profit making or, in the very least, is not incompat- ible with rational business practices. Yet nobody has really established that assertion as an undisputed fact. Some studies support the idea, but there is also much evidence to the contrary.

Levi's own experience illustrates the contradictions in the theory that humanistic values and profit making can bind synergistically. The principled instincts Robert Haas acted on when he made his executive decision to withdraw from China, for instance, have been subjected to a reinterpretation on the grounds that the resulting policy of withdrawal sacrificed the company's competitiveness in one of the world's most important markets. Likewise, the company's sincere effort to maintain paternalistic employment practices for American blue-collar workers—a tradition established by Haas's great-grandfather and great-great-granduncle—have been deemed contrary to the company's overall competitiveness in today's global economy.

You have to ask, then, whether doing the right thing fails the feasibility test when it simply doesn't cost out. Taking the matter of moral ambivalence from the whole to the particular, can a clothing contractor in Indonesia or Saipan be expected to adhere to the labor standards of the Levi Strauss code of conduct when the act of granting his seamstresses the privilege of collective bargaining undermines his competitive cost structure? Here's the ignoble truth: For any business, socially responsible practices are justifiable and sustainable only when there's a consensus among managers and owners that the long-term benefits—such as protecting a brand image, complying with the law, avoiding litigation, or enhancing efficiency through employee loyalty—outweigh the short-term costs.

The problem with this formula is that the benefits are mostly intangible and theoretical, while the costs are glaringly clear-cut and quantifiable. The right thing to do is always going to be subject to interpretation, depending on the moral views of whoever is involved in the decision. Situational ethics set the rules of behavior. This cynical truth is inescapable, whether the company is privately held as a virtual public trust or listed on a stock exchange and susceptible to bullying by the shortsighted demands of craven shareholders for higher dividends. That's why Levi Strauss may never be the same again. That's why other American corporations, large and small and across the industrial landscape, may face the prospect of losing an extremely valuable model for ethical behavior in the future.

| | |

As soon as sales showed signs of seriously hemorrhaging, Levi Strauss started taking steps to streamline operations, selling off its Brittania Sportswear unit and killing a partnership with Stride Rite to make shoes. In 1997 it began planning the reduction of its U.S workforce. The original intention was to trim the payroll by 20 percent, but as the situation deteriorated more radical steps were deemed necessary. First, the company cut 1,000 of its 5,000 white-collar jobs in the United States. Then, in three steps over the next two years, it eliminated 13,286 blue-collar jobs in North America and closed four owned-and-operated plants in Europe, cutting 1,560 more jobs. By the time all the separations were completed, Levi Strauss had slashed its 1996 global workforce of 37,500 employees by some 43 percent. Its U.S. employment had been nearly cut in half, practically overnight.

The drastic downsizing followed a failed—some former Levi managers have said "bungled"—attempt to improve productivity at U.S. plants. Starting in 1992, the company began a program to revitalize its factories with the "team concept," which was in vogue among manufacturing consultants as an innovative method of "empowering" workers and at the same time cutting down on the loss of efficiency caused by repetitive stress injuries. Instead of the old piecework system, in which one worker would perform a single task all day and be paid on the basis of meeting or exceeding quotas, the team concept grouped several operators into a collaborative effort to produce whole garments, rotating tasks to avoid monotony and reduce injuries. Early difficulties with the new style of production prompted John Ermatinger, then head of U.S. manufacturing, to warn his plant managers in 1994, prophetically, that if they did not reduce costs by 28 percent by the end of 1997, they'd face uncertain consequences.

By the time the teamwork system of production had been introduced to all of Levi's domestic plants in 1997, however, it was obvious that the innovation, intended as a humane policy to promote efficiency, had backfired. Productivity was below levels achieved under the old piecework system. Highly skilled and more nimble workers complained bitterly that their pay had been reduced because work was bogged down by slower teammates. Anger, stress, and frustration on the factory floor had risen to the boiling point, with workers fighting and blaming each other for problems. "It's just not the same company anymore," Herb Etheridge, a former production manager, told *The Wall Street Journal*. "The perceived value of the individual and the concern for people just is not there."

Robert Haas, quoted in the same article, conceded that the team-work concept caused tensions and unhappiness, adding: "Ours is a culture of experimentation and innovation and novelty, and we're not always successful." Making matters worse, glitches with a new computer system as well as lapses in management controls under-mined the only demonstrable success achieved by the teamwork approach, which was a faster turnaround time in churning out com-pleted garments for shipment in response to specific orders. But clothing too often sat on trucks outside the factories instead of moving efficiently into Levi's internal distribution system, causing reliability problems for irritated retail customers.

Levi's biggest retail account, J. C. Penney, reportedly suffered a forty-five-day delay in the delivery of an order for its back-to-school line in 1998. These sorts of distribution delay problems no doubt helped propel a new trend toward private brand blue jeans in the retail industry, delivering a coup de grâce to Levi's dwindling mar-ket share and its costly domestic production. J. C. Penney was among several of Levi's most important retail outlets that turned from cus-tomer to competitor, eliminating the middleman and selling jeans made cheaply by their own overseas contractors, guaranteed to re-plenish their shelves on time. The store still carries Levi's brand blue jeans but undercuts the price by about $10 a pair with its private brand Arizona jeans.

| | |

When Levi Strauss & Co. reached its zenith in sales in 1996, Robert Haas borrowed $3.3 billion from a consortium of banks and threw in another $1 billion from the company's cash reserves to complete a second stage of the leveraged buyout he and his family had started eleven years earlier. In the 1985 transaction, a new Haas family-controlled entity, Levi Strauss Associates Inc., acquired most of the publicly held shares that the family didn't already own, taking the company semiprivate and removing it from the New York Stock Exchange. At the time, the $1.6 billion deal was described as the largest leveraged buyout in history. This first transaction got myopic securities analysts off Haas's back and gave him free rein to exercise his visionary long-term "values-based decision making" that was the centerpiece of his management philosophy. But it still left a small amount of Levi stock—about 4 percent of total outstanding shares—in the hands of employees, requiring the private company to comply with disclosure obligations under Securities and Exchange Commission regulations.

Haas has not explained why he felt compelled in 1996 to take the stock out of the hands of his employees and consolidate total control among a select core of like-minded family members by buying out many of his relatives. Knowledgeable inside sources maintain the only possible explanation was greed; the transaction was a means for the family to take money out of the company at the top of its value. The $4.6 billion transaction—technically a recapitalization—made the company a completely private entity under the ownership of Haas's new vehicle, LSAI Holdings.

The deal had a peculiar string attached: The board of directors was asked to stipulate that Haas; his uncle, former CEO Peter Haas; his cousin Peter Jr.; and F. Warren Hellman, Levi's investment banker and a distant Haas relative, would create a four-member "voting trust" retaining total control of the company's managerial operations for fifteen years. A bitter family feud erupted around a dispute over the new voting trust, pitting Haas against his aunt Rhoda Haas Goldman, who controlled 13 percent of the shares. "The voting trust came out of the blue," said one individual close to the controversy, who asked not to be identified. "It just didn't make any sense." Goldman cast the only abstaining vote on the deal when it went before the twelve-member board of directors. Adding tragedy to the unpleasant business, she died of a heart attack while vacationing in Hawaii a week later, at the age of seventy-one.

This was the year of Levi's peak in revenues, so the price paid for outstanding stock was generous at $265 a share. Employees now deprived of their stock ownership plan were mollified by the promise of an extraordinary incentive program that would give each of them—more than 37,000 people in 60 countries—a bonus equivalent to their annual salary in the year 2001, provided the company reached the goal of a cumulative cash flow of $7.6 billion over a six-year period. If *Fortune*'s information is correct and 1998 cash flow was $1.1 billion, the company is right on target. Anyone on the company rolls in 1996 and subsequently laid off was still vested in the plan. A debt-ridden Levi later reneged on the bonus.

It is no easy chore for an outsider to fathom all the permutations of motivations and intent behind the Haas family's two-phase leveraged buyout of Levi Strauss, not to mention its effects on the health of the company. It raises some intriguing questions, however. Would Levi Strauss & Co. have benefited by remaining subject to the discipline of the stock market had it remained a publicly traded company? Conceivably it would have abandoned its U.S. workforce much earlier and joined the bandwagon of other apparel manufacturers shifting production overseas. Pesky securities analysts certainly would have nagged Haas and his chief financial officer about declining market share, and that element of transparency would have had the positive effect of shaking the company out of its fateful complacency.

The pressures of Wall Street's overarching value system—profit maximization—also might have coerced Levi's into compromising its principles and leaping into the amoral vortex of globalization much sooner. By the same token, a company constrained by Wall Street values might never have given the world Levi's ground-breaking code of conduct, which since 1992 has set a benchmark for the ethical behavior of multinationals across the industrial spectrum.

Another question is whether Haas's determination to snatch up employee stock holdings was ultimately bad for business because of potentially corrosive effects on employee morale and productivity. The move was at odds with the company's rhetoric on the fundamental precepts of social responsibility. Can employees be "stakeholders" when their privileges as shareholders have been taken away? No doubt the cash windfall enjoyed by the more than 1,200 employees who owned stock, not to mention the prospect of the 2001 bonus, muted the pain of disfranchisement. But after decades of sincere rhetoric about motivating and "empowering" loyal employees, this must have been a harsh message—another telltale sign of Levi's ambivalence about its idealist principles when the money side of things doesn't quite add up.

For the record, Levi Strauss described the purpose of the transaction, inscrutably, in its 1996 annual report as "designed to create a newly refocused Company which would be dedicated to remaining privately held and managed with an explicit commitment to achieving superior financial returns while operating in a values-oriented manner." Whose values the document did not specify. Robert Haas spoke to the logic of privatizing the company in his 1999 interview with *Fortune,* saying that if Levi Strauss had remained publicly traded, "I wouldn't be CEO because I wouldn't want to work in the company." His passion for Levi Strauss would be diminished, he said, "if I had to deal with the kinds of frivolous and unproductive distractions that many of my peers at public companies have to deal with."

The glossy business magazine was unforgiving in its assessment of Haas's passions, ridiculing his attempts to orient his business priorities to the kind of moral compass that had been guiding Levi's family CEOs for generations. The article ran under the title "How Levi's Trashed a Great American Brand: While Bob Haas Pioneered Benevolent Management, His Company Came Apart at the Seams." Popping out of the mean-spirited text of the article are such snide declaratives as "Levi Strauss is a failed utopian management experiment" and "Levi's wasn't just a garment company committed to social responsibility. It was a politically correct organization that happened to be in the garment business."

When it was publicly traded, Levi Strauss was a venerable Fortune 500 company. It had not been long since *Fortune* lionized Robert Haas and his management philosophy in gushing tones in the 1997 article "Levi's: As Ye Sew, So Shall Ye Reap." The more recent article, however, viciously trashed a company whose legend the magazine had once popularized. No wonder that Levi Strauss was gun-shy about the news media to the point of deep distrust, compulsively shielding access to its inner sanctum. This goes straight to a final, lingering question about how transparency will figure into Levi's future. The completion of the buyout in 1996 had the effect of shrouding Levi's "values-oriented" ethical policies, as well as its business operations, in a pained aversion to bright light. The company that once championed the stakeholder philosophy of corporate social responsibility could now exercise almost total control of the information available to external stakeholders in the community at large.

Consider the number of news releases posted on the Levi's corporate World Wide Web site during the first six months of 1999: a total of three. One, in January, announced Peter Jacobi's plan to retire as president; in February there was one disclosing the latest drop in annual sales, with scant elaboration or details; and another brought tidings of the latest round of factory closings and layoffs. In 1997, the first year after going totally private, the company posted a total of seven news releases electronically, reaching out to the public about once every two months.

In theory, any private company is entitled to communicate with the community as it pleases, free of regulatory requirements. There is nothing improper per se about Levi's reticence. But it doesn't seem quite right, either, for a self-proclaimed leader in social accountability. The effects on the balance sheet of the $3.3 billion debt from the 1996 recapitalization, for example, is impossible to know. Dribs and drabs of scattered information appear in the legal and financial press but resist being pieced together. The role of Warren Hellman, a prominent San Francisco financier and philanthropist, is hardly clear. Hellman and a former partner were involved in the 1985 leveraged buyout as investment bankers, and he secured a stake in the new entity, LSAI Holdings, the year before it absorbed Levi Strauss & Co. in 1996—making him a significant shareholder and more or less explaining his exclusive seat on the four-person voting trust. Hellman, like Haas, did not respond to requests for an interview.

Things were going badly enough by 1998 that the company executed the critical first step of its top management reorganization, going outside of the ranks to install a new chief financial officer to take a rational look at things and get its house in order. It recruited William B. Chiasson, who had served in senior positions at Kraft Foods Inc., Baxter Healthcare Corp, and Arthur Andersen & Co. By the time Peter Jacobi announced the decision on his retirement at the beginning of 1999, a major management shake-up was well under way, and it still hadn't fully resolved itself at the time of this writing.

In a surprising development in September, Haas and his fellows on the voting trust decided to replace Jacobi with Philip A. Marineau, a seasoned marketing executive from the beverage industry. The choice of Marineau made perfect sense: what Levi Strauss needed more than anything was marketing sophistication to rebuild its tattered brand. But Marineau's new title—CEO—was a shock. It meant that Haas would be stepping aside, under pressure from the board, giving the reins of day-to-day management to a total outsider. The move was unprecedented in the company's long history, and it demonstrated how desperate the situation was. Haas would remain in power—at least until the voting trust expired in 2011— but told employees in a memorandum announcing the recruitment of the "world-class brand builder" that he had not intended to give up his CEO job for a couple of years.

Marineau, the story goes, was courted through the executive search firm Spencer Stuart as the best candidate for Jacobi's position as president and chief operating officer, but he had refused to join Levi unless he got the CEO title as well. Marineau, fifty-two, had made a name for himself as a marketing savant at Quaker Oats Co. by turning Gatorade, the salty sports drink, from a small concern into a billion-dollar brand. But he took the fall for the troubled performance of the company's Snapple fruit juice unit and left Quaker Oats under a cloud in 1995 after twenty-three years at the company, having lost a shot at the top job. After serving less than a year as president of Dean Foods Co., a food-processing and milk distribution company in the Chicago area, Marineau joined PepsiCo Inc., where he headed the $11 billion North America division and distinguished himself as a capable marketer. Once again, however, he was passed over as heir apparent to the CEO job.

There was no way of predicting how long this hired gun from Pepsi would preside over the resurrection of Levi Strauss & Co. or how effective he might be at restoring the lost magic of the Levi's brand. One would have to assume that Marineau had been brought in to be a merciless cost cutter and given a mandate to make painful decisions that would turn the company around. Any speculation that Marineau, fresh from the cola wars, had nuanced convictions on human rights or corporate social responsibility would be a meaningless exercise. Not surprisingly, Levi's vice president for communications, Dan Chew, declined to make Marineau available for an interview on the topic.

Chew offered a glimpse of official insight into Marineau's attitude about Levi's core values by citing, in a terse E-mail message (he did not return phone calls), two sentences from an in-house video interview he had conducted with the new CEO. Asked to talk on the topic of "corporate culture," Marineau replied: "Well, I share the values that Levi Strauss & Co. practices and espouses, and I believe that you really have the opportunity to be a performance-oriented business and have great social values and be a great place to work. The opportunity to lead and be a part of a place that has these values and at the same time has a performance ethic is great as well."

In a characteristic display of its inscrutable style of media management, the company did not issue a press release announcing Marineau's appointment. Instead the news was announced internally and cautiously released. Official interviews were arranged only with selected newspapers and apparel industry trade journals "because of time constraints and relationships with those publications," Chew explained.

| | |

No matter how you interpret the chaotic story of management problems at the company, the integrity of Levi Strauss's ethical tradition was severely tested by financial deterioration at the end of the 1990s. The fact that Robert Haas will be overseeing the company as chairman for another decade, if not running the operations himself, is a consolation. Ordinarily it takes a strong-willed CEO with an unclouded vision to instill the principles of social responsibility in any corporation, private or public. But if Marineau lacks the interest or passion to play that leadership role during his tenure, Haas may retain considerable authority to influence the corporate culture.

There's no guarantee, however, that the principles Haas inherited and reinvigorated will be sustainable for long. The biggest blow against the company's values comes from the long-term equation of succession at the top. For the first time in the company's 147-year history, there was no family member being groomed—or even in sight—to take over at the helm.

Handing the mantle from generation to generation had been a proud ritual started by the Bavarian immigrant Levi Strauss, continuing to Robert Haas's grandfather Walter A. Haas. The first Haas at Levi's helm presided over a struggling company's transformation into a successful national brand. Then he passed it on to his two capable sons, Walter Jr. and Peter, both professionally trained in business with MBA degrees from Harvard University.

Walter Haas Jr. was the bold leader who stood firm on integrating Levi's plants in the Deep South, who kept the old Valencia Street factory alive out of a sense of obligation to minority workers, and who sought the counsel of a Methodist theologian at the Berkeley Theological Union on how to institutionalize his family's unique ethical legacy. It was Walter Jr. who took the company public in 1971 with a cheeky disclosure in the prospectus advising investors of the company's commitment to social responsibility. He turned Levi's into a global brand, using cash from the initial public offering to finance expansion in Europe and Asia. He also embarked on a diversification binge into peripheral product lines like skiwear and belts that would put the company in financial straits by the time his oldest son, Robert, took over at the helm.

Before following in the footsteps of his father and grandfather, the younger Haas showed signs of straying from the business life, eschewing the drudgery of bookkeeping and statistics courses to major in English literature at the University of California's Berkeley campus. He graduated as valedictorian in 1964—the year that the Berkeley free speech movement raged and became a catalyst for campus political protest nationwide. Coming of age in this political firmament, Haas felt passionately about social injustice: he marched in civil rights demonstrations and joined the Peace Corps, volunteering two years as an English teacher and a physical education coach in the Ivory Coast. The prodigal son took another detour after completing business school at Harvard, seemingly in search of his political soul. He spent a year as a White House Fellow during the final days of the Lyndon B. Johnson administration and tried his hand at political campaigns, working for presidential hopeful Eugene McCarthy before knuckling down and joining the consulting firm McKinsey & Co. He didn't report for duty at Levi Strauss until 1973—he and his father had never openly discussed the idea before then. It was perhaps a tacit understanding.

After eleven years of grooming by his uncle Peter Haas and interim CEO Robert Grohman, Robert Haas took over the management of the family firm in 1984, at the age of forty-three. At the time, the company was undergoing serious financial trauma, the kind that would be repeated in the late 1990s. Demand for blue jeans was flattening out after the boom of the 1970s, and Levi's sales and profits had been erratic over a period of several years. "Our sales were dropping, our international business was heading for a loss, our domestic business had an eroding profit base, or diversification wasn't working, and we had too much production capacity," Haas would later tell the *Harvard Business Review*. "I had no bold plan of action. I knew values were important but didn't have the granite tablets that I could bring down from Mt. Sinai to deliver to the organization."

Haas came on like gangbusters, closing 27 plants and laying off 10,600 workers by 1990—nearly a third of his workforce. He divested the bloated company of many of its subsidiaries in order to consolidate around the core denim brand. All the while he continued to espouse his convictions about the importance of the softer side of management, where the dignity and sense of empowerment of his employees was paramount. Skepticism that Haas could turn the company around prevailed among the pundits in the financial community at the time—much as it does today.

Yet Haas got the best of his naysayers in the first round. A year after becoming chief executive, he pulled off the initial leveraged buyout that made the company semiprivate and effectively got the shrill critics off his back. Marketing the brand aggressively overseas, Haas presided over a decade of phenomenal growth—until things fizzled in the late 1990s. Under the leadership of the Haas clan, the folksy blue jeans maker became a colossus with greater revenues than any other apparel maker, admired for its innovation and distinguished—almost immortalized—by a tradition of balancing profits with the family's tradition of values.

There was no one to receive the mantle now. Robert's younger brother, Walter J. "Wally" Haas, was elected to the board of directors of Levi Strauss Associates in 1995, but he had spent his career as an executive in the Oakland Athletics Baseball Company, which their father bought in 1980 partly out of a civic duty to prevent the team from leaving the community and sold just before his death at nearly seven times the purchase price—an apt illustration of the Haasian concept that good values can generate profits. Wally rose to become CEO of his father's baseball team, but he had never been involved in the management of Levi Strauss. Nor had their sister, Elizabeth Haas Eisenhardt, a lawyer who took time out to raise children after marrying an Oakland Athletics executive. Robert's younger cousin Peter Jr. spent seventeen years at the company in a variety of senior positions and sits on the board's voting trust, but he is preoccupied with philanthropic work. No one from the sixth generation of Walter Jr. and Peter Sr.'s grandchildren had begun apprenticeships at the firm. Robert's teenage daughter is an accomplished equestrian whose passion is for horses, not the blue jeans business. She was accepted at Harvard in 1999 but planned to put off enrollment to compete in the U.S. Olympic trials.

The fact that Robert Haas would be the last heir to Levi Strauss to run the day-to-day operations of the family brand was partly a sentimental matter and would not necessarily affect the ability of the company to restore itself to health in business. Yet the severance of the line may have a more profound impact on the company's ethical tradition and its humanitarian concerns, which have hinged since its earliest days on strong family leaders making a "commitment to commercial success in terms broader than merely financial measures."

||||

Conservatively speaking, the prognosis for long-term profitability at Levi Strauss & Co. was guarded at the time of the company's second major business crisis in fifteen years. Scant information was available to outsiders on which to base a credible forecast, and since public shareholders were out of the picture, financial journalists no longer could claim access to information as surrogates of the public. Securities analysts would no longer be able to pore over balance sheets and corporate filings or have access to management. Since their clients wouldn't be able to invest in Levi Strauss anyway, they had limited interest in tracking the fortunes of this storied firm. Levi was relevant as a struggling competitor to public apparel makers, but not as a home team.

Levi Strauss had retracted into a shell, leaving its critics as well as its loyal admirers guessing about its future. Company officials did not feel obliged to make themselves available for more than cursory remarks to local and national news media. And when they opened up for closer scrutiny by magazine reporters in 1999, they felt "burned" by the results, according to company insiders.

The lack of solid information didn't deter business pundits from pondering the company's fate. "You can never predict whether a company will get its act together in the fashion and marketing industry," said Carol Emert, a business reporter at the *San Francisco Chronicle* who covered Levi's on her retail beat. "Anyone whose sales fall by 15 percent is definitely in a downward spiral. But nobody can predict whether they can turn that around or not." *The New York Times* canvassed a range of opinions about Levi's prognosis, soliciting comments from consultants and financial analysts. "We talk about life cycles in business, and it seems Levi's is at the very end of the road with some of these problems. Somewhere in the life cycle they fell off the curve, and management didn't catch it," UCLA business professor and corporate crisis management consultant

Sanford Sigoloff told the *Times*. "It's pretty hard to recover, and it's clear that management is reaching for pretty catastrophic measures at this point. They are cutting costs, taking losses, moving to off-shore manufacturing—crisis management. They face a long fight back."

In a stinging rebuke, the credit-rating agency Moody's Investor Service had downgraded the company's Eurobonds and commercial paper in November 1998. Richard Mercier, senior vice president of finance at Moody's, told the *San Francisco Business Times* he had no access to Levi's numbers but observed that the company relied too heavily on distribution through department stores, where young people do not shop; he predicted that shrinking market share in blue jeans would continue to cut into profits and that a turn-around would take several years.

| | |

A rededication to the now cardinal value of being "cool" in the eyes of capricious adolescents and young adults in their early twenties was the high-stakes strategy Levi's took in its first struts toward redemption in the marketplace. It created the marketing position of "urban networker," for instance, paying young employees to penetrate the cultural scenes of major cities and persuade trendsetters to wear Levi's Dockers khaki pants—even giving the pants away—in an effort to seed brand coolness. Levi's put energy into the "Silver Tab" line of jeans products, cut baggy and offered in myriad styles and made available for purchase at a new "Levi's Online" Internet store. Electronic commerce was a bold leap for a company that had for years been locked in to a rigid pattern of relationships with retailers.

The company had a rough start in the on-line business, though. It was so slow to get going, it was beaten to the punch by an interloper who registered the "levi.com" World Wide Web address, and the company had to sue in court to recover that designation. Eventually, an aggressive "levi.com team" would send out electronic mail solicitations to browsers of their cyberstore, such as this scintillating message: "Hey Karl, Hot sand, hot skin, hot looks. Click here (http://replynow.net/levi-r/r.asp?id=89910490 &group=1PP) to see the latest ways to go bare from levi.com." (In August 1999 I did make a purchase from the company's Web site: a new pair of Levi's 505 zipper-fly blue jeans for $36 plus tax and shipping. I was not terribly surprised to see "Assembled in Mexico" in fine print on an inside label. Every other pair of Levi's jeans I had owned said "Made in USA" on the exterior trademark patch above the right rear pocket.) Suffering from high costs and poor sales, the company announced in October 1999 it would shut down its e-commerce operations after Christmas.

Levi Strauss extended the direct-marketing strategy to the traditional "bricks and mortar" world of retailing in 1999, opening its first major owned and operated sales outlet since it tested the waters in 1991 with a more modest effort in Columbus, Ohio. The company had assiduously avoided retailing since it closed its historic dry goods establishment earlier in the century. Now Levi's publicists described the new flagship store in downtown San Francisco as a "multisensory shopping experience," providing "innovative customization services and experiences that don't exist in any one place, anywhere else in the world." The twenty-four thousand-square-foot space, designed to look like an industrial loft, was supposed to be a "pulsating world of Levi's fashion, music and digital audio and visual images." A tub of hot water allowed customers to observe the almost forgotten ritual of bathing in a pair of shrink-to-it jeans to mold them to their bodies. The store offered high-tech body scanning to custom tailor the clothing for sale, as well as hand-painting fabric ornamentation and embroidery. Hip young shoppers were expected to be drawn to the on-site music shop, live disc jockeys, and interactive art gallery. "The store is more than a retail space, it's an engaging environment where kids can hang out," said Gary Magnus, concept and development director.

Levi Strauss started sponsoring independent film festivals and pop music concerts in a continuing effort to etch the Levi's logo on the jaded retinas of young shoppers. The company launched a "Levi's Fuse '99" summer concert tour featuring rock bands such as the Goo Goo Dolls, Sugar Ray, and Fastball. To get better results from its $90 million advertising budget, it switched ad agencies to TBWA/

Chiat Day, which convinced Levi's management it needed something called "viral communications" to reach its customers. Levi's inaugurated a new brand management team of young creative directors and designers and youth marketeers to crack the code of coolness and find new ways of making and selling its clothing.

A new "viral" ad blitz Levi Strauss unveiled at the end of 1998, the "What's True" campaign, betrayed a deep sense of foreboding and confusion bordering on desperation within the company's inner executive sanctum. In an awkward attempt to appeal to the teenage niche market, Levi's took a stab at capturing the imagination of the street culture with TV spots and billboards proclaiming such in-your-face "truths" as "Teachers Make Great Pets" and "Best Friends' Moms Are Usually Sexy." Robert Holloway, vice president for Levi Strauss's "youth category," is quoted by one of the company's on-line press releases as saying: "Young people are bombarded with messages every day that are steeped in pretense. With this campaign we're trying to provide a respite from that pretense and offer them a platform from which they can speak about their lives."

It is a contemporary twist on the naughty James Dean legend, which Helen Bulwick, a retailing consultant and business school lecturer at UC Berkeley, thinks goes way too far. "The biggest brand damage is being done by Levi's itself. Just look at their TV ads, featuring young punks and dropouts as customers—it looks like a drug scene," Bulwick said. "What kind of customer are they going after? It raises great doubts about Levi's role in the community. One kid in the commercial is talking about getting out of going to school. They've become a bit schizophrenic in their strategies. They're struggling."

The publicity windfall of James Dean wearing the Levi's product in a popular motion picture, entirely unprompted, was not likely to happen again. So the company took matters into its own hands and sponsored the 1999 movie *The Mod Squad,* a big-screen version of the kitschy television series of the late 1960s, in which maverick young undercover cops wore bell-bottom trousers and gaudy flower-pattern shirts with ridiculously long collars, the mod fashion rage of that aesthetically questionable era. It was a vacuous movie that got panned mercilessly by film critics and snubbed by audiences. Yet genuine Mod Squad designs were available for sale in a corner of Levi's on-line emporium, long after the movie's artificial and ephemeral buzz had dissipated. It was a desperate bet on retro grooviness, which failed to mitigate, in the minds of the street culture's arbiters of cool, the indelibility of Levi's stodgy old work pants image.

| | |

Sales of Levi's traditional clothing were nothing to scoff at, despite the panicky attempts to pander to the young. In the mid-1990s worldwide revenues from the sale of Levi's jeans and jeans-related products was $5.2 billion, accounting for a whopping 78 percent of its total revenues, according to the company's last publicly available annual report. The breakdown for sales by product line was under wraps in subsequent years, but the picture is clear: Denim remains the life and soul of the company, no matter how well its khaki Dockers or retro bell-bottoms are doing. The best estimate was that more than 80 percent of Levi's jeans were still being sold in department stores, some of which, like J. C. Penney, had turned themselves into competitors by launching their own brands of blue jeans, taking full advantage of the high profit margins offered enticingly by low-wage production overseas. The global economy made doing things like this easy, and disloyalty to a longtime supplier like Levi's was a minor consideration for department store chains that were fighting for their own survival. So-called private label blue jeans—such as Canyon River, sold by Sears, and J. C. Penney's Arizona brand—had made rapid gains in the market, surpassing Levi's dwindling share to account for some 20 percent of the jeans sold in the United States in 1998, according to the New York–based retailing consultant Tactical Retail Solutions, Inc.

The domestic market for blue jeans, in terms of the number sold, had shrunk from 502 million pairs in 1981 to 412 million pairs in 1998, according to the NPD Group, which also tracks the apparel business. But the dollar value of the market was still growing, with sales of $8.3 billion in 1998.

While Levi's piece of the blue jeans pie collapsed from 31 percent in 1990 to 16.9 percent in 1998, its longtime rival VF Corp., maker of the Lee and Wrangler brands, grew from 18 percent to 25 percent. A glib VF, with $5.5 billion in sales, sized itself up against Levi Strauss by claiming to be the "world's largest publicly owned apparel maker." High-end designer jeans brands such as Calvin Klein, Guess, and Tommy Hilfiger, advertise heavily for name recognition but commanded only 7 percent of the market.

For Levi Strauss, the ultimate comeuppance came at the hands of Gap Inc., the ubiquitous emporium that got its start in life in a single storefront in the neighborhood of San Francisco State University selling Levi's brand clothing and rock-and-roll records to the turned-on youth market of 1969, two years after the summer of love. The pop caricatures from the *Mod Squad* TV series might have shopped at this store, whose name alluded to the "generation gap" that observers of pop culture fussed about back then. Founders Don and Doris Fisher and CEO Millard "Mickey" Drexler went on to become Levi's nemesis, sourcing clothing competitively from overseas contractors and creating a retail empire of some 2,500 outlets under the Gap, Banana Republic, and Old Navy brands. Hot-selling blue jeans made in Mexico under the Gap's label claimed 5 percent of the U.S. market, adding insult to the injury of Levi's declining share. More important, Gap's sales had ballooned by 39 percent to $9 billion in 1998—the principal reason Levi Strauss could no longer claim to be the world's largest apparel brand. It had been eclipsed, in a single year, by one of its old retail outlets.

To its chagrin, Gap Inc.'s phenomenal success placed it squarely in the crosshairs of human rights activists taking aim against the apparel industry. Gap was one of the earliest companies to draft a code of conduct covering contractors, but it had the usual problems with compliance, and it was heavily exposed to the stigma of bonded labor on Saipan. The company also had lots of centrally located storefronts that could be easily picketed for local television news stations. By most accounts, Gap's labor practices were no worse and no better than the rest of the apparel industry. But to maximize public awareness of their cause, the human rights community needed a brand that symbolized the sins of the entire industry, much as Nike was the whipping boy for sneaker makers. The notoriety that Levi's managed to avoid when it was at the top of the heap now visited Gap with a vengeance.

It was fair game for financial pundits to pick at the mistakes Levi Strauss & Co. made over the years in its marketing strategies, or lack of them. But as the company's declining business performance drew attention, its vaunted ethical practices also came under the microscope. Conventional wisdom, as reflected in the news media, quickly seized on Levi's idealistic mission statement and the unconventional values it articulated, as though a malignant tumor had been discovered that begged for surgical removal.

Under the spell of Levi's 1987 "aspiration statement," the theory goes, Levi's managers were subjected to supposedly untenable practices such as building consensus, observing mutual respect and tolerating a diversity of opinions. The mission statement had "devastating impact on company effectiveness," wrote Carol Emert, the *San Francisco Chronicle* reporter, in her story about the resignation of Peter Jacobi in January 1999. Emert said, with a slight tinge of professional embarrassment, that she later received a kind note from Levi's public relations manager Dan Chew complimenting her on the accuracy of her coverage. "Staff were afraid to debate company strategy because arguing violated the Aspiration Statement," she had written. "On issues in which no consensus could be reached, all too often, no action was taken." Haas himself told Emert that the mission statement spawned a "dysfunctional" culture and that it was undergoing "fine tuning." It's important to note that Haas chose the phrase *fine tuning,* not total repudiation.

Yet the pundits had Levi Strauss on the defensive. *Fortune* sneered at the excesses of the Customer Service Supply Chain initiative, a task force that evidently ran amuck under a misguided interpretation of "aspirational" principles in an effort to improve the efficiency of the company's distribution channels. Hal Espen, writing for *The New York Times Magazine,* ridiculed the company's "devotion to values" as something that creates "an open-ended temptation to spend vast amounts of time discussing personal accountability, seeking feedback, taking required week-long courses in ethical decision-making, and participating in exhaustive evaluations of colleagues and supervisors." There was nothing in the mission statement, he adds, about "acting ruthlessly to save the company in the event of a crisis." Espen's article focused on the company's renewed efforts to market the putative coolness of its brand. His negative spin on the company's traditional values seemed to reflect the attitudes of the young Levi's marketing executives Espen spent time with and whom he portrayed sympathetically as, well, really cool.

What exactly was this highly maligned aspiration statement, and what did it say? The document was part of a chain of written policy proclamations that had begun with the ethics codes drafted in the 1970s and led up to the Global Sourcing Guidelines of the early 1990s. In its original form it was a verbose treatise encouraging the creativity and innovation among employees. It said much about the diversity of views and nothing about a straitjacket of political correctness. This was Robert Haas's attempt to institutionalize Levi's unique ethos, much as his father had tried to institutionalize its ethics in the 1970s. "When we describe the kind of Levi Strauss & Co. we want in the future, what we are talking about is building on the foundation we have inherited: affirming the best of our company's traditions, closing gaps that may exist between principles and practices, and updating some of our values to reflect contemporary circumstance," read the statement's preamble.

It goes on to exhort Levi's managers to practice leadership that "epitomizes the stated standards of ethical behavior" and "provide greater recognition—both financial and psychic—for individuals and teams that contribute to our success." The aspiration statement praises diversity—in the race and gender of personnel as well as in their ideas. "Differing points of view will be sought; diversity will be valued and honesty rewarded, not suppressed."

Sounds like an ideal corporate culture, the kind of place where the best and brightest—or any self-respecting person—would want to work. The problems apparently resulted from the way this inspirational mission statement was grafted into the corporate bureaucracy. An ability to manage "aspirationally" became an important criterion for evaluating the performance of Levi's executives. As much as one-third of a manager's raise, bonus, and other financial rewards was based on the vaguely defined aspirational quotient.

"Giving people tough feedback and a low rating on aspirational management means improvement is necessary no matter how many pants they got out the door. Promotion is not in the future unless you improve," Haas explained in a 1990 interview with the *Harvard Business Review*. The process, however well intentioned, was ripe for arbitrary application and abuse, despite the massive amount of time and energy that went into educating executives. Nearly every other week the company ran off-site training sessions on the so-called core curriculum of executive leadership behavior—all supervised by one of the company's top eight officers.

Levi Strauss may well have exhausted itself with its ethics, but that's no reason for critics to make light of the honorable intent behind them or for the company to entertain the idea of abandoning them.

By the middle of 1999 indications were that Levi Strauss did not intend to turn its back on its values—it just wanted to understate them. In late May the company revised its mission and aspirations statements with a more tersely worded document that tones down the prior focus on corporate social responsibility. It deleted the old headline "Responsible Commercial Success." Gone was the bold promise at the heart of the company's old statement of its mission: "We will conduct our business ethically and demonstrate leadership in satisfying our responsibilities to our communities and to society." A single line now describes the mission, "to achieve and sustain commercial success as a global marketer of branded apparel."

Bob Haas's "values drive the company" philosophy had survived in the text, somewhat muted, but still there in black and white. The new language of the company's "aspirations" celebrates the "traditions and values that we have inherited and that continue to lead us to commercial success." Among these are "honesty, promise-keeping, fairness, respect for others, compassion and integrity," which "guide our conduct and actions even when we are confronted by personal, professional and social risks or economic pressures."

Clarence Grebey, the former Levi's spokesman who played a role in the revision, explained that the aspiration statement was altered to make it more succinct, but that its "spirit" hadn't changed.

Indeed, the rambling document was edited down from 1,069 to 393 words. Grebey said things had gotten out of hand in the past because the old statement was too long and confusing and vulnerable to misinterpretation. Originally the idea of "empowerment" meant to be accountable and to make decisions independently. But it was later interpreted by some executives as having the right to participate in every decision, slowing things down. "Complacency set in," Grebey said.

| | |

It was no coincidence that the policy deliberations that created Levi's landmark code of conduct governing its terms of engagement with overseas contractors and foreign host countries were steeped in the very kind of consensus-building, values-oriented, touchy-feely style of management that was now under attack. The framework used in drafting the code, and later implementing the code in a decision on China policy, was something the company called the "principled reasoning approach." In essence, this was designed to address situations in which ethical concerns needed to be balanced against business interests. The idea, according Levi's human resources department guidelines, was to "protect against self deception, self-interest and expediency and to ensure consistency and fairness in decision-making."

The six steps of the principled reasoning approach are mapped out on a somewhat esoteric company document that suggests an ongoing process of reevaluation. Written in a bubble at the top of the page is "Problem Identification," with two arrows pointing downward to "Stake Holders" on the left and "Principles" on the right. Stakeholders and principles join in an arrow pointing down the page to "Solutions," which then spins in a circle of arrows with "Implementation" and "Consequences" and back to "Solutions" again. Arrows then point along broken lines snaking back up to the "Problem Identification" bubble at the top of the page, which starts the process all over. The principled reasoning approach is a perpetual motion machine, which no doubt would leave Dilbert, the comic strip antihero, totally dumbstruck.

But if you think seriously about virtuous behavior, from almost any perspective, this chart is about as close as you can get to what taking responsibility is really all about. Since a rigid moral compass is impractical, Levi Strauss had designed a map of how the company would navigate the topography of situational ethics, under which it aspired to do business in good conscience. Haas conceded in his 1990 interview that the process slows down decisions. "We challenge ourselves more explicitly to give some factors more weight than we did before—especially the impact of a plant closing on the community."

The relevance of all the high-minded rhetoric about social responsibility—the ethics codes, the elaborate decision-making procedures, the graphical representations of the company's spiritual soul—is now open to question as Levi Strauss struggles to resurrect itself from decline. The rhetoric itself is dispensable, as long as the senior executives who run the company remain constant to the underlying principles. As Levi Strauss slips into silence about the values it once articulated with confidence, admiring the company's goodness will become a matter of faith. "My belief is that these people are sincerely principled and true believers in their principles," said David Baron, a professor at Stanford University's Graduate School of Business, who teaches ethics and has supervised extensive case study research on the company. "But they're dealing with difficult issues now. I think they are still guided by principles and the culture of the company. My view is that they try to lead by example. I'd expect them to do these things, cautiously and quietly."

Unfortunately, a cautious and quiet Levi Strauss—succumbing with resignation to the amoral tides of globalization—leaves the international business community without a beacon of strong leadership at a time when it needs positive models of ethical policy more than ever. There appears to be no other company with the credibility to fill that role. The noble idea that business can somehow regulate itself through voluntary measures and make social responsibility compatible with profits, a concept that Levi Strauss was influential in propagating, is a vulnerable one. It could fade away like last fall's fashions unless it is vigorously and openly defended. The political hot potato of corporate human rights policy—covering such basic tenets as taking responsibility for labor standards and avoiding complicity with political repression—is going to be at the very bottom of any business agenda unless there's a good reason to make it a priority.

Ethics have a price, to be set by the arbitrary invisible hands of the marketplace unless some visible hand intervenes—an irate public, a government regulation, or a strong-willed chief executive who can convince him- or herself and persuade the board of directors and the ranks of middle managers that you cannot put a price on doing the right thing.

Chapter Seven

|||

Manchurian Candidates

Then the King will say to those at his right hand, "Come, O blessed of my Father, inherit the kingdom prepared for you from the foundation of the world; for I was hungry and you gave me food, I was thirsty and you gave me drink, I was a stranger and you welcomed me, I was naked and you clothed me, I was sick and you visited me, I was in prison and you came."
—Matthew 25:34–36

It was never entirely clear why security agents detained Xiu Yichun, a senior manager at Royal Dutch/Shell Group's Chinese subsidiary. She was arrested in February 1996 on charges of obtaining "state secrets," presumably on behalf of her foreign employer, which was then negotiating a deal to build an oil refinery with one of China's state-owned energy companies. Police also arrested Ms. Xiu's counterpart at China National Offshore Oil Corporation on the same charges. The Hong Kong news media speculated that the trouble had something to do with sensitive information about the financing and environmental impact of Shell's $6 million joint-venture project.

When asked what was behind this disturbing development, all Shell would say was that its employee, a Chinese national, did not violate the law. The Anglo-Dutch company did its best to shield news of Xiu's arrest from the media, fearing that high-profile publicity could only endanger her chances of release. Very possibly Shell didn't know much anyway. China's judicial system reserves the right to act in total secrecy, in commercial as well as in political and criminal prosecutions. Xiu's case makes one thing painfully clear, however: Despite laudable progress in the sphere of economic reform, China's security apparatus wields immense and arbitrary powers to arrest and detain its citizens. It's not just troublemaking political dissidents who fall prey to this Orwellian terror. Legitimate business-people—and sometimes foreigners as well as Chinese—are at the mercy of a system that is strong on police powers and appallingly deficient in due process and the rule of law.

Ms. Xiu was eventually released and reunited with her daughter in March of the following year, after being held incommunicado for thirteen months. She had been tried in secret, convicted, and given a suspended sentence on the mysteriously vague charges before the court. Shell's quiet diplomatic efforts, and its influence as a major private investor, may have spared her from a far worse fate.

For Shell, the case caused some deep trepidation, as well as embarrassment. At the time, the company was under severe rebuke by international human rights groups for supposedly not acting boldly enough to intervene with Nigerian authorities in the summary trial and execution of a local political activist, Ken Saro-Wiwa. He had criticized Shell's Nigerian subsidiary and the military government for causing environmental degradation in his native Ogoni tribal territory. The dissident was hanged along with eight fellow Ogoni activists just three months before the shock of Xiu Yichun's arrest in Beijing.

Shell maintains that it did indeed speak out publicly on Saro-Wiwa's behalf and that former chairman Cor Herkstroter sent a personal letter appealing to the brutal Nigerian dictator General Sani Abacha "to show clemency on humanitarian grounds." Still, human rights and environmental activists insist the company failed to intervene aggressively enough to use its considerable political leverage in Nigeria to save the lives of the Ogoni nine. Calls went out for a boycott of Shell and an embargo on Nigerian oil.

Before all this took place, Shell might have been characterized as the Levi Strauss of Europe. It had been working seriously on human rights and other issues of corporate social responsibility for many years. It articulated its Statement of General Business Principles as early as 1976—leading the trend in its industry—and was further along at developing realistic policies to implement its ethics code than many other major multinationals. As an oil company, it felt it didn't have much choice. The business is long-term, with investments in international oil concessions that can go on for decades as local government leaders—despots as well as democrats— rise and fall. "The natural course of events can place Shell companies in a position where they are paying taxes to a government which is an international pariah," Robin Aron, head of external relations for Shell International, said in an interview published by the organization Ethics in Economics. "Factories can be moved out, but oil wells cannot. Therefore, Shell companies rarely disinvest; they stay and try to contribute as meaningfully and as positively as possible."

Like Levi Strauss, Shell is a natural target for criticism because it talks about principles that it probably will never be able to live up to. Its vision of "constructive engagement," hell or high water, can be at odds with its business mission. Whether it considered its critic Ken Saro-Wiwa and his Ogoni people as "stakeholders" or not in its scheme of corporate responsibility is open to question. In the case of its Chinese executive, there's no doubt the company did everything it knew how to protect her. If Shell considers itself truly engaged *constructively* in China, shouldn't it be making quiet inquiries about other victims of arbitrary arrest—dissidents and religious leaders as well as businesspeople? Better not hold your breath.

The problem with the idea of large multinational investors using their considerable influence to alter the situation in a despotic regime is that it can be hard to tell who has influence over whom, especially when huge sums of money are involved.

When Levi Strauss announced its plans to recoil from China, a mandarin at the Foreign Ministry sniffed, "So what!" To China, the world's largest branded apparel maker was just one of many foreign suitors, and its absence would hardly be noticed. Likewise, had Shell been bellicose about the arrest of its employee, the Chinese side could very well have found another joint-venture partner among rival international oil companies eager to expand their piece of the action. In countries like China and Indonesia, foreign corporations are just as likely to be exploited by authoritarian regimes as they are to exploit the country's resources.

188 | LEVI'S CHILDREN

It can also be a trade-off, as in the case of Motorola, which went against the tide in 1989—when most U.S. business was retreating apprehensively from the China market after the Tiananmen massacre—to invest heavily in the fledgling Tianjin Free Enterprise Zone. Beijing got a critical endorsement of legitimacy from a major multinational; Motorola got the rare privilege to operate a wholly owned production facility, establishing a platform to constructively engage the people of China by taking the domestic market by storm with its pagers and cell phones. It was a brilliant business move, but a high-stakes gamble with the company's social accountability image. At the time, however, Motorola was mostly a chip-making gizmo company in the eyes of the public, as opposed to the high-profile consumer brand it became in the 1990s. It's hard to imagine the company making a decision like that today, without carefully weighing the risks to its brand equity before jumping into the laps of a regime with fresh blood on its hands. The pretext of constructive engagement is a far more effective shield for a corporate reputation when nobody's really watching.

Talking about constructive engagement, however, is meaningless without first thinking about the circumstances under which multinationals must operate. An agenda of good intentions that would satisfy critics and shareholders alike in an autocratic country like Indonesia, for instance, can be a recipe for disaster in China, a nation whose legal practices are beyond the looking glass. To a certain extent, Indonesia tolerates the existence of local independent NGOs, and a company like Levi Strauss could conceivably work with this civil-society resource to promote the protection of labor rights among the contractor workforce in Java, making its code of conduct more than just lip service. To do so in China's Guangdong province would be technically legal—but practicably impossible, because there are no local NGOs.

There's always an easy out. Investors and foreign companies that source goods in China can cite the theory of passive constructive engagement, claiming that a hygienic seal insulates their business operations from the political realities that fester around them. They come on their own ethical terms to do business quietly and legally and need not sully themselves by getting involved in politics or intervening in the domestic affairs of their host country. Hear no evil, see no evil, speak no evil—and sniff no odor of hypocrisy. On the ground, however, they must immerse themselves in a swamp of legal and ethical inconsistencies, which may not immediately threaten profits or brand reputations but will entangle them in a condition of moral accountability. There is no way to operate in China, or any other country where pervasive human rights violations are part of the political ethos, without being engaged in the system. The question then is whether the corporation is engaged passively, condoning the wrongdoing, or engaged interactively, taking at least some responsibility for the problems and trying to help make progress toward solutions.

|||

The truth about the arrest of the luckless Shell employee is that her case was unusual only in that it involved a high-profile multinational investor and a top state-owned enterprise. Further down the food chain, stories abound in China of businesspeople being arbitrarily detained and arrested in murky commercial disputes. The vast majority of these cases occur at the provincial and county levels, where corruption among local Communist Party cadres, police, and court officials is notorious. The victims are typically Chinese entrepreneurs who find themselves out of political favor or outmaneuvered by unscrupulous business partners with better *guanxi*, connections or patronage ties, to officialdom.

The phenomenon of arbitrary detention was so hopelessly out of control in the early 1990s that central authorities in Beijing issued nationwide circulars to local law enforcement agencies, warning them in vain to stop these illegal arrests. No accurate data is available that could measure the trend, but anecdotal accounts of the detention of businesspeople continue to emerge, despite cleanup campaigns and formal reforms. The draconian "shelter and investigate" statute, by which police can hold suspects indefinitely while gathering evidence, was abolished from the criminal procedure law at the beginning of 1997, but foreign legal observers are skeptical about the prospects for real change. It is commonly believed that not just crooked cops, but corrupt prosecutors and court officials are involved in this incorrigible pattern of abuse. Legal technicalities don't get in the way of convictions in China, where there is no presumption of innocence.

Occasionally, ethnic Chinese businessmen with passports from Hong Kong and Taiwan—even some U.S. citizens—find themselves caught in this trap. James Peng, a Chinese native with an Australian passport, is perhaps the most celebrated case. Peng got caught up in a nasty dispute with his politically well-connected business partners, including the niece of the late patriarch Deng Xiaoping, and he was sentenced in 1995 to sixteen years in prison on embezzlement charges—even after the court repeatedly sent the indictment back to prosecutors for lack of credible evidence. Peng, who was abducted from a luxury hotel in the Portuguese colony of Macao and taken across the border during his arrest, insists he was framed.

"If they want to put you in jail, they can do it. No matter what the charge is," said Philip Cheng, a Hong Kong businessman who is still petitioning Chinese officials to clear his name after his arbitrary detention in 1993. "But if you pay money to a judge, you can win your case," scoffs Cheng, a U.S. citizen and former journalism professor.

Cheng was ensnared in a dispute with his Chinese partner, Hunan Arts and Crafts Import and Export Co., with whom he'd set up a joint venture making motorcycle helmets for export. There had been a misunderstanding about a shipment of goods that Cheng refused to pay for because of defective workmanship, Cheng said. When he went to the interior city of Changsha in Hunan province to negotiate a settlement—the Chinese partner demanded $165,000—Cheng was abducted from his hotel. About six men in uniform took him by military jeep to another hotel in a "dark place," where he was "thrown into a small room" and held and interrogated under duress for three days. "They didn't beat me up, but they surrounded me and pushed me around," recalls Cheng. His American passport had been confiscated, and he was denied the use of a phone. In desperation he wrote a message asking for help, addressed it to a local friend, and slipped it to one of his guards, a young man who seemed sympathetic. On the fourth day, a Chinese judge visited and transferred him to a larger room in another hotel, where he spent the next two months under house arrest. "I was so lucky I had a U.S. passport," Cheng said. "If I was a Hong Kong or a Taiwanese citizen, I might have died there."

Only when he was allowed to relocate to the coastal Chinese city of Zhuhai—a special economic zone bordering Macao where his company, Zhuhai Golex, was based—did Cheng learn the official charges against him: violating a commercial contract. Finally his passport was returned and Cheng was allowed to travel freely in March 1994, after a high official in Beijing intervened in his case. "According to Chinese law, what happened to me should not have happened. But nobody cares about the law in China." Cheng still does business on the mainland out of Hong Kong, but only through his sons and other intermediaries. "I don't want to go back there again," he said. "I'm scared."

Cheng's account of his ordeal cannot be independently corroborated beyond a few press reports. But the frustration and terror in his face as he tells his story from his cluttered office in the Kowloon district of Hong Kong gives it a certain authenticity. He believes ethnic Chinese foreign businessmen are continuing to be harassed by arbitrary detentions in China, but that few cases ever come to light because victims wish to avoid public embarrassment and settle by quietly paying "ransom" for their freedom.

Indeed, a slew of troubling cases popped up in news reports in the 1990s. There was the odd tale of Vasily Ladicenko, the Russian businessman from Irkutsk, who was arrested over a disputed $100,000 debt and permitted to leave China only after a colleague replaced him as a virtual hostage. In another case, Troy McBride, a Miami businessman, told reporters he had been held "commercial hostage" in a hotel room in Hefei, capital of Anhui province, where he went voluntarily to negotiate a disputed $500,000 debt with Chinese partners. A stock analyst from SG Warburg Securities was arrested for conducting routine economic research, sending a chill down spines in the financial community. Xi Yang, a Hong Kong journalist with the *Ming Pao* newspaper, was detained and sentenced to twelve years in prison for "stealing and spying on financial services of the state." His crime was writing stories about China's plans to raise interest rates and protect gold holdings—information that might be considered legitimately relevant to foreign investors trying to fathom the Chinese economy.

As the trend persisted it generated outrage in the Hong Kong Legislative Council, which held hearings on the matter during the nervous years before the British colony was to return to Chinese sovereignty under a shaky agreement conditioned on continued political autonomy for the territory. Robin Munro, the tenacious investigator based in Hong Kong for Human Rights Watch, compiled an alarming report titled "China: The Cost of Putting Business First," which put the problem in these terms: "There are telling signs that the same factors that produce serious abuses of human rights in China are also detrimental to trade, including a flouting of the rule of law that leaves businesspeople and economic reformers increasingly vulnerable to the types of arbitrary detention customarily meted out to dissidents, and strict controls on politically 'sensitive' economic data."

On balance, the risk is relatively minimal that foreign expatriate businesspeople, or their Chinese employees, will be subject to arbitrary arrest in garden-variety commercial disputes. But a strong argument can be made that the wide pattern of corruption in Chinese jurisprudence and the official paranoia about the free flow of economic information, which many of these cases reveal, has a definite impact on the bottom line for business. Accurate and timely information is the lifeblood of traders and investors, as important as having confidence that they can conduct business fairly under the rule of law.

| | |

Perhaps the most eloquent advocate of the argument that human rights violations are bad for business—and that business should do something about that—is John Kamm, a stocky, owl-faced, and slightly graying China trader who has testified repeatedly before Congress on the matter. Kamm is no ordinary businessman, and his incredulous colleagues have let him know that for some time, warning him that his consulting business in China can only suffer as a result of his outspoken views—and his provocative activism on behalf of political prisoners. But Kamm is unbowed. "I think the arbitrary abuse of power used to jail dissidents is the same obstacle to successful business in China," he said.

Since the early 1990s Kamm has made it a practice to take time off from his business trips to China to pursue his quixotic quest: cajoling information from Chinese officials about political and religious dissidents imprisoned in the Laogai, China's version of the Gulag. In his one-man campaign, he's made discreet inquiries about hundreds of prisoners of conscience, most of them obscure and unmentioned in the mainstream news media. Kamm doesn't bother with the more celebrated dissidents who are featured prominently in the Western news media and often get exploited as pawns in the Sino-U.S. diplomatic dance, released or rearrested or deported as bargaining chips. His effort on behalf of the anonymous inmates has shown clear results, with dozens of the prisoners on the lists he's submitted to the Chinese Justice Ministry being paroled or having their sentences commuted. "I came to the understanding that the simple act of asking about a prisoner, that in itself constituted a powerful act of intervention," Kamm said. "It gave him a name."

Kamm's crusade started in 1990, when he was a vice president for Dallas-based Occidental Chemical Corporation (OxyChem), running the company's business in China and serving a term as president of the American Chamber of Commerce in Hong Kong. He cast the die with an audacious question when he attended a banquet hosted by Zhou Nan, head of the Hong Kong branch of Xinhua— the Chinese news agency that served as an unofficial diplomatic mission in the British enclave for the People's Republic of China. Zhou was a doctrinaire, hard-line Communist cadre who was dispatched to Hong Kong after his predecessor at Xinhua sought political asylum in the United States during the tumult of the Tiananmen protests the previous year. When Zhou raised his glass for the welcoming toast, Kamm did something very unbusinesslike: he brazenly asked the top-ranking PRC official in Hong Kong: "Why don't you release Yao Yongzhan?" Yao was a Hong Kong student jailed in Shanghai for political activities during the Tiananmen incident. The intervention enraged Zhou and created a brouhaha among the ranks of the Chamber's timid membership, but the student was released within weeks.

Kamm realized that while businesspeople could not necessarily change the system in China, they had an incredible potential to influence the outcome of specific human rights cases. An ardent opponent to the threat of revoking China's MFN trade privileges, Kamm went to Washington representing the Hong Kong Chamber and argued against the sanctions in testimony to Congress. He also pledged to "use my relationships and the goodwill that my position engendered in Beijing not to improve my business, but rather, to intervene on behalf of prisoners believed to be imprisoned for the nonviolent expression of their political and religious beliefs."

There was no turning back now. A Princeton- and Harvard-trained Sinologist who had been doing business with China since the early 1970s, Kamm left OxyChem to devote more time to his Prisoner Information Project. He became an independent consultant to U.S. chemical companies doing business in China and would combine his business trips with visits to officials in the Chinese justice system to ferret out information about the status of specific political prisoners. The single prisoner names he adopted soon turned into lists, and his lobbying efforts started consuming so much time that his business suffered. Kamm was able to continue his crusade with the financial backing of prominent Hong Kong tycoon Sir Gordon Wu, head of the property development giant Hopewell Holdings and the philanthropist who in 1995 gave $100 million to his alma mater, Princeton University.

Businesspeople are uniquely qualified to do human rights work in China, Kamm reasons, because they have "local knowledge and, most important, they have trust." He framed this fundamental idea of engagement when he spoke at a 1995 seminar sponsored by the Commission on Security and Cooperation in Europe, the organization that spawned the Helsinki accord. "Remember, when the officials of these governments see a businessperson walking in the door, they don't see an enemy. They see someone with whom they think they share common interests. If they see a human rights advocate coming in the door, a member of Congress, or a journalist, the defenses go right up," Kamm told his audience. "It's up to the businessman to figure out how to use that trust."

Kamm has had some bumps in the road, with the Chinese side cutting off its cooperation whenever Sino-U.S. relations sour over human rights issues or ties to Taiwan. In early 1999 Kamm anticipated a major breakthrough—the Justice Ministry had notified him they would release a "basket" of information on more than one hundred political prisoners he'd inquired about—when Beijing cut him off again. This time thin-skinned officials cited the introduction of a U.S.-sponsored resolution at the UN Human Rights Commission in Geneva, criticizing China's human rights record. He was lobbying friends in Congress to help him get the deal back on track when, on the night of May 7, a U.S. bomber with an outdated map fired missiles at the Chinese embassy in Belgrade during the Kosovo air war, not realizing the target was a diplomatic compound. Three Chinese journalists inside were killed in the tragic blunder. Angry anti-American protests erupted in Beijing, and the Chinese government suspended its dialogue with the United States on human rights. As the tenth anniversary of the June 4, 1989, Tiananmen massacre was nearing, America was the new villain for many Chinese students, not their repressive government, and Kamm's program went into a chill.

Kamm sat in his office at the top of San Francisco's Nob Hill, in an ornate 1920s building where he also has lived with his wife and two sons on a separate floor since leaving Hong Kong in 1995. He was antsy and waiting for the phone to ring, hoping to find out more about the congressional testimony he was supposed to deliver on May 18, until the hearing before the Senate subcommittee on Asian and Pacific affairs was overtaken by events and canceled. Kamm, forty-eight years old and dressed casually in polo shirt, cardigan sweater vest, and black Levi's jeans, rambled passionately on about his story, digressing into the minutiae of his encounters with certain Chinese officials and the drama of individual prisoners he's helped.

He recalled one of his first major cases back in 1991, the Li brothers, labor activists who were tortured in prison until Kamm had a chance encounter with a member of the Chinese state council in

Hong Kong and meeting with a supreme court judge in Beijing that led to a promise of their release. Then he described how he returned triumphantly to Hong Kong and issued a press release on the deal, only to learn the Chinese had reneged on the promise. Kamm was disconsolate and sank into a deep depression. His brother was visiting from New Jersey, where they had grown up in a suburban, middle-class setting as sons of a prosperous traveling whiskey salesman and a high school teacher, raised Catholic. On Sunday the brother dragged him to church—Kamm hadn't attended mass in years—and it was there that he experienced an epiphany of faith that has driven him like a madman ever since. The sermon was about the dying woman on the shore who was cured by touching Jesus' robe and the official's daughter he brought back from the dead. "I felt a surge in my body," Kamm recalls. "The hairs on my arms stood up." When he got home from church he received a phone call from a human rights activist, informing him that the Li brothers' family had just been told their sons would soon be released from prison. "It was like being hit by a thunderbolt."

The tale of one independent businessman on a human rights crusade may appear to have little relevance for the huge corporations that do business in China or in other repressive regimes. But John Kamm's practices map out a strategy for interaction with officials of an authoritarian government that can put substance behind the rhetoric of constructive engagement.

It's far from certain whether American companies will rally to support Kamm's new nonprofit organization, Dui Hua, or "Dialogue" in Chinese, which will carry on with the Prisoner Information Project and also examine human rights conditions in the United States. Financial support from tycoon Gordon Wu has been cut back since the Asian financial crisis dealt a blow to Hong Kong's economy, and Kamm is raising foundation grant money to get his NGO off the ground. He's not hopeful about corporate largesse from China investors—the taboo on confronting Beijing and the risks of jeopardizing their business weigh heavily on the managers of these enterprises. Kamm aims to persuade them that it is in their own interests to raise questions about political prisoners and labor laws as they meet with Chinese officials in the course of conducting their business affairs. Yet he has no illusions about the challenges he faces. "Companies have indicated to me that while they think what I'm doing is admirable and noble, they could never get close to the project," Kamm said. "I tend to be sober about the prospects for corporations taking the lead on human rights issues."

||||

A harrowing landscape awaits Levi Strauss & Co. once it acts on its decision to reverse course in China and explore the options of expanding production and investing in marketing opportunities. In addition to the unabated pattern of political repression and human rights abuse that made the company wary in the first place, however, the bloom was off the rose for international business in China at the beginning of the new century. The fanaticism that attended the flood of inbound investment has been muted with worries about China's economic stability amid the financial malaise infecting its neighbors. The mind-boggling market of more than a billion consumers was no longer the seductive mirage it had once been.

In what appeared to be a combination of cold feet and revised strategy, Levi Strauss made a point of saying—soon after announcing its policy change in 1998—that the company was in no particular hurry to expand in China. Part of the problem had to do with the voodoo of macroeconomics. China was holding firm on its refusal to devalue its currency, which it might have done to regain competitive parity with the region's other low-cost producers, whose currencies had fallen precipitously. So it became a relatively more expensive place to source production. Making clothing in China for domestic consumption still made sense, once the company was ready to combine that effort with a marketing plan for domestic consumers. But exporting from a production platform in China to moribund regional markets was not a good idea for now.

Another factor stalling Levi's advance into China was a new trend in the apparel business. China was still a great place to source textiles, but it was too far away from the home market for finished clothing. As Levi focused on competing more effectively in the fast-changing fashion industry, it needed quicker turnaround time among the stages of design, fabrication, and delivery to the fickle youth-oriented emporiums of North America. Replacing and expanding production overseas following Levi's massive layoffs in the U.S. workforce would have to happen in nearby Latin America and the Caribbean to meet the demands of just-in-time merchandising. Not only would response time be much quicker, but the benefits of the North American Free Trade Agreement (NAFTA) would be considerable.

NAFTA would be less of a factor in the balance of competitive advantage once China gains entry into the World Trade Organization—an almost certain outcome that will offer easier access to the U.S. market and eliminate the politically charged annual agony of renewing its most favored trade privileges, which are accorded automatically to WTO members. In any event, China will remain an extremely important production center in the garment sector, as well as in a range of other industries that produce exports for the U.S. market. In the rag trade it is a particularly valuable source for fabric production—a business that requires heavy capital investment in looms and other machinery that cannot be moved around as easily as sewing machines, which Chinese and Korean compradors are packing up in Asia and taking to more promising Latin American labor markets.

When Levi Strauss's inevitable expansion in China does come, the company and its path-breaking code of conduct is going to be under intense scrutiny by human rights and labor organizations, journalists, and scholars. Whether or not the company chooses to uphold its long tradition of corporate social responsibility, the story of Levi's in China is bound to become one of the defining tales in the annals of economic globalization. Levi's will be able to slip quietly into new situations in Latin America, but in China its penchant for extreme privacy is much more likely to be taken to task with demands for greater accountability and transparency. The human rights community did not ask Levi Strauss to pull out of China—indeed, very few Chinese political dissidents have ever advocated corporate withdrawal as a means of leveraging political reform. But when the company expands its presence in the People's Republic, there are high expectations—articulated by such prominent organizations as Amnesty International—that Levi Strauss will take leadership and serve as a positive model for constructive engagement.

The biggest stumbling block for Levi's "terms of engagement" in China is not going to be the human rights environment—that problem has been eliminated by the 1996 revision of its Guidelines for Country Selection, which watered down the terms. What gives the company pause is the problem of labor standards. According to Chinese law, workers are supposedly free to form independent trade unions, but in practice, the state criminalizes the activities of independent union leaders. Levi's code technically requires that workers enjoy the right to free association, and that simply is not possible in China today. "If we're going to contemplate expanding in China, that's going to be a major issue," said company spokesman Clarence Grebey.

Gare Smith, the State Department human rights official who joined Levi Strauss as its vice president for external affairs in early 1999, quickly went to work on trying to resolve this contradiction. He saw that the basic gap between Levi's code and conditions in China could not be resolved without changes in the way the Chinese government implements its own laws. "One of the challenges any company operating in China faces is the government's failure to respect the freedom of association," Smith said.

An opportunity to take action on the issue came in March 1999, when Chinese labor minister Zhang Zuoji came to Washington to meet with U.S. labor secretary Alexis Herman, a meeting that had been agreed upon during President Clinton's summit in Beijing the previous year. Herman invited representatives of several U.S. companies to join the meeting, including Liz Claiborne, Reebok, Levi Strauss, and the U.S.–China Business Council. Smith was the most outspoken of the businesspeople, and he pressed Zhang on why China does not honor its legal guaranty for the freedom of association. The minister responded that it does indeed enforce the law, but that some parts of China have been slow to come into line. Smith asked why the central government doesn't step in and force local compliance with the labor law, and Zhang said there was no need to do that; change would come in time. When Smith asked why labor leaders who tried to form independent unions had been jailed, the minister said China had to enforce its criminal laws as well as its labor laws. Zhang then quickly turned the conversation to trade issues and talked about the importance of foreign investment in China.

||| |

Interactive constructive engagement was something that Levi's China Policy Group did a lot of deep thinking about back in 1993, when it was assessing China's fitness as a place to invest and do business under the company's new Global Sourcing Guidelines code of conduct. They used the principled reasoning approach, the byzantine method of decision making that financial pundits later would ridicule, blaming it for the inefficiencies of management that contributed to the company's decline. Nonetheless, these deliberations provided an extremely valuable prism for evaluating the moral issues in the Chinese market, using the stakeholder concept to take into account the tenets of corporate social responsibility as well as relevant financial imperatives. This was no laughing matter.

Internal company documents indicate that the panel went far beyond the fig leaf approach of passive constructive engagement, realizing that the problematic conditions in the market would not go away automatically just because Levi Strauss and other companies established a presence in China. The Levi's executives considered a list of "elements of constructive engagement," which they would refer to as "ECE" in deliberations. The list included such standard concerns as nondiscrimination and the right of free association but also ventured boldly into more controversial terrain.

Constructive engagement in connection with "emergency human rights aid" and "support for human rights organizations" were both marked as something that "applies through the actions of LS&Co." in cases of sourcing products in China. So was the category of "human rights improvement," though this was modified to say, "applies through the actions of LS&Co. liaison/employees as appropriate." No such qualifications in these categories were cited for the options of direct investment, however, indicating a higher level of responsibility to intervene should the company go beyond sourcing in the market and risk its assets.

Behind the shorthand on this document are some innovative ideas on how to act responsibly in China. Most members of the panel backed the idea of hiring a full-time employee to promote human rights. They wanted to ban political activity at the workplace—apparently to counteract the pernicious influence of the Communist Party apparatus on worker rights. Training in ethics and company values was also explored. So was a plan to avert the punitive anti-maternity sanctions that employers are expected to administer under China's one-child policy.

Banning a "permanent military presence" at the manufacturing site was deemed inapplicable for Levi's sourcing arrangements, but it was an issue of concern in the case of direct investment. The military question came up, undoubtedly, because a significant part of China's garment industry was connected with or owned by the People's Liberation Army—not a business partner that many consumer brand companies would be comfortable with so soon after the Tiananmen massacre. (President Jiang Zemin has since ordered the military to get out of business, but many analysts are skeptical about the practicality of enforcing that decree because the PLA is so deeply entrenched in the economy.)

The China Policy Group considered five options for recommendation to CEO Robert Haas and the executive management committee:

1. Don't engage in any business activity in China.
2. Engage in business in China in a manner that actively supports the improvement of human rights—in direct investment but not sourcing.
3. Engage in business in China in a manner that actively supports the improvement of human rights—in sourcing but not direct investment.
4. Engage in business in China in a manner that actively supports the improvement of human rights—in both direct investment and sourcing.
5. Engage in business in China, but don't worry about human rights.

The panel apparently wanted to consider ending its troublesome sourcing arrangements in China while keeping open the option of investing directly in production, which would give it greater control over conditions at the plants.

In keeping with the terms of engagement already outlined in the company code of conduct, the choices were evaluated for the costs they would impose and the benefits they might yield. For example, how would staying in China affect the Levi's brand name? What would it cost to transplant existing production from China to other markets, and what opportunities would be missed if Levi's abandoned China instead of building brand identity and consumer loyalty in a market with such tremendous potential?

In the end, the China Policy Group was divided in its recommendations. The majority advocated the point of view that Levi Strauss could best serve its obligations—social as well as financial—by staying in China while actively promoting human rights protections through the "elements of constructive engagement." When the executive management committee deadlocked on the decision, CEO Haas stepped in and decided in favor of the minority opinion. Levi's was to begin a phased withdrawal from China, subject to revision should circumstances change.

Five years later, when the company aired its second thoughts on the matter, there was a gaping hole in Levi's new China policy: the China Policy Group no longer existed. The careful deliberations of that task force used in the first decision were nowhere in evidence. Planning for the initiative to reverse the policy was a more informal process that came out of the public affairs department in San Francisco and the Asia Pacific regional headquarters in Singapore.

Until Gare Smith arrived on the scene, it appeared that any of Levi's semiautonomous business units was free to explore opportunities in China without regard to the elements of constructive engagement that were conditional in the 1993 policy recommendation. The principled reasoning approach had been dismissed as nonproductive and inefficient during the remaking of the company in 1999. Smith's brief involvement at the company seemed to allay concerns that the original framework for constructive engagement had entirely lost its validity, at least for the time being.

| | |

Since the mid-1990s the focus of the human rights debate, as far as international business was concerned, had gradually shifted from the emphasis on engagement with rogue regimes to preoccupation with safeguarding labor standards. Implementing, monitoring, and enforcing compliance with the terms of engagement codes, which cropped up like dandelions after Levi Strauss took the lead in 1992, became the priority. Anybody who could be shamed into leaving Burma had already pulled out; the big oil companies were holding their ground in Nigeria, which had a new government and was showing the promise of democratic reform anyway. Putting diplomatic pressure on China to improve its human rights record seemed a daunting cause, now that commercial relations were of paramount importance. Chinese dissidents weren't asking for economic sanctions, but they wanted multinationals to do the right thing once they came to China.

There is a single crucial link that puts corporate codes of conduct stipulating labor standards on the same page as the broader political issues of democratization and human rights protections. It is the simple, seemingly innocuous item that virtually all these corporate codes contain: the right to free association.

It's a sleeper clause, which many corporations feel they must insert in their codes to follow the prevailing fashion but hope they will never have to get serious about enforcing. Free association, of course, means workers getting together to advance their common interests in improving their condition. This implies organizing into unions or forming collective bargaining units that will demand such things as greater compensation, fairness in hours and overtime wages, job security, and workplace safety.

Though this right is enshrined in the laws of the United States and most industrialized nations and is a fundamental precept of international human rights and international labor laws, it remains an uncomfortable issue for many entrepreneurs and industrialists. Union activism is still vilified by a significant spectrum of conservative economists, politicians, and business owners and managers in America, often perceived as an impediment to productivity, free-market efficiency, and competitiveness in the global economy. That's why you would close your plant in Michigan and reopen it in a right-to-work state in the American South, to hold down labor costs and minimize the threat of strikes. It's also a good reason to shut down your garment factory in Tennessee and move production to Mexico or the Dominican Republic.

Unfortunately no one is in a position to guarantee the right of free association to the cannon fodder of globalization, those low-wage transient workers at contractor factories who make the global division of labor an efficient economic model in the first place. Guaranteeing the freedom of association for these workers is in its essence an incendiary idea. It is subversive, as human rights should be according to the doctrine of the UN's Universal Declaration. If workers are free to congregate and build alliances independent of state or corporate control, the gathering of people with common political interests follows naturally. Allowing the exercise of human rights in the economic sphere risks an osmotic spread of networking skills into the world of politics. New grassroots networks can emerge that challenge the orderly status quo.

From the point of view of authoritarian governments, the discipline, the harmony, and the stability of society are jeopardized by the very existence of independent trade unions. It's not always necessary for these regimes to send in their troops to quash labor unrest, as South Korean authorities did with such vicious determination during the dying gasps of military dictatorship or as occurred under autocratic rule in Indonesia. The companies can take care of these matters on their own, in a tacit understanding with the state. In the apparel and shoe industries, the comprador-contractors—who are obliged now to comply with the codes of their international clients—have strong vested interests in keeping unions out of their factories. The higher the cost of wages or overtime pay or workplace safety mitigation, the lower their profit margins.

This rational business model goes bust when a customer won't pay more for the product but demands compliance with labor standards that say union organizers demanding higher wages can't be harassed, penalized, or fired. In most developing countries the export sector has the blessings of officialdom in holding the line against union activity and wage inflation, even when local laws nominally guarantee the right to free association and collective bargaining. In the global division of labor, it's against the interests of the state to see light manufacturing—a critical catalyst to economic development—pick up and move to a country offering lower wages.

The real subversion begins, however, when freedom of association for labor works its catalytic effect on the growth of a pluralistic civil society. Consider the case of China, which has crushed the fledgling Democratic Party and the Falun Gong religious cult by jailing its leaders. China has no interest in seeing workers exercise their rights to free association, which its laws nominally guarantee. The Communist Party leadership has solved that inconvenient problem by creating the All China Federation of Trade Unions, which acts as the eyes, ears, and muscle of the state in coopting the formation of independent trade unions at the factory level. Authoritarian states do not want independent trade unions, and they don't want the kind of civil societies that spawn viable opposition forces.

| | |

The freedom of association dilemma is one reason why Western organized labor is often the power behind some of the most vociferous of the human rights activists investigating the operations of multinational corporations. It's no accident that the international campaign of outrage against Nike Inc.'s questionable labor practices was ignited, almost single-handedly, by a labor lawyer—Jeffrey Ballinger, a representative of the AFL-CIO in Jakarta, Indonesia. Ballinger is an old-fashioned firebrand reminiscent of a bygone era in American labor history when Sacco and Vanzetti were folk heroes to the workingman. Ballinger, in his mid-forties, has an intensely loquacious and brightly affable mien, the kind of advocate you might write off as a gadfly—until you realize that his quixotic charge against Nike ended up shaking heaven and earth for the sneaker-making industry.

It all started, Ballinger said, during an expatriate softball game in Jakarta back in 1988 when a Nike executive on his team told him, in a cryptic reference to Ballinger's mission as a labor investigator: "I'm your worst nightmare." Ballinger followed up on the tip and said he found indications of rampant abuse in the contractor factories where Nike and the big sports brands had their shoes made. Taiwanese managers punished errant workers by forcing them to do strenuous calisthenics; Korean bosses beat their employees and learned enough of the Indonesian language to verbally abuse them, calling them "dogs" in the local vernacular. "Young Javanese girls are the least likely people to complain about anything," Ballinger said. "So we tried to legitimize the process of complaining. My strategy was to focus on one company in one country and reduce their wiggle room so they couldn't claim they'd fixed the problem." Thus begun the whipping-boy strategy of holding Nike accountable for the sins of the entire sports shoe industry. Ballinger got thrown out of Indonesia in 1992 after he started a postcard campaign demanding enforcement of Indonesia's labor code.

Ballinger continued his anti-Nike crusade after moving to Turkey, communicating with local Indonesian NGOs and sending information packets to the international media. "By 1993, Nike knew its contractors were lying to them," he said. "By 1996, they knew exactly what was going on in those plants." Teaming up with the advocacy group Global Exchange and other allies, Ballinger continued stoking the fires of an unrelenting campaign that spread to college campuses and broadened its scope from Indonesia to Nike operations in China and Vietnam. A call for a boycott of Nike products went out. Garry Trudeau lampooned Nike's bungled attempts at damage control in his Doonesbury comic strip.

The company remained essentially in denial throughout this maelstrom, at first dismissing any responsibility for the welfare of workers employed by its contractors, then launching an aggressive public relations campaign to deflect criticism of the conditions at the plants. Nike retained auditing firms like Ernst & Young and Price Waterhouse to get a professional appraisal for its internal use—though one damaging report was leaked to activists and the press. For public consumption, Nike asked Andrew Young, former UN ambassador and an eminent leader of the civil rights movement, to investigate the company's compliance with its code of conduct in a whirlwind tour of the plants. Young's report, released in 1997, was widely dismissed by the advocacy community as an embarrassing whitewash.

It wasn't until sales and profits starting falling in 1997 that the company changed its tack. Fashion trends in the sports shoe industry were changing, so it was impossible to say how much of Nike's downturn in sales could be attributed categorically to the boycott campaign, but it was clear the onslaught of negative publicity wasn't helping. Nike insiders suggest that founder and CEO Phil Knight was a stubborn holdout against taking a conciliatory approach to Nike's detractors, while his own subordinates lobbied for a more open accountability. "His personal stake in his reputation and in Nike's reputation obscured his vision," explains one Nike executive. Ballinger, the activist, likes to tell the story of how Knight displayed his contempt for his critics while attending a 1996 Rose Garden ceremony for the White House's antisweatshop initiative, the Apparel Industry Partnership. He proclaimed, "We're not going to change economic history"—throwing cold water on the sanguine rhetoric of the event. "Phil Knight was the perfect target," said Ballinger.

Finally, a seemingly born-again Knight swallowed his pride and made a stunning about-face in May 1998, announcing plans to work cooperatively with NGOs on the independent monitoring of Nike's code of conduct at overseas plants. He revealed plans to adopt the rigorous standards of the U.S. Occupational Safety and Health Administration (OSHA) at the contractor factories serving the Nike brand, raise the minimum age requirement to eighteen, and expand programs that offer education and microfinancing for workers. Knight assumed a role in the effort to hammer out an agreement in the Apparel Industry Partnership, the White House antisweatshop task force he'd disparaged in the Rose Garden ceremony. Nike was the major corporate sponsor of the Business for Social Responsibility's annual convention in 1998. It was now positioning itself among the true believers.

Nike restructured its management team, naming a new vice president, Maria Eitel, to head a "corporate responsibility" division. The company moved its point man on the controversy, Dusty Kidd, a former journalist brandishing the title of "director of labor practices," from the corporate communications department to Eitel's newly created strategic policy-making unit. The public relations assignment for handling the controversy fell upon Vada Manager, a savvy veteran of Levi Strauss who had served as an executive assistant to Robert and Peter Haas. By all appearances, the company had begun to move responsibility for resolving human rights problems out of the damage-control modality and graft it into its core business operations.

| | |

The contrast couldn't be greater between the way Nike responded to allegations of labor abuse, tardily and reluctantly, and the way Levi Strauss managed to head them off at the pass, quietly and smugly. Levi's managers had anticipated the potential aspersions that could be cast against their brand reputation well before the issue of corporate complicity with labor abuse exploded into a cause célèbre for human rights activists. The late company patriarch, Walter Haas Jr., had worried about the stigma of sweatshop production way back in the early 1970s, when he pondered whether to keep the historic San Francisco factory in operation.

Indeed, the dynamic within the management of the two companies was poles apart: Levi's Robert Haas felt obligated to inculcate a philosophy of social responsibility in his management ranks, while Nike's Phil Knight was managed from the bottom up by his subordinates on the issue. Both organizations were aiming for a viable balance between ethics and profitability, between brand protection and competitiveness, but they came at it from different directions.

It's also informative to compare how the two companies have handled the matter of transparency. Nike is publicly traded and downright logorrheic with its news releases and public pronouncements, as though it aims to drown the public—and its detractors— in information. The *swoosh* logo of its brand has been etched in the minds of consumers through a strategy of omnipresence in the environment, attached to billboards and flaunted by top professional athletes and made compelling by clever television advertising. Nike lives and dies by publicity. When it changed its policy on labor monitoring, it unveiled the news with great fanfare calculated to maximize media coverage, centered on a major policy speech by its CEO at the National Press Club in Washington. Nike invited journalists to visit its contractors' factories in Asia.

Levi Strauss, in contrast, is a fiercely private company that tightly controls access and manages its information flows in a practice of reticence and ambiguity. It has a brand that has been such a mainstay in American popular culture, it hasn't needed to pander to consumers or overwhelm them with exposure to the company logo. It established a policy of withdrawal from China without issuing a single press release, instead letting the news leak out. Then it quietly reversed that policy, granting low-key interviews to selected journalists in Hong Kong. Levi Strauss declined to identify its contractors overseas, let alone entertain the idea of allowing a journalist or an NGO investigator to visit one. A company official strongly rebuked me, for instance, for the mere act of contacting Levi Strauss executives in Hong Kong to request information about production in China.

| | |

A foreign investor or a multinational corporation doing business in China faces a seemingly insurmountable challenge when it comes to enforcing a code of conduct that mandates the freedom of association for Chinese workers. There's no problem getting a union on the factory floor, but a technicality is involved: Authorities require the unions to be officially sanctioned under the umbrella of the All China Federation of Trade Unions, which acts as a Communist Party apparatus. Having the ACFTU represent the workforce brings party surveillance and the vestiges of a semitotalitarian state into your factory: pregnancies can be monitored, for example, in the enforcement of the government's one-child policy. The union can just as easily repress a young female worker as act as an advocate of her needs. Often, however, there's no union in sight. The rule of law in China has gained some considerable formal authority in recent years, but the application of the regulatory system for economic activities remains informal and, in many cases, arbitrary.

A shoe factory catering to Nike in Dongguan, near the southern city of Guangzhou (formerly Canton), provides a useful example. The Dongguan Wellko Shoe Factory is owned, its managers say, by South Korean investor J. K. Liu—with strategic financial participation by Hutchison Whampoa Ltd., a Hong Kong company belonging to supertycoon Li Ka Shing, who is renowned for his influential political ties in Beijing. Wellko employed some 5,500 workers (median age 22.5), mostly young women who earn a starting base pay of about $44 a month. It is a transient workforce, fed by the inexhaustible supply of economic migrants from the hinterlands, whose average period of employment is less than two years.

S. Y. Cha, a Korean manager at the plant, said he can't recall hearing about labor unrest at the factory and has no knowledge of wildcat strikes reported by human rights activists in Hong Kong. "There have been no strikes," Cha said. "There was a day in 1998 when workers showed up late. We interviewed them and found out they were confused about how production bonuses were being paid." When workers complain, he said, it's usually about the food—the girls who come from all over China find Cantonese cuisine doesn't measure up to the regional cuisine back home. But Cha confesses a "personal opinion," that he harbors a bias against organized labor, having experienced the trauma of militant union activity in his homeland. "I know the necessity of labor unions," he said, "but personally my opinion of unions is negative."

Indeed, there was no labor representation at the plant in early 1999, despite the fact that the central government's labor code requires one for purposes of collective bargaining. Officials at the local labor office waived the requirement, Cha said. "The labor law is open to interpretation and autonomy at the local level," explains Todd McKean, Nike's senior compliance official for Asia Pacific, a Chinese-speaking son of missionaries who lives in Guangzhou. "I think labor unions in China are a joke. It's a Party apparatus. My concern is whether a factory has a procedure set up to allow the free association of workers and over time communicate with management about their grievances." Nike's code of conduct, translated into Chinese, is plastered on all the walls throughout the factory.

The code states that Nike "seeks partners that share our commitment to the promotion of best practices and continuous improvement" in, among other things, "management practices that recognize the dignity of the individual, the rights of free association and collective bargaining, and the right to a workplace free of harassment, abuse or corporal punishment." A more explicit section of the code said Nike binds its partners to "specific standards of conduct," prohibiting such exploitative practices as using forced labor, employing children, and cheating workers on wages.

Ballinger, the anti-Nike critic, asserts that the company has pursued a calculated strategy of doing business with authoritarian regimes and avoiding unions since it moved its production from high-wage Japan in the 1960s to Taiwan and South Korea—both military ruled at the time. In turn, when those societies began undergoing democratic reforms, Nike's Taiwanese and Korean contractors took their machinery and their business to competitive labor markets in Southeast Asia and China. It is no coincidence that authoritarian regimes offer the lowest wages, as well as labor peace, he argues.

It's impossible to draw conclusions from circumstances at one plant—or even a dozen plants—that would reveal the truth about the complicated picture of labor practices in a country as huge and diverse and in as rapid transition as China. In all respects, the young women at the Wellko plant seem cheerful, well treated by their employers, and well protected from workplace hazards by Nike's code of conduct. The contractor has found a way to absorb the more than $300,000 expense of installing, at Nike's demand, a ventilation system that improves air quality for line workers involved in the gluing process. "If we can improve relations with Nike and get more orders, that's our compensation," said Cha. Along with all Nike subcontractors, this one has switched from using noxious glues containing chemical substances to safer water-based glues.

Nike's McKean brushes off the allegations of labor troubles at the plant made in a 1997 report by two Hong Kong advocacy groups, Asia Monitor Resource Center (AMRC) and the Christian Industrial Committee (CIC). He challenges the credibility of the methodology used in the research—random interviews of workers outside the factory gates. The report alleges that Wellko employees complained of marathon shifts—many as long as eleven hours a day—to meet production quotas. "The Labor Law and Nike's Code of Conduct both clearly state that coerced labor is not acceptable, yet workers in Wellko are forced to work long hours or they will be subject to termination," said the report, which also alleges that Wellko employees who went on strike in 1997 were fired. McKean dismissed the claims, stressing the improvements made at the plant in the past year.

The installation of the ventilation equipment was part of Nike's new policy of accommodation with its human rights critics, a policy that also included working with NGOs in the independent monitoring of the Nike code. McKean said arrangements are being worked out in places like Indonesia to work with independent groups to monitor its code, including local NGOs. But he said China wasn't ready for this process yet. There may be some credible institutes and university-affiliated groups with expertise, but there are no independent nongovernmental organizations in the international definition in this tightly controlled society. Working with Hong Kong–based NGOs, McKean believes, is not a solution to the problem.

Meanwhile the nervy human rights advocates in Hong Kong—who held their ground after the British colony became a semiautonomous Special Administrative Region of the People's Republic on July 1, 1997—continued to crusade against labor abuses linked to foreign companies operating in China. In 1998 AMRC and CIC reopened their investigation of the toy industry in China, which makes approximately 80 percent of the world's toys, probing factories producing for such major brands as Mattel, Fisher-Price, Hasbro, Disney, and McDonald's. The report cites problems ranging from child labor to cafeteria food poisoning to the termination of strikers and concludes that wretched conditions in Chinese toy factories had not improved significantly since it began its research on the industry: "It is important to make clear that the systematic violation of workers rights continues unabated." In 1999 CIC released a critical report on Disney's clothing production in China, alleging violations of the company's own code of conduct.

The next battlefront is the electronics industry, suggests Eli Chan, associate director of the CIC. Chan doesn't think corporate codes of conduct are the answer to China's labor problems, because they are applied from the outside, not bargained for from within. "A code of conduct has got to be more than just words. It's got to create some sense of understanding by the workers about what their rights are," Chan said. "Five years ago nobody would have imagined that codes of conduct would be as popular as they are today. It's almost like a company has to have a code of conduct or it's out of fashion. But business is not trying to improve the fate of the workers with these codes. What they're really afraid of is that workers will stand up and bargain."

Indeed, the advancement of labor rights was never a particularly popular cause in Hong Kong's rough-and-tumble capitalist culture, so it makes sense that it will be a long time coming in mainland China under the tutelage of Hong Kong free-market entrepreneurs. "When I first came to Hong Kong in 1962, all the sewing work was done by children," said Ira Kaye, a prominent apparel industry sourcing agent based in the territory, in an interview before his death in 1999. "The thing that made Hong Kong what it is today was the combination of the Shanghai industrialist and the Cantonese worker, who was willing to work twenty-four hours a day, spend all his money at the racetrack, and then work overtime to get it back. That's what's going to happen in China."

Your basic profile of an apparel contractor in southern China would be a Hong Kong Chinese businessman who might have fled the Communists as a refugee in 1949, then discovered he had to move his factory to the mainland after labor in Hong Kong became too expensive some twenty years ago. You'll find a great deal of ambiguity in his attitudes about freedom—the refugee mentality is preoccupied with seeking security and an accommodation with the status quo just as much as it is with escaping persecution. "There are different standards of human rights," said one of Hong Kong's most influential compradors, who asked not to be named. He's a business community leader who heads a family-run apparel contracting business that he describes as having a turnover of "more than $100 million"—apparently a lowball figure—with plants in

China and Mexico. "In this part of the world, especially if you go into a developing country, you cannot demand the same standards," he said. "So-called democracy and freedom in China is limited—there should be more freedom. But if you push too hard, you don't get results. We need to be a little more patient and wait for things to develop naturally."

| | |

During the chaos of the massive student protests on Tiananmen Square in May 1989, a small band of young men set up camp on the corner of the great plaza, across from the Gate of Heavenly Peace. They looked older and more streetwise than the students, who apparently had eyed them with suspicion and barred them from the student-only zone around the Monument to the People's Heroes in the center of the throng. Even at arm's length, however, their presence on the square signaled a sea change in the meaning of the protests from student activism to an inchoate united front including other elements of society. These were laborers, not intellectuals. It was what the authorities feared most, and indeed, increasing expressions of sympathy from the broader community forced the hands of Beijing's hard-line leaders to crush the protests with troops in the predawn hours of June 4.

The designated spokesman for the scrappy band of labor activists was a gaunt-faced young man named Han Dong Fan, a railway electrician. He was an impressive figure on the square, placing himself at great risk by agreeing to be identified by foreign journalists, to have his face appear on television newscasts and his name recorded in dispatches. A student might be indulged for demonstrating, but a worker joining the pro-democracy protests was by definition "counterrevolutionary"—the Communist Party's term for seditious activity, which can range from writing a letter expressing an unpopular viewpoint to speaking out in public against government policies.

A decade later Han explained what took him to the square. Interviewed in a Hong Kong restaurant, Han recalled a long personal history of disappointment in the Chinese system, dating back to his days in the army. He said he yearned to be just like Comrade Lei Feng—the apocryphal model soldier lauded for his selfless virtue in Maoist propaganda—until he spoke out about corruption in his platoon. That naive gesture cost him a promotion and blacklisted him from the Communist Party, which he repeatedly tried to join out of zealous idealism, only to be rejected.

With no place to hide, Han ended up turning himself in to the authorities after the violent crackdown on protesters, and he spent nearly two years in prison—without a trial—accused of being a "black hand" in the prodemocracy movement. He contracted tuberculosis in jail and said he was tortured with acupuncture needles by a sadistic prison doctor who refused to give him medicine, accusing Han of faking his illness to avoid "cooperating" with his jailers. "I'll never forget the look in the doctor's eyes—the man was scared," Han recalled. "In a Chinese jail, the first thing to do is forget that you're a human being. If you do, you'll get treated better." A defiant Han did not forget his humanity; he went on a hunger strike. Because of his public exposure during the Tiananmen protests, his name went on a list of prisoners of conscience monitored by international human rights advocates, and he was released on medical grounds. "When [the authorities] found out I was dying, they didn't want me to die in jail," said Han, who eventually sought political asylum in the United States and now lives in Hong Kong. He chose to remain a thorn in the side of the mainland after the British colony surrendered to Chinese sovereignty.

Han is the host of a controversial talk show dedicated to labor issues aired by Radio Free Asia, a U.S. government–funded broadcasting service that transmits Chinese-language news programs into the mainland, a cousin to the Voice of America. He gets improbable phone calls from workers all over China; some of these callers he interviews and puts on the air. His informants report widespread labor unrest in Chinese factories and express frustration at the futility of trying to form independent and free-trade unions. Employees at foreign-invested enterprises are no exception. "I can say for sure that if workers in a foreign-owned company engage in trade union activities, the first trouble will be with the company, not the government. They'll get fired," Han said, now speaking confidently in English. "How can these people think about human rights when they don't have a job?"

Han publishes his views in the *China Labour Bulletin* and collaborates closely with the Asia Monitor Resource Center and the Christian Industrial Committee, the two NGOs that criticized the labor practices of the likes of Nike and Disney. They all seem to agree on one basic view, that labor standards in China will not improve in a significant manner without independent free-trade unions. Corporate codes of conduct, if adequately monitored, can be effective in adding pressure for change, but they will never be a solution by themselves.

Trini Leung, an official at the Hong Kong Federation of Trade Unions who studied the labor movement in China in her dissertation research at Hong Kong University, laments that there's a limit to what a foreign company can actually do to change things. "We have yet to see one single example where management encourages trade union activity. At best they don't attack the organizers," she said. "For a company that goes into China and talks about free association and collective bargaining, irony is perhaps a better word for this than hypocrisy."

True labor rights for Chinese workers may be a lost cause for the foreseeable future, but no major multinational corporation operating in China, or in any other authoritarian society, can afford to sweep these issues under the rug any longer. The company's leaders may not share in the recognition that local violations of human rights ultimately damage their own freedom to conduct business, and they may not subscribe to the belief that they have moral responsibility for the welfare of the contract workers who help make their business profitable. But they must wake up to the fact that their policies and their company's behavior are going to be examined relentlessly by the international human rights community in the years to come. There is no turning back the clock to the days when business practices overseas were out of sight and out of mind—confidential and protected from the public's gaze.

CHAPTER EIGHT

| | |

Ethics by Stealth

Believe nothing, no matter where you read it, or who said it, no matter if I have said it, unless it agrees with your own reason and your own common sense.

—Siddhartha Gautama

The Dominican Republic is as good a place as any developing country to examine the impact of the global economy on traditional society. What happens when a big American company like Levi Strauss comes to this poor Caribbean island nation and places large orders with apparel contractors to have its branded clothing made, cheaply and efficiently, for American consumers? If the business of outsourcing production to contractors cannot be clarified in this setting, so close to the U.S. mainland, then monitoring the phenomenon in faraway lands would seem an impossible task.

Only in relatively recent times has the Dominican Republic experienced the brutal demographic pattern that uproots farming folk from the land and draws them to the cities, where—if they're lucky—they secure low-wage industrial jobs. Instead of scratching the soil to grow cash crops like coffee, cocoa, and sugar cane as their parents did, destitute people are forced by the dictates of the marketplace to gravitate toward the opportunities of the free trade zones, where employment in a sewing factory is a prize for a young woman.

This nation of 7.7 million Spanish speakers enjoys a fairly stable and nominally democratic political system and has not drawn attention to itself with the kind of turmoil that has blighted Haiti, its neighbor on the island of Hispaniola. But the Dominican Republic suffers all the indignities of economic dislocation and erratic development. It aches from a rising income disparity between the descendants of Spanish colonists at the top and the impoverished descendents of African slaves at the bottom. As much as 70 percent of the population lives below the poverty line, and two-thirds of the residents of Santiago, the capital, make their homes in shanty towns. The economy subsists largely on tourist dollars from groups of European visitors, remittance dollars wired home from economic migrants in the United States, and illicit dollars from the underground trafficking of narcotics.

A coveted job at a factory in the free trade zone that makes clothing on contract for Levi Strauss & Co. pays a minimum of four hundred Dominican pesos a week, or about $32; diligent seamstresses can double that amount if they work hard and long enough. On the scale of things, the sewing factories catering to Levi Strauss in the Dominican Republic are first-rate. They are clean and well maintained, they provide suitably safe environments, and workers seem to be generally well treated, according to human rights advocacy groups that participated in a study of the company's code of conduct monitoring process in 1998.

But the workers at these facilities, the investigators found, were blissfully unaware of their labor rights under Dominican law. They had no idea that Levi Strauss was ostensibly concerned with their well-being and knew nothing about the company's code of conduct that requires their managers to afford them the right to free association.

Indeed, the NGO participants who interviewed the workers as part of the pilot study, Evaluation of Levi Strauss & Co.'s Terms of Engagement Process, discovered that Levi's code of conduct monitors did not bother to talk to workers during periodic inspections of the plants. This was some six years after the code was first published and four years after the company was humiliated in Indonesia, where a Levi's inspector failed to detect the horrific practice of strip-searching female employees until the local media reported on the women's complaints to the Indonesian government. Levi's Dominican Republic study supports what some human rights critics have been saying about the company for years: It may have an admirable, groundbreaking code of conduct protecting the rights of workers on paper, but the monitoring and enforcement of compliance with that code is fatally flawed because the company has not made it a formal practice to talk directly to the workers whose interests are at stake.

"The Terms of Engagement Process must include interviews with employees and department managers in order to collect data about the working conditions," recommended the NGOs, which were carefully selected on their qualifications to participate in the pilot study. "Not enough attention is paid throughout the process to workers. They have poor knowledge of the Terms of Engagement and its implementation." Another recommendation: "Given labor union–related difficulties that have prevailed in the free trade zones, in the Global Sourcing & Operations Guidelines brochure, additional text should be included to emphasize the right to free association of workers." A company official explains that interviews with workers are conducted routinely during the audits, but they are not part of a formalized process.

More specifically, the NGO investigators point out in the body of their report to Levi Strauss that when they interviewed a sample of forty workers at the four plants in the study, "none of the interviewees knows what a code of conduct is. Most know they work for Levi's, though no one in this firm has approached them to explain the contents of the code of conduct." The provision in Levi's Terms of Engagement that states the company will do business only with partners that allow the "right to free association" apparently would mean little to these young women, however, even if they knew about it. "Most workers have no knowledge of the Dominican Labor Code," the NGO report said. "They state they have been explained their duties and responsibilities, but not their rights. In general, they feel distrustful in this regard. They have no idea whether their rights have been violated by the companies they work for. None of these belong to a union, nor see the need to belong to one and, furthermore, they do not exist in the free trade zone plants. They also think these unions are unnecessary and harmful for the interests of free zone workers and that only union leaders profit. This union rejection matter also seems to be part of the free zone culture."

The experiment in the Dominican Republic was a far cry from the open and independent monitoring that the human rights advocacy community is demanding to hold multinationals accountable for their codes of conduct. Instead representatives of OXFAM-Great Britain and three local Dominican Republic NGOs were invited to participate as consultants in a study that was designed to evaluate Levi's in-house monitoring process; they weren't asked to participate in the process itself. In the company's words, this was "in the spirit of continuous improvement," a continuation of the various changes the company has made to the code since its inception. In the "Program Overview" document that describes the project, the company said it is "in full agreement with the spirit and the content of the recommendations received and intends to implement the recommended improvements with our contractors worldwide. Levi Strauss & Co. intends to share its progress in implementing these improvements with the NGOs."

Levi Strauss conducted a second pilot study in the Philippines in 1999 but did not immediately release its results. The company had scheduled another study of its contractors in Tunisia and was considering the possibility of trying the experiment in China as well, but it canceled those projects when it decided in mid-1999 to join a collaborative monitoring program with other apparel industry leaders through the Fair Labor Association, which grew out of the Clinton administration's Apparel Industry Partnership.

In an unusual display of transparency, Levi Strauss presented the findings of its Dominican pilot study in an open session of the annual Business for Social Responsibility forum in November 1998. "You've just got to be completely transparent in these kinds of communications. Don't be afraid to take risks, and don't be afraid to venture into the unknown, because you might learn something that will make you better," Michael Kobori, the Levi's executive in charge of the pilot study, told his colleagues during a panel discussion.

Kobori left Levi Strauss several months later to join BSR's human rights department, in his words, "to be more effective." But the fact that Kobori was allowed to make a public presentation of the rather unflattering results of the Dominican study hinted at coming changes within the organization. Specifically, an influential faction of Levi's executives who adamantly opposed independent monitoring of the company's compliance with its code of conduct, many of them based overseas, were beginning to lose their sway over corporate policy.

Tucked away at the end of a thick file of annexes to Levi's Dominican Republic report—but curiously on the record—was what appeared to be a dissenting opinion from a local feminist organization participating in the study, the Research Center for Feminist Action (CIPAS). The organization recommends that Levi's code compliance "should be reinforced by an independent monitoring system or an accompanying critical observation."

In May 1999 Clarence Grebey, then director of global communications, insisted that the company had absolutely no intention of allowing an independent monitoring of its code. But within a matter of months Grebey would leave the company—his job had been eliminated in a restructuring of his department, colleagues explained—and Levi Strauss would agree to take the first steps toward independent monitoring under the rules of the Fair Labor Association.

| | |

Levi's fundamental aversion to transparency appeared to have been a major factor in its initial decision to shun the Apparel Industry Partnership. The presidential task force brought apparel makers into a high-profile deliberation with labor and human rights activists to combat the scourge of sweatshops. The effort was born in August 1996, a year after the shocking news of the El Monte "virtual slave labor" case and shortly after controversial legislation was introduced on Capitol Hill that would hold manufacturers and retailers legally liable for conditions under which their contractors operate. The Clinton administration offered the voluntary AIP process as an alternative to the intrusive regulatory measures proposed in the bill.

Certainly the prestige of Levi Strauss, the leader in corporate social responsibility and the innovator of the first global code of conduct, would have contributed considerable momentum to the AIP when it got off the ground. Levi's protégés at BSR were involved in the program, which grouped eighteen separate companies, unions, and NGOs. Yet Levi Strauss executives believed they didn't need to participate in the AIP consultation because they were satisfied that their internal procedures for monitoring the company's code were doing the job. One former executive cited a "cost-benefit" consideration, questioning whether the AIP process would significantly alter public perceptions and improve Levi's brand protection beyond what it already had in place. "Our position is that there's not a one-size-fits-all solution," said Grebey, the former Levi's spokesman. "We have a proven track record with our [Global] Sourcing Guidelines and Terms of Engagement. We think that solution has worked for us and continues to work."

Levi's snub of the AIP was a delicate matter. The task force's high visibility in its deliberations, seeking maximum publicity for its efforts, didn't match Levi's traditionally low-key manner of practicing corporate social responsibility. Glitzy Kathie Lee Gifford, the group's celebrity mascot by dint of her own complicity in sweatshop scandal, was not exactly Levi's style. Neither was the in-your-face pluck of Nike, which needed the AIP to restore its tattered reputation. There was also the question of unions and messy politics in the AIP collaboration. "One of the criticisms of the task force is that it could fall victim to being politicized," Grebey explained. "So many interests are at the table."

But there was more at stake for Levi Strauss than a mere distaste for hyperbole and open political debate. Because the AIP included representation by unionists and human rights activists, the question of independent external monitoring of code compliance was under negotiation from the very beginning, a condition that Levi's had consistently opposed. Also, the code of conduct that AIP was developing as a common instrument for the industry contained specific language referring to the "right of free association" and "collective bargaining." Levi's terms of engagement literally did not go that far. Its code did not mention collective bargaining at all, and it downplayed the reference to the freedom of association by not citing it as a separate item under the list of specific standards, as the NGO report in the Dominican Republic study points out.

The company's position is that the right to collective bargaining is implied by the mere mention of freedom of association. Certainly it is serious about the matter; otherwise its new human rights manager, former diplomat Gare Smith, wouldn't have posed embarrassing questions about jailed labor leaders in his conversation with the Chinese labor minister. But perhaps the ambiguity of Levi's written code is no accident—the lack of clarity makes it far more practical to apply in the union-loathing demimonde of overseas apparel contracting. However, without the elements of independent monitoring and transparency, outsiders would find it impossible to determine whether or not Levi's code and its auditing system is in fact successful in resolving labor problems.

The AIP concluded its deliberations with much fanfare in November 1998, announcing, after two years of contentious debate, an agreement to set up an external monitoring system for overseas factories, creating the Fair Labor Association to oversee its implementation sometime in the year 2000. But the agreement was not unanimous, having emerged from negotiations conducted by a rump AIP—only nine of the original eighteen members of the group signed on. Most conspicuously absent from the accord was UNITE, the garment workers union, which had pushed for more stringent independent monitoring requirements and a commitment by manufacturers to pay a "living wage" to workers. Also dissenting were the Interfaith Center on Corporate Responsibility, the AFL-CIO, and the Retail, Wholesale and Department Store Union.

The living wage issue was fast emerging as a major cause—and stumbling block—for organized labor. It was a buzzword, spouted ad nauseam without a great deal of clarity on what the concept actually entailed. There was an obvious reason to oversimplify the idea—nothing can chill the passion of a human rights battle like a didactic discussion of macroeconomics. Currency exchange rates, purchasing power equity, commodity prices, inflationary trends, median housing costs, and caloric intake—these are all part of the grim determination of what a poverty-abating living wage might be in the plethora of economic subsystems where sweatshops flourish. Lift up the rock of the living wage issue, and your eyes will glaze over before your blood boils. Yet the living wage took on a certain sanctimony as shorthand for economic justice, and the concept actually made significant inroads on the U.S. domestic debate over fair wages.

Another issue that drove the unions out of the AIP process was the lack of a mechanism addressing countries like China and Indonesia, where independent trade unions are repressed. "This agreement's not very good," Mark Levinson, UNITE's director of research, told *The New York Times*. "The agreement allows companies to produce in countries that systematically deny worker rights, and it allows them to do that without requiring them to say anything to protect rights in those countries."

Signing on to the initial AIP agreement on November 4, 1998, were Liz Claiborne, Nike, Reebok, Phillips Van Heusen, BSR, the Lawyers Committee for Human Rights, the National Consumer League, the International Labor Rights Fund, and the RFK Memorial Center for Human Rights. Following the announcement, Kathie Lee Gifford, L. L. Bean, Nicole Miller, and Patagonia agreed to join. Michael Posner, director of the Lawyers Committee for Human Rights and a key player in the deliberations, characterized the agreement as the "first step" toward gaining higher wages in the industry.

Although only a handful of early joiners jumped on the bandwagon, the Fair Labor Association got a boost when some fifty U.S. university administrations signed up, attempting to assuage the campus uproar over alleged sweatshop abuses by college logo licensees. For many of the campus activists, however, that wasn't enough. Protests continued to snowball, with "knit-ins" demanding a living wage for workers, more comprehensive independent monitoring, and open disclosure of factory locations, in addition to protections for free association. These were the four pillars of the advocacy position that defined the campus debate and drove the fury of the antisweatshop campaign.

The AIP's moderate caucus was able to reach an agreement after making some major compromises in the FLA's compliance monitoring regime. Oversight and accountability hinged on reporting requirements to the FLA, where labor and human rights NGOs were to sit on the board of directors and could theoretically cry foul if the auditing process was tainted. Although companies were encouraged to work with local NGOs in the monitoring process, the external monitoring itself could be conducted by accredited professionals such as employees of accounting firms, who may be bound by nondisclosure agreements to protect proprietary interests. One of the most divisive issues was the frequency of external monitoring. The agreement calls for companies to supplement a program of internal labor auditing with independent external monitors for 30 percent of contractor plants in the initial three years after adopting the association's code of conduct. That ratio would level out to 10 percent in each subsequent year, which detractors said would leave huge gaps in accountability. Locations of subcontractor factories audited under the FLA process would be disclosed to the organization's board, which reserved the right to make all findings public. But the process fell short of the complete transparency and open accountability demanded by the most radical human rights activists.

Jeffery Ballinger, the indefatigable Nike critic—now a research fellow at Harvard's Kennedy School of Government studying the Turkish constitution—snapped back at the AIP agreement in a letter to the editor published in *The New York Times:* "Voluntary codes of conduct and periodic inspections may lead to marginal improvements in the working conditions of workers making famous-label apparel," he writes. "But the federal government has ignored its major responsibility in this area: workers rights. For example, in Asia and Central America workers are still not allowed to fight for better conditions by forming independent trade unions. The main reason is that officials of major apparel firms shift production as soon as workers begin to gain some bargaining power. The promise of a reliable 'no-sweat' label is still a long way off."

Levi Strauss pulled off another one of its surprising about-face maneuvers in July 1999 when it announced it had joined the Fair Labor Association. Gare Smith, who had pushed hard for the move since his arrival at the company, explained the decision this way in a prepared statement: "Joining the FLA enables us to build on our many years of experience in promoting a safe and healthy work environment through adherence to our stringent code of conduct.

We are excited to join forces with our industry colleagues and non-governmental organizations in a concerted effort to bring positive change to workplace conditions globally."

It remains to be seen whether the Fair Labor Association, brokered by the White House and the Department of Labor and now backed by the considerable weight of Levi Strauss, can enlist enough members from the apparel industry to create a critical mass and make the experiment work. How it will be accepted by the labor and human rights and campus advocacy communities is yet another question. Despite Levi's belated endorsement, the Apparel Industry Partnership could prove to have been another elaborate exercise in the empty rhetoric of sweatshop abatement.

| | |

Amid all the sound and fury generated by the debate over human rights and corporate social responsibility, a single riddle stands out above the others: Is there a systemic solution that can change the way in which multinational corporations conduct their business, with a minimal standard of social accountability, in the amoral superstructure of economic globalization?

Any business with its antennae intact must realize that it is in its best interests to maintain a basic level of decency and humanity in its operations. The alternative is to face potentially ruinous publicity and risk damaging the critical asset of its brand image. But the appropriate policy response to the human rights challenge is never very clear. It's easy enough to adopt a terms of engagement code citing lofty principles, but getting caught out of compliance with this code can be almost as bad as not having one in the first place. Accusations of negligence can quickly turn to charges of hypocrisy and duplicity. There are simply not enough guideposts out there to show how to implement the codes and, in doing so, balance the vital interests of profit making against the obligations of meeting vaguely defined societal needs. Letting that balance go out of kilter to the detriment of the bottom line can potentially undermine a company's ability to put its principles into practice, as the story of Robert Haas's Levi Strauss might suggest.

Practicing a reactionary damage-control style of public relations in a guerrilla war with human rights activists is a losing proposition, as the saga of Nike's recalcitrance shows. Conversely, an industry making concessions under pressure on a case-by-case basis does little to change the overall pattern of the social ills in question. Invariably, the child labor and the union busting and the jailing of labor leaders will pop up somewhere else, an incorrigible phenomenon in an economic system where market forces are global and the legal protections are local—and highly corruptible.

By default, the agenda is being driven by aggressive human rights watchdog groups. They play a healthy role in the evolutionary process of advancing human rights in the global marketplace, prodding corporations through exposure and negative publicity to face up to problems they might otherwise ignore. But there are not enough human rights watchdogs in the world to keep the activities of all the major corporations and their suppliers under ad hoc surveillance. The breadth and depth of the companies' operations is so vast, and their contractual relationships so ephemeral, it is an impossible task. By no fault of their own, these human rights zealots do not have the necessary resources to do much beyond gathering intelligence and pointing fingers. As advocates they are admirable; as policy organs they tend to be poorly equipped. And the punishment meted out by the human rights spotlight is too arbitrary to sustain any systemic reform by itself. All it can do is make scapegoats out of symbolic offenders, like Gap and Wal-Mart and Shell Oil, in the belief that society will be shocked, shamed, or otherwise motivated to find solutions to the underlying problems.

"Without public pressure on the companies, revealing the real conduct inside the factories, there can be no long lasting systemic change" said Joshua Karliner, executive director of the Transnational Resource Action Center, the pugnacious NGO. "But any solution has to have the participation of international civil society. There needs to be some sort of oversight of corporate activity in the global economy. How that comes about is a huge challenge."

At this point, an outraged citizenry might be disposed to turn to its government to seek redress for all these terrible wrongs being exposed. But there are limits on how far legislators in one country can reach into sovereign territory abroad to fix the social problems of globalization. Perhaps the greatest obstacles are the market forces themselves, which create powerful countervailing lobbying pressures at home. For instance, the 1993 anti-MFN legislation against China was skillfully coopted by the Clinton administration, under pressure to accommodate rational business interests. An initiative to legislate cross-industry principles for investment in China was subsumed by the administration's machinations on human rights policy the following year and quickly fizzled into a voluntary and virtually invisible document called the "Model Business Principles." Again, in 1996, the energy behind the post–El Monte legislative initiative to make companies legally responsible for their contractors was diverted into the AIP process. And the effort to enact federal labor reforms in Saipan has been torpedoed by powerful free-marketeers among Republican lawmakers.

The legislation that banned U.S. private investment in Burma in 1997 was the one exception that proved the rule, but even that is viewed by some as a watered-down compromise. Cynics characterize the Burma sanctions as a conciliatory bone thrown to the human rights advocacy community, aimed at taking the heat off the China policy. In any event, the U.S. Congress has not been able to muster the political will to legislate solutions for human rights problems in the economic sphere.

The absence of legislative options creates a moral void, which is partly being filled by innovative litigation. Gregory J. Wallance, a New York corporate litigator writing in a law journal on the class action suit alleging Unocal's complicity in forced labor in Burma, argues that the case is troubling because the judicial doctrine that might emerge cannot set orderly rules for companies to follow. Only a regulatory statute can do that, he reasons. The same might be said about the Saipan lawsuit against U.S. apparel manufacturers and retailers. The threat of joint liability for the misdeeds of a business partner in one specific case does not provide a coherent set of standards to follow in a variety of different situations.

Wallance argues that Congress should consider passing legislation that would regulate human rights standards for companies in the same way that the Foreign Corrupt Practices Act of 1977 regulates ethical standards for U.S. businesses operating overseas. The idea seems reasonable enough. If private industry cannot regulate itself effectively, or can't be held in check adequately by an international network of watchdog NGOs, why shouldn't government step in to take responsibility by providing regulatory answers? Wallance, after making the clarion call for congressional action, concedes he has limited expectations. "I think it's hard to say whether it could happen," he said in a terse E-mail message. "Plausible but not probable is where I come out." His ambivalent faith in the legislative solution typified the pessimism of many observers and activists.

"The Foreign Corrupt Practices Act came into being at a time when government was expanding its regulatory responsibilities, but now we're in a time of government contraction," said Alice Tepper Marlin, executive director of the Council on Economic Priorities, an NGO that ranks companies on social responsibility and offers a certification process for labor practices. "It seems highly unlikely that the federal government will ever take on responsibility for these issues. One of the reasons we chose to step in is that we saw there would not be a legislative solution." She adds, however, that if business were to widely recognize the risks of being held liable for poor working conditions, "then they would see it is in their own interests for governments to enforce labor regulations. Otherwise they have to be the policemen, and that can be expensive. They'll lobby with the question 'Why should we have to do government's job?'"

The case of the Massachusetts selective purchasing law for Burma provides a critical example of the maddening complexity that lies ahead for legislative answers. On one level, its constitutionality is under doubt because a state is mucking around in the realm of foreign policy, the exclusive reserve of the federal government. But more onerous for the Massachusetts law is the challenge in the court of the World Trade Organization, which administers the rules that member nations negotiate for fairness in international commerce. The state's anti-Burma economic sanctions law, alas, appears not to abide by those multilateral rules—which were not in place when Massachusetts legislated a similar selective purchasing law for South Africa during the apartheid era.

Multilateral treaties, like those establishing the WTO and the North American Free Trade Agreement, offer tremendous benefits to international trade. They also accelerate the process of globalization, which depending on your point of view can be bad as well as good. While there's no doubt that the growth of trade creates jobs and generates new wealth, globalization has a tendency to leave an array of social and human rights problems festering unattended in its shadows. Unfortunately the multilateral ethos behind the dream of the global economy has little tolerance for efforts by individual nations to set their own terms for involvement in the system. "Unilateralism" is a dirty word.

The Massachusetts law can also be construed as "protectionist," the most mortal of sins. Likewise, the arguments of labor activists, who grouse about job flight to *maquiladora* sweatshops in Latin America under NAFTA, are bereft of moral authority because they stink of protectionism. Lost in the polemics of this dialogue is the question of humanitarian concern and social responsibility for the people who must toil in those factories or lose their jobs to the prosecution of global competitive advantages.

| | |

If finding a solution for the injustices of globalization is stalled on account of the infallibility of multilateralism, then it follows that the solution itself must be multilateral. In that light, UN secretary general Kofi Annan's proposal to involve international business in a Global Compact on human rights—giving a "human face" to globalization—offers a vague hope that something might be accomplished.

George Kell, an economist in the UN secretary general's office in New York, said drafting a set of specific human rights and labor standards for business in a global code of conduct is not in the works. Memories of the ideological squabbles within the UN over such issues as the distribution of wealth and job creation during the cold war era are too fresh. "The climate is not right for a code of conduct," he said. "Back in the 1970s and 1980s the UN advocated codes for transnational corporations and for technology transfers, and it became very political." The UN apparatus would have been inadequate to the task of enforcing such a code in any event.

Instead, the Global Compact will take the form of a discussion about the need for a voluntary "convergence of values" that would create "one level playing field" for international business operations where human rights, labor, and the environment are concerned. "The whole thing is a balancing act," he said. "Developing countries fear protectionism. We're trying to make the case that while we need open markets, we also need to move forward on these other areas of human rights and social rights and the environment. Rather than destabilizing trade, we're encouraging corporations to work with UN institutions toward solutions."

Annan and Mary Robinson, the UN's high commissioner for human rights, began meeting with business leaders in the summer of 1999 to spread the word on the basic principles of the Global Compact. There are nine of them, according to a UN document posted on the Internet, specifying among other things that business should "support and respect the protection of internationally proclaimed human rights within their sphere of influence" and "make sure they are not complicit in human rights abuses." Other principles address such labor rights as free association and the abolition of child labor and admonish businesses to "promote greater environmental responsibility."

The agenda is not a radical one. It's highly unlikely the UN will be putting teeth into a compliance mechanism for whatever the program might evolve into. But even if the issue gets wrapped in the timid mumbo-jumbo of UN-speak, there's bound to be some benefit in Kofi Annan's Global Compact. As an exercise in moral suasion, it could help turn the tide against stragglers in the international business community who still hope that the human rights challenge is going to go away and leave them in peace to concentrate solely on profit maximization. The prestige of the program's UN imprimatur may prod Japanese corporations out of hibernation on international human rights issues, pointing them in the direction of a true convergence on international values, and at the same time offer theoretical support for fledgling human rights NGOs in Japan.

Robinson, the human rights high commissioner and former president of Ireland, reminded businesspeople attending a conference in Interlaken of the "enhanced role which business plays in modern society" since the collapse of the Communist bloc and the gradual decline in power among governments. "We live in an age of mergers and giant corporations, of multinational companies which dominate whole segments of the global market," she said. "The phenomenon of globalization has shifted many of the vital decisions that affect people's lives from the cabinet room to the boardroom. The actions of companies, often taken far away, can have a huge impact on national economies, particularly those in the developing world. Business leaders wield more power than ever before."

Organized business has been guarded in its reaction to the UN's modest proposal, making it clear in at least one high-level pronouncement that profitability has to come first before social responsibilities can be addressed.

"Business accepts the challenge and is eager to cooperate with the UN and other public-sector bodies to embrace all three areas" (human rights, labor, and the environment), said Marie Livanos Cattaui, secretary general of the International Chamber of Commerce (ICC). "Alongside them, however, we must place a fourth value—the economic responsibility incumbent upon any company to its customers, to its employees, and to its shareholders. Fulfillment of that responsibility is the key to the other three, for without it companies cannot remain in business."

Cattaui also makes the point that companies are not capable of taking responsibility for systematic remedies to the problems. "Business should not be called upon to meet demands and expectations that are properly the preserve of governments," she said in an ICC statement. "The private sector cannot, for example, ensure that the rule of law reigns in a given country, that all citizens have access to education and enjoy freedom of speech, that wealth is fairly distributed, and that there is an adequate social safety net for the old, the sick, and the jobless."

Cattaui goes on to articulate the glory of the classic model of laissez-faire capitalism, describing the benefits of globalization and couching the question of corporate responsibility in terms of *pas-*

sive constructive engagement—"globalization has already become a powerful force, spreading high standards and best business practices throughout the world." Yet she does not respond meaningfully to Annan's appeal for a more proactive approach: "Don't wait for every country to introduce laws protecting freedom of association and the right to collective bargaining," Annan had admonished the business community. "You can at least make sure your own employees, and those of your subcontractors, enjoy those rights." Like Leon Sullivan in the case of South Africa, Annan is asking business to transcend local law in a subtle act of human rights subversion.

That's not likely to happen, of course, unless the act of subversion by individual companies has some sort of international framework to legitimize these practices. Again, the ICC's Cattaui is skeptical. "No master plan created the global market, and no master plan can give it a human face."

Why can't the WTO get into the act? If Kofi Annan were able to sell his vision of converging values of commercial and corporate social accountability to the WTO, real systemic changes could begin taking place in the international human rights scene. The long, drawn-out process of negotiating and institutionalizing such values into a concrete set of global rules would be a painful one, however, and the chances of this happening are almost nil. Already the UN and the International Chamber of Commerce have gone on record in a joint statement opposing the idea because the expanded regulatory role for the WTO "would expose the trading system to great strain and the risk of increased protectionism."

Riotous street protests outside the December 1999 WTO ministerial meeting in Seattle, where advocacy groups were shut out of the dialogue, symbolized the impasse. Inside, delegates from developing countries adamantly rejected a proposal by President Clinton to include labor issues in the agenda.

Perhaps the emergence of a global cop with jurisdiction over such economic practices as official corruption, labor exploitation, and environmental degradation is a mere fantasy, as is the UN's Global Compact on shared values. But it's all worth dreaming about.

| | |
Epilogue

It is a sober conclusion to make, but the world probably will never be able to agree on a multilateral structure that could govern the behavior of transnational corporations. Without a common set of rules on a common set of values, corporations are left to their own devices to make policy decisions on how to manage the human rights challenge in their business operations. Voluntary codes of conduct are already de rigueur for many industries, so the next stage will be figuring out what to do about complying with them, now that companies have legions of human rights activists nipping at their heels.

One thing is certain. It's not just the apparel firms and the shoe-makers and the toy companies that will struggle with these choices. The human rights challenge is going to expand rapidly across manufacturing industries to shake up the high-technology sector and eventually reach deep into the service sector as well. Because the semiconductor industry is subject to such erratic business cycles and is already highly exposed to the vagaries of globalization, it is extremely vulnerable to the scandals that have afflicted low-tech industries. Clean rooms, the dust-free facilities where silicon wafers are fabricated into computer chips, can also become sweat-shops in terms of hours and wages. The *San Jose Mercury News* published in 1999 an alarming investigative series on the wide-spread practice of piecework assembly of integrated circuits out-side the corporate production facilities in Silicon Valley. This work was being performed in many cases by Vietnamese immigrants on their kitchen tables, allegedly in violation of state and federal labor laws.

Manufacturers of personal computers, like the makers of blue jeans, are relying increasingly on outsourcing as they struggle in a consumer market where retail prices are being driven down by intense competition. Compaq Computer Corporation, for instance, cut its workforce in Singapore by 1,600 jobs—62 percent of its payroll—in August 1999, contracting out the local production to reduce costs. Troubling questions about how companies like Compaq monitor the labor standards at the factories of their foreign contractors are bound to emerge sooner or later. Likewise, contract software production from Seattle to Bangalore offers a wealth of opportunities in the hunt for labor abuse. Mom-and-pop foundries in Brazil subcontracting to parts suppliers who cater the big automakers in Detroit and Japan are ready and waiting for the human rights searchlights.

Said Alice Tepper Marlin of the Council on Economic Priorities: "We need to wake up the sleeper industries. There are a lot of companies out there that are at risk of having their brand reputations compromised—they just don't know it yet."

Tepper Marlin has a vision for what to do until a better solution for safeguarding human rights in the workplace comes along. She developed something called "Social Accountability 8000," a rigorous certification process that provides manufacturers with something akin to the Good Housekeeping Seal of Approval when their factory operations comply with strict standards. Tepper Marlin is the author of the consumer advocacy book *Shopping for a Better World,* a guide to social accountability measurements for U.S. companies. Her corporate rankings became a valuable resource for the social responsibility investment advisory industry, which boomed along with the South Africa divestiture movement, serving church pension fund managers and other politically or socially sensitive investors.

Tepper Marlin started the Social Accountability 8000 project in 1996, working closely with corporations, UN agencies, and other NGOs over an eighteen-month period to develop procedures and technical standards. She borrowed heavily from established ILO standards but also innovated new criteria for the human rights elements such as child labor. Tepper Marlin's new organization, the

CEP Accreditation Agency (CEPAA), trains and supervises the auditors—all employees of three big European industrial auditing concerns—who perform the inspections for member companies. The application process is costly, slow, and demanding. A year after the program got off the ground with its first certification in May 1998 of a U.S. factory belonging to Avon Products Inc., CEPAA counted eight multinational corporations as members, mostly European, and had certified some fifteen plants that passed the stringent "corrective action requirements." Reebok and Toys "R" Us were in the fold, but Tepper Marlin still has a lot of marketing to do. The prospect of consumers seeing products on store shelves with Social Accountability 8000 seals is a long way off.

Tepper Marlin's program, along with the AIP's Fair Labor Association, is part of a broad spectrum of nongovernmental organizations and institutions that are gearing up to help companies navigate the uncharted waters of social accountability in the global marketplace. It's an impressive list. The Ethical Trading Initiative in Europe is bringing together business leaders, government officials, and human rights advocates into a consultative process. Business for Social Responsibility is making great strides in training and education in the field and advising individual companies on strategies for human rights policies. The Minnesota Center for Corporate Responsibility's work with the Caux Roundtable, the trilateral grouping of business leaders, is exemplary. Business leaders should know that dealing head-on with the challenge of human rights does not have to be isolated or confrontational. Despite the explosion of protest at the WTO meeting, doing battle with hostile activists is not exactly what this game is about anymore.

Global Exchange, the aggressive human rights NGO in San Francisco that chastised Levi Strauss on its China policy reversal, offers a good example of how things are changing. The group has resurrected the abortive effort to impose model business principles on U.S. companies with operations in China, but this time around it is taking a conciliatory approach to the task. So far it has enlisted the support of Mattel, Reebok—and, yes, Levi Strauss. One week before the tenth anniversary of the Tiananmen massacre, the three companies signed on to the "U.S. Business Principles for Human

Rights of Workers in China." This document commits them to a tough code on labor standards, as well as a promise to work cooperatively with human rights groups to ensure compliance—a strong hint at independent monitoring—and "more broadly to promote respect for these principles in China," suggesting a duty to engage interactively with the Chinese on human rights. It was clearly a positive development. The project may not solve China's labor rights problems, but it points the way to positive collaboration among companies and their harshest critics. "It's an experiment for us," said Medea Benjamin, Global Exchange's executive director. "It's not our usual practice of bashing companies on the head."

| | |

There's significant hope out there that corporations and social advocates can find a middle path. That's why the story of Levi Strauss & Co. is so incredibly important in coming to terms with human rights in the global marketplace. The company is not a perfect model, neither in its business strategies nor in its social responsibility practices. But it has the distinction of trying harder and far longer than any other multinational corporation to do the right thing. It is a company whose iconic brand resonates deeply and emotionally in the minds of many people around the world, and a company that hard-edged cynics truly want to believe in. In the convoluted conversation about balancing corporate success against the human rights challenge, a troubling question arises: If Levi Strauss can't do it, who can?

There aren't many candidates out there of Levi's stature that could exercise the kind of leadership that is badly needed at this time. Levi Strauss is one of the very few major companies in the apparel industry that has not been indelibly branded a scoundrel by human rights critics. In the sporting goods industry, Reebok has aggressively positioned itself in the avant-garde on human rights, but the company is vulnerable to criticism that it exploits that position for crass marketing purposes. Mattel may be on the right road, but no company in the toy industry can stand up to intense scrutiny of its record on sourcing practices in China. One wouldn't even think of turning to a company like Microsoft for exemplary values of corporate social responsibility—founder Bill Gates hadn't really discovered the concept of philanthropy until a fellow multibillionaire, media baron Ted Turner, shamed him into it in a public challenge. (Not to be outdone in philanthropy as in business, the fiercely competitive software mogul responded by setting up a $17 billion charitable foundation, the nation's largest.)

In a debate that has fueled itself with an unrelenting negative focus on corporate scapegoats, it is now more important than ever to strike a balance by paying attention to positive models. Levi Strauss, by default, has for years been the single "good" example cited when journalists and scholars examine the allegations against the other companies under siege. With recent events, however, Levi's has lost its aura of unblemished innocence, and it has become a much more complicated—and valid—model to draw lessons from. It's no longer a matter of simplistic comparison: Nike, bad; Levi's, good. The truth has always been that both of these companies have practiced business while swimming in a turbid sea of situational ethics—though their priorities and values may have been quite different. Striving to understand how a Levi's-inspired model might work in conducting business guided by principles, however, remains an essential task for any serious student of corporate social responsibility.

The problem here, again, is that Levi Strauss and the family that owns and runs it could be much more accommodating if they wanted to be. At odds with the company's claim of including the interests of outside "stakeholders" in its commitment to social responsibility, Levi Strauss has fastidiously shrouded itself from public view. There may be some very good reasons for this obsession with secrecy—its private corporate status, its family tradition of not taking credit for doing good deeds—but the net effect is that the company practices its ethics by virtual stealth. Other companies cannot learn from the leader if they're not allowed to see and hear how it makes decisions. And no company can claim to practice social responsibility without making a genuine commitment to transparency.

"We are an anomaly, especially in the eyes of the business press and the financial community," said Clarence Grebey, the former Levi Strauss official in charge of global communications who, for the most part over an eighteen-month period, chose not to speak to me. Repeated requests for interviews with Levi's executives went unanswered. "We are one of the most well known businesses in the world, and we're a market leader in almost every market we operate in—and we're a private organization. That's frustrating for people whose job it is to extract information and interpret it for their audiences."

One former Levi's executive attributes the company's attitude toward publicity to a family trait that goes all the way back to founder Levi Strauss himself. He described the Haas family as "very old money," a creature of elite San Francisco society, which values a low-key approach to philanthropy and shuns celebrity. The former executive, who asked to remain anonymous—for reasons other than modesty—cites the example of Water Haas Jr., who in 1989 was completely befuddled when his Oakland Athletics team won the World Series championship. Levi's patriarch found it painful to speak to the media and refused to take any credit for the victory. Any other baseball team owner would have gloated; Haas deferred to the players and coaches.

This is an admirable family trait, indeed, but it is an anachronism in today's world of open business communication, where true corporate accountability is not possible without a high degree of transparency. The biggest threat to undermining Levi Strauss's long and remarkable tradition of social responsibility is this enduring knee-jerk impulse for privacy and information control.

Encouragingly, there have been some positive signs that Levi Strauss may be thinking about opening up. Its recruitment of diplomat Gare Smith to head its human rights and social responsibility policy process was the right idea. Smith is extroverted, confident, and effusive, a personality that collides with the prevailing culture of reserve at Levi's. Smith, who wrangled openly with the Chinese labor minister weeks after coming onboard, had tried to steer the company away from its lone-wolf approach to seeking solutions for labor and human rights problems. He presided over the company's joining of the Fair Labor Association, which would appear to have involved a major policy reversal with the explicit acceptance of at least a minimal level of external monitoring and transparency.

Smith describes the somewhat cryptic but inspirational mandate given to him by Robert Haas shortly after he arrived at Levi Strauss. The chief executive strolled into his office informally, leaned against a bookshelf, and said: "I want you to think about where the field is going to be twenty years from now. Work backward from that point to ensure that we are in a leadership position and moving toward the ethical principles we value."

The philosophy of aspiration seemed alive and well at Levi Strauss, and Smith said he's confident it will survive under his new boss, the outsider CEO Philip Marineau. Now all that is needed is the kind of transparency that will allow the company's stakeholders and its fellow corporate travelers around the world to follow its leadership and draw inspiration from common values.

| | |

The story of Levi Strauss and its human rights policy already provides grist for evocative case studies in business school ethics courses. No doubt these will be updated and reexamined once the air clears on the company's positions on such issues as external monitoring and its investment plans in China. Many of the knotty ethical dilemmas confronting the company are likely to remain unresolved, however. There will be no correct answers to the professor's exam questions.

If market trends continue, the students will be wearing blue jeans from the Gap, or maybe Tommy Hilfiger. But there's a good chance that the professor will have grown up wearing Levi's and will still have a few faded pairs in the drawer and will still identify the brand with a certain nostalgic idealism. That might explain the impulse to teach business ethics in the first place, instead of a course like Merciless Downsizing 101. To be sure, Levi Strauss could be part of the syllabus of either course now, but let's presume it will be better remembered for ethics than its plant closings.

We may be living in a era of unmitigated greed, but the subject of human rights is gradually working its way into the mainstream curriculum of major American business schools, taken up by some very distinguished scholars. It's difficult to say whether ambitious

MBA graduates are going to take ethics and human rights seriously once they enter the job market. It won't be easy to consider oneself an agent of social change while being tantalized by lucrative compensation packages for entry-level management jobs. Nor can it be said that many of their parents' generation, the Levi's-wearing sons and daughters of the 1960s counterculture, placed a priority on saving the world during their inevitable accommodation to the practical realities of life.

Nevertheless, one can find Levi's children packed into conspicuous demographic bumps—baby boomers all—in urban populations all around the world. They matured out of social mutiny decades ago to join the Establishment they once derided. They have passed, quietly, into middle age. They now hold a huge stake in social equilibrium, having assumed positions of responsibility and power in business, government, and the professions. Many may have stopped buying Levi's jeans in favor of other brands that offer a more comfortable fit to their bulging bottoms. Evidence from the marketplace also suggests that a significant number of these old denim comrades have maintained brand loyalty by buying Levi's Dockers and Slate's, even if this less casual attire carries no implicit message of political consciousness.

| | |

In the absence of some kind of moral compass redefining the values of multinational corporations from within, American business risks the real possibility that society will impose its values from the outside.

Scandal exposés and consumer boycott campaigns targeting alleged offenders can be expected to remain largely symbolic, without clearly quantifiable effects on sales. But they can also tarnish a brand name irreparably and sour consumer attitudes to the point where companies experiencing declining sales may never know for sure what hit them. The kind of civil litigation that puts teeth into environmental justice may well become common in the human rights and labor fields, as the Unocal and Saipan cases suggest. Local selective purchasing laws are on the rise and will become a significant nuisance for companies with sloppy human rights policies, even if the laws don't stand up in court. The antisweatshop movement on university campuses has tremendous explosive potential to drive public policy, exactly as campus activism did during the antiapartheid movement and the Vietnam War era. There's already a code word for this: Seattle.

Finally, there's always the potential that a new administration and a new Congress will respond more attentively to public pressure for legislative remedies. When enough American consumers wake up to the fact that they are as much to blame for the social injustices of globalization as the multinationals that pander to their demand for cheap goods, then things might begin to happen. With a strong push from an educated and motivated electorate, the economic sanctions placed on Burma could become an important precedent for future regulation, to be refined and improved upon, instead of an isolated and cynical diversionary tactic.

The odds are fairly good that in the next few years Levi Strauss will emerge from its current business crisis on financially sound footing, having reclaimed some lost market share and resurrected its appeal to younger consumers. The brand name has such incredible resilience and authority, it's almost impossible to imagine a scenario of continued rapid decline. What's more difficult to predict, however, is whether the company will keep alive the core ethical conviction of five generations of the Strauss-Stern-Haas family—the belief that true success in business involves much more than just seeking profits.

If that flame goes out, it would be a devastating loss for the world. Because if Levi Strauss can't do it, then maybe nobody can.

NOTES

|||

PROLOGUE

p. 2 'The Chamber's special guest that morning . . .': James Mann, *About Face: A History of America's Curious Relationship with China from Nixon to Clinton* (New York: Alfred A. Knopf, 1999), pp. 302–3.

CHAPTER ONE

p. 6 'The story of what happened next has been told . . .': Richard Baum, *Burying Mao: Chinese Politics in the Age of Deng Xiaoping,* (Princeton: Princeton University Press, 1994), pp. 275–91.

Personal observations in Beijing and Shanghai, China, May–June 1989.

p. 8 'The atrocity has since been conceptualized . . .': See Daniel Jonah Goldhagen, *Hitler's Willing Executioners: Ordinary Germans and the Holocaust* (New York: Alfred E. Knopf, 1996).

p. 9 'In what may prove to be the last act of German War reparation . . .': Edmund L. Andrews, "Germany Accepts $5.1 billion Accord to End Claims of Nazi Slave Workers," *New York Times*, December 18, 1999.

p. 9 'The moral tone of the document's preamble . . .': The United Nations Universal Declaration of Human Rights, Adopted and proclaimed by General Assembly resolution 217 A (III) of December 10, 1948 (United Nations Web site: www.un.org/Overview/rights.html). *See Appendix B.*

p. 9 'The Declaration was a radical document . . .': Henry J. Steiner, "Securing Human Rights: the first half-century of the Universal Declaration and Beyond," *Harvard Magazine,* October 1998.

Henry Steiner, personal interview, Cambridge, Massachusetts, November 1998.

p. 11 'It is important to note the extent of sharp disagreement . . .': See Franklin and Eleanor Roosevelt Institute (Web site: www.udhr.org/history/frbioer.htm).

p. 12 'Amnesty International, the London-based . . .': Amnesty International USA, *United States of America: Rights for All,* (London: AI Publications, 1998).

p. 14 'UN secretary-general Kofi Annan articulated . . .': Kofi Annan, Statement to the World Economic Forum in Davos, Switzerland, January 31, 1999, United Nations press release, February 1, 1999.

George Kell, telephone interview, New York, May 1999.

p. 16 'Whatever the UN did on business and human rights . . .': Transnational Resource & Action Center, "Key UN Agency Solicits Funds From Corporations," TRAC press release, March 12, 1999 (TRAC Web site: www.corpwatch.org).

Amit Srivastava, personal interview, Tokyo, January 1999.

Joshua Karliner, telephone interview, San Francisco, May 1999.

p. 16 'Host Charlene Hunter-Gault sets the scene . . .': Rory O'Connor and Danny Schechter, "Globalization and Human Rights," PBS Documentary, (Globalvision Inc., 1998).

p. 18 'Most notable among these efforts . . .': Shepard Barbash, "Dunn Deal," *Stratos,* September/October 1997.

Bob Dunn, telephone interview, January 1998, and personal interview, San Francisco, September 1998.

Aaron Cramer, personal interviews, Berkeley, October 1997 and San Francisco, July 1998.

p. 20 'Peter Liebhold, one of the curators of a groundbreaking exhibition . . .': Peter Liebhold, personal interview, Washington, D.C., April 1999.

p. 21 'One critical reference point for the emerging . . .': David P. Baron, *Business and its Environment* (Upper Saddle River, New Jersey: Prentice Hall, 1992), pp. 515–22.

p. 24 'The Business Roundtable released a statement . . .': Baron, ibid., pp. 522–5.

'Consider the perennial problem of graft . . .': Jere Longman, "Head Of Olympics Expels 6 Members In Payoff Scandal," *New York Times,* January 25, 1999.

p. 25 'Evidence suggests that this law . . .': Ed Cray, *Levi's,* (Boston: Houghton Mifflin, 1978), p. 230.

p. 29 'Levi Strauss, it should be noted . . .': Gare Smith, telephone interview, San Francisco, August 1999.

p. 30 'Humanity cannot live without a moral yardstick . . .': Charles McCoy, personal interview, Berkeley, December 1998.

p. 30 'When Levi Strauss moved out of the old building . . .': Cray, op. cit., 238–41.

p. 32 'The senior manager in charge of quality . . .': Cray, ibid., pp. 127–9.

Harriet Nathan, 1973 interview with Walter A. Haas, Jr., *Levi Strauss & Co.: Tailors to the World,* Regional Oral History Office,

The Bancroft Library, (University of California, Berkeley, 1976), pp. 4–5.

p. 32 'Haas was not joking, however . . .': Levi Strauss & Co., Prospectus: offering 1,396,000 Shares of Common Stock, Lehman Brothers and Dean Witter & Co., March 3, 1971.

p. 33 'Indeed, Walter's son Robert . . .': Robert Haas, "Risks, Innovation and Responsibility: a Business Model for the New Millennium," speech to Business for Social Responsibility conference, Los Angeles, November 6, 1997.

'Levi Strauss, the man, was not a prospector . . .': Cray, op. cit., pp. 1–15.

Hambleton, Ronald. *The Branding of America: From Levi Strauss to Chrysler,"* (Dublin, New Hampshire: Yankee Books, 1987), pp. 21–5.

Sondra Henry, *A Biography of Levi Strauss: Everyone Knows His Name,* (Minneapolis: Dillon Press, 1990).

See also "Biographies: Founder" on Levi Strauss & Co. corporate Web site (www.levistrauss.com).

Chapter Two

p. 38 'She scaled a high stucco wall . . .': "Jena" (accompanied by attorney William M. Livingston), personal interview, Los Angeles, August 1995.

Peter Liebhold and Harry R. Rubenstein, "Between a Rock and a Hard Place," *Labor's Heritage* (George Meany Memorial Archives), Vol. 9. No. 4, Spring 1998.

Karl Schoenberger, "Escapee Sparked Sweatshop Raid," *Los Angeles Times,* August 11, 1995.

p. 40 'This new and illicit twist on the game of globalization . . .': Paul J. Smith, ed., *Human Smuggling: Chinese Migrant Trafficking and the Challenge to America's Immigration Tradition* (Washington, D.C.: Center for Strategic & Intl Studies, 1997).

Steven A. Holmes, "Arrests Made In Smuggling of Immigrants: Mohawk Land Used On New York Border," *New York Times,* December 11, 1998.

p. 41 'The Los Angeles Jewish Commission on Sweatshops . . .': Report by the Los Angeles Jewish Commission on Sweatshops, Los Angeles, January 1999.

p. 43 'In 1996 the seven defendants pleaded guilt . . .': E-mail communication with Julie Su (Asia Pacific American Legal Center), Los Angeles, December 1998.

William Livingston, telephone interview, Glendora, California, November 1998.

Henry Ong, telephone interview, Los Angeles, March 1999.

p. 44 'The Smithsonian Institution enshrined . . .': Peter Liebhold and Harry Rubenstein, personal interview, Washington, D.C., April 1999.

p. 45 'Testimony to the abominations of El Monte . . .': Virtual exhibition: "Between A Rock and A Hard Place: A Dialogue on American Sweatshops 1820 to the Present," National Museum of American History, Smithsonian Institution (Smithsonian Web site: www.si.edu/nmah/ve/sweatshops/start.htm).

p. 47 'The Levi Strauss Foundation was the tenth largest . . .': *Foundation Giving: Yearbook of Facts and Figures on Private, Corporate and Community Foundations* (The Foundation Center, 1998). In the Center's 1999 survey, the Levi Strauss Foundation had slipped in ranking to No. 13, with $121.9 million in assets at the end of 1997 (Foundation Center Web site: http://fdncenter.org/grantmaker/trends/top50assets.html).

"Apparel Maker Wins First Ron Brown Award for Corporate Leadership," *Business Wire,* February 11, 1998.

p. 48 'Unfortunately for Haas and the many . . .': David Cay Johnson, "At Levi Strauss, Big Cutbacks, With Largesse," *New York Times,* November 4, 1997.

p. 49 'Levi Strauss was still haunted . . .': Sheila Contreras, "Chale con Levi Strauss & Company: No Justice, No Jeans," *sub(TEX),* Austin, Texas, Vol. 1, No. 6, April 1995.

Peter Thigpen, personal interview, San Rafael, California, February 1999.

Miriam Ching Louie, telephone interview, Oakland, March 1999.

p. 51 'Levi Strauss later found itself in another . . .': Verdicts: Delgadillo v. Levi Strauss & Co., *National Law Journal,* February 23, 1998.

p. 52 'But this generosity could not resolve . . .': Steve Gregory, telephone interview, Centerville, Tennessee. May 1999.

p. 53 'That line had changed 180 degrees . . .': Carol Emert, "Levi's to Slash U.S. Plants: Competitors' Foreign-Made Jeans Blamed," *San Francisco Chronicle,* February 23, 1999.

Leslie Kauffman, "Levi Is Closing 11 Factories; 5,900 Jobs Cut," *New York Times.* February 23, 1999.

Levi Strauss & Co., "Levi Strauss & Co. To Close 11 Of Its North American Plants," press release, February 22, 1999.

Bruce Raynor, "UNITE Statement Regarding LS&Co. Announcement of Plant Closings," press release, February 22, 1999.

p. 56 'Levi Strauss never promised it would go bankrupt . . .': Levi Strauss Associates Inc., Annual Report for fiscal year ended November 26, 1995 (Form 10-k, U.S. Securities and Exchange Commission).

Justin Adams, David P. Baron, "Levi Strauss & Co. Global Sourcing Guidelines," case study S-P-12, Graduate School of Business, Stanford University, July 1994. David P. Baron et al., "Levi Strauss &

Co. Terms of Engagement Audits," case study S-P-14, Graduate
School of Business, Stanford University, July 1994.

Jane Palley Katz, Lynn Sharp Paine, "Levi Strauss & Co.: Global
Sourcing (A)," Case study 9–395–127, Harvard Business School, Harvard University, November 29, 1994.

David Baron, personal interview, Stanford, December 1998.

p. 57 'The allegations went as follows . . .': Frank Swoboda, "Levi Strauss
to Drop Suppliers Violating Its Workers Rights Rules," *Washington
Post,* March 13, 1992. Alicia Brooks, "Saipan Factories Socked by
OSHA for Labor Violations," *United Press International,* March 31, 1992.

Frank Swoboda, "Saipan Firm Agrees to Pay Back Wages," *Washington Post,* May 22, 1992.

p. 65 'Complaints of inhumane living conditions . . .': Office of Insular
Affairs, "Federal-CNMI Initiative on Labor, Immigration & Law
Enforcement In the Commonwealth of the Northern Mariana Islands,
Fourth Annual Report," U.S. Department of the Interior, 1998.

Philip Shenon, "Saipan Sweatshops are No American Dream," *New
York Times,* July 18, 1993.

Terry McCarthy, "Abused in the U.S.A.," *Time,* February 9, 1998.

Thomas Korosec, "Our Man in Saipan," *Dallas Observer,* February
19, 1998.

p. 67 'Meanwhile, Levi Strauss & Co. continued quietly . . .': Sweatshop
Watch, "First-ever Lawsuits Filed Charging Sweatshop Conspiracy
Between Major U.S. Clothing Designers and Retails, Foreign Textile Producers" (Web site www.sweatshopwatch.org), January 13,
1999.

Steven Greenhouse, "18 Major Retailers and Apparel Makers Are
Accused of Using Sweatshops," *New York Times,* January 14, 1999.

Glenn Schloss, "HK Firms in $7.8b Sweatshop Suit," *South China
Sunday Morning Post,* January 24, 1999.

p. 67 'The U.S. Equal Employment Opportunity . . .': Carmencita Abad,
telephone interview, Oakland, May 1999.

Robert Collier, "Apparel Firms Settle Suit on Sweatshops," *San
Francisco Chronicle,* August 10, 1999.

p. 69 'Levi Strauss said it wasn't targeted . . .': Clarence Grebey, telephone
interviews, San Francisco. January 1999 and May 1999.

'By midyear, four of the retailers named . . .': Robert Collier, "Apparel Firms Settle Suit on Sweatshops," *San Francisco Chronicle,* August 10, 1999.

p. 70 'Levi Strauss has escaped the negative publicity . . .': Medea Benjamin,
personal interview, San Francisco, July 1998.

Global Exchange, et al., "Sign-on Letter to Levi Strauss & Co. CEO
Robert Haas," June 24, 1998.

Medea Benjamin, "A Riveting Announcement," *San Francisco Bay Guardian,* June 10, 1998.

p. 71 'Levi Strauss was not entirely off the hook . . .': Jacques Bertrand, "For Independent Monitoring of the Levi Strauss Code of Conduct, Noveca Industries: a Case Study in the Philippines," October 1996, Canadian Catholic Organization for Development and Peace, Montreal.

Committee for the Defense of Human Rights in Honduras and Federation of Independent Workers of Honduras, "Workers in Honduras: An Examination of Working Conditions in Several Plants Producing Goods for Levi Strauss & Co.." September–November 1995.

Rachel Sylvester, "22p an Hour by Fashion Factory: Credibility Gap." *Sunday Telegraph,* January 28, 1996. Jacques Bertrand, telephone interview, Montreal, August 1998.

p. 73 'The Dutch antisweatshop advocacy group . . .': Nina Ascoli, ed., "Case File: Levi Strauss & Co.," Clean Clothes Campaign of the Netherlands, report presented to conference Workers and Consumers Rights in the Garment Industry, Brussels, April 30, 1998.

Patrick Neyts letter to Ineke Zeidenhurst of Clean Clothes Campaign, rebutting the CCC report, Levi Strauss & Co. document, undated.

E-mail communication with Nina Ascoli, May 1999.

Dutch Clean Clothes Campaign Web site (www.cleanclothes.org).

G. Pascal Zachary, "Exporting Rights: Levi Tries to Make Sure Plants in Asia Treat Workers Well," *Wall Street Journal,* July 28, 1994.

CHAPTER THREE

p. 78 'Burma has two kinds of mosquitoes . . .': Aung Naing Oo, "Burma's Time to Choose: A Worsening economy creates an explosive situation," Viewpoint, *Newsweek,* October 2, 1998.

Bertil Lintner, *Outrage: Burma's Struggle for Democracy* (London and Bangkok: White Lotus, 1990).

Personal interviews with Burmese citizens requesting anonymity in Rangoon, Bangkok, Tokyo and in Northern California.

Human Rights Watch/Asia, "Burma: Entrenchment or Reform?," Vol. 7, No. 10, July 1995.

Business for Social Responsibility, "A Guide to Human Rights and Rule of Law Issues Affecting Business Operations in Burma," Business for Social Responsibility Education Fund's Human Rights Program, January 1997.

p. 81 'The company explained it this way . . .': Simon Billenness, "Beyond South Africa: New Frontiers in Corporate Responsibility," *Business and Society Review* (Management Reports, Inc.), June 22, 1993.

p. 82 'Ironically, since Levi Strauss . . .': National Labor Committee, "U.S. Apparel Imports from Burma Soar, Despite Increased Repression and Sanctions," November 17, 1998 (www.nlcnet.org/burma/impots.htm).

p. 83 'Firms such as Motorola, Eddie Bauer . . .': Seth Mydans, "Pepsi Courts Myanmar, Preferring Sales to Politics," *New York Times,* February 22, 1996.

p. 83 'Unocal had earned the disapprobation . . .': Sheri Prasso and Larry Armstrong, "A Company Without a Country: Unocal Says it Won't Leave Burma, but it may De-Americanize," *Business Week,* May 5, 1997.

John Imle, personal interview, Los Angeles, April 1994.

p. 84 'In 1997 a judge in California ruled . . .': Gregory J. Wallance, "Fall-out From Slave-labor Case Is Troubling," *New Jersey Law Journal* (American Lawyer Newspapers Group), December 8, 1997.

p. 85 'The $5.5 billion international oil giant . . .': "Human Rights and Democracy: A Discussion Paper," Unocal Corp. (Web site:www.unocal.com/responsibility/humanrights).

p. 86 'For multinational corporations, . . .': Karl Schoenberger, "Motorola Bets Big on China," *Fortune,* May 27, 1996.

p. 88 'Soe Min Aung, a local businessman . . .': Soe Min Aung, personal interview, Rangoon, October 1998.

p. 89 'This was a time when most of the American . . .': Fred A. Avila, personal interview, Rangoon, October 1998.

p. 90 'Japanese multinationals will be the ones . . .': "Suzuki to Set up Joint Venture to Make Vehicles in Myanmar," *Nikkei Weekly,* October 19, 1998.

Akinori Seki, personal interview, Tokyo, October 1998.

p. 92 'Tokyo broadened its small but uninterrupted . . .': Personal interviews with Akira Chiba and Hisanaga Tomikoka, Foreign Ministry, and Hiro Hisazawa, Ministry of International Trade and Industry, Tokyo, September 1998; and diplomatic sources in Rangoon, October 1998.

p. 94 'In Japan, effective NGOs devoted to international . . .': Simon Billenness (Franklin Research & Development Corp.), telephone and personal interviews, Boston, August and November 1998.

Schu Sugawara (PD Burma Japan). Personal interview, Tokyo, September 1998.

Barbara Warner, "Japan's Growing Nonprofit Sector Responds to Government Shortfalls, *Japan Economic Institute Report,* June 5, 1998.

p. 94 'Japanese companies are not bothered . . .': Aron Cramer. personal interview, San Francisco, July 1998.

p. 96 'Tokyo-based Pacific Asia Resource Center . . .': Pacific Asia Resource Center, "Nike: Just Don't Do It: Mienai Teikokushugi," PARC Booklet 6, *Gekkan Oruta,* July 10, 1998.

Yoji Sato (Asics Corp.), telephone interview, Tokyo, February 1999.

Ben Watanabe, telephone interview, Tokyo, February 1999.

p. 97 'One Japanese group that may rise . . .': Shinichi Sakuma, personal interview, Tokyo, February 1999.

Mika Iba, trans., "Asian NGO Charter on Transnational Corporations," TNC Monitor Japan, Tokyo, November 1998.

p. 98 'Meanwhile, Japanese companies are not immune . . .': Billenness interview.

p. 99 'The views on the Burma question expressed . . .': Kenichi Omae, "1997: Year of Transition," *Asia Week* (special issue), December 1997.

Donald M. Seekins, "One Trip to Myanmar and Everyone Would Love the Country: Japan Incorporated Rolls Out a Big Gun," *Burma Debate,* Vol. V, No. 1, Winter 1998.

p. 101 'The problem is that when UN secretary general . . .': Japan Federation of Economic Organizations, "*Keidanren Kigyo Kodo Kensho* (Keidanren Corporate Code of Conduct)," Keidanren document.

p. 102 'Canon Inc., which has positioned itself . . .': Ryuzaburo Kaku, personal interview, Tokyo, October 1998.

Akihiro Tanaka (Canon), telephone interview. Tokyo, February 1999.

Ryuzaburo Kaku, "The Path of Kyosei," *Harvard Business Review,* July/August, 1997.

Joe Skelly, "Interview: Ryuzaburo Kaku," *Business Ethics,* March/April 1995.

Caux Roundtable, "Principles for Business," 1994 (Minnesota Center for Corporate Social Responsibility Web site: www.stthmas.edu/mccr).

p. 103 'When Kofi Annan proposed . . .': George Kell interview.

p. 104 'But things are happening in Japan today . . .': Mitsuko Shimomura, personal interview, Tokyo, January 1999.

CHAPTER FOUR

p. 108 'Five years after the Tiananmen Massacre . . .': Mann, *About Face,* op. cit.

Warren Christopher, *In the Stream of History: Shaping Foreign Policy for a New Era* (Stanford: Stanford University Press, 1998), pp. 152–64.

p. 109 'The atmosphere in the elegant banquet hall . . .': Mike Chinoy, "Christopher Talks Settle Down to Polite Tone," *CNN* (Transcript # 497–2), March 14, 1994.

Daniel Williams, "U.S. Softens Trade Stand with China: Human Rights Steps Would No Longer Be Spelled Out," *Washington Post,* March 14, 1994.

p. 113 'Yet by the U.S. State Department's reckoning . . .': U.S. Department of State, "China Country Report on Human Rights Practices for 1997," Bureau of Democracy, Human Rights and Labor, January 30, 1998.

p. 120 'At the time, damning reports were coming . . .': Abraham Wu, David P. Baron, "Levi Strauss & Co. in China," case study S-P-13, Graduate School of Business, Stanford University, July 1994.

Timothy Perkins, et al., "Levi Strauss & Co. and China," School of Economics and Business Administration, St. Mary's College of California (Case 5: Council for Ethics in Economics, Columbus, Ohio) November 1995.

p. 122 'Put to the test of Levi's stringent code . . .': Kennis Chu, "Levi's Delivers Blow to MFN Hopes," *South China Morning Post,* May 2, 1993.

p. 123 'In a speech some years later Haas . . .': , Robert Haas, "Risks, Innovation and Responsibility: a Business Model for the New Millennium," speech to Business for Social Responsibility conference, Los Angeles, November 6, 1997.

Thomas C. Hayes, "Hard Decisions Ahead for the New Chief of Levi Strauss," *New York Times,* April 15, 1984.

p. 124 'Officials in Beijing were quick to dismiss . . .': Geoffrey Crothall, "Beijing Plays Down Levi's Pull-out," *South China Morning Post,* May 7, 1993.

Kent Chu, "Levi Says Pull-out Not Due to Rights," *South China Morning Post,* October 29, 1993.

p. 124 'Close examinations of Levi Strauss's decision . . .': Gavin Power, "Behind Levi's Decision to Leave China," *San Francisco Chronicle,* May 17, 1994.

Joanna Ramey, et al., "Levi's Turning Its Back on China May End Up as MFN Ammunition." Women's Wear Daily, May 5, 1993.

Wu, op. cit.

Perkins, op. cit.

p. 125 'Company president Peter Jacobi . . .': Mark Landler, "Reversing Course, Levi Strauss Will Expand Its Output in China," *New York Times,* April 8, 1998.

Levi Strauss & Co., "Talking Points On Conducting Business In China," press release, April 8, 1998 (Corporate Web site: www.levistrauss.com).

p. 126 'What was left unmentioned by Jacobi . . .': *See Appendix A.*

p. 127 'The scrappy San Francisco-based advocacy . . .': Greg Frost, "Human Rights Groups Assail Levi Strauss Over China," *Reuters,* April 10, 1998.

Harry Wu, telephone interview, Milpitas, California, April 1998.

William F. Schulz, "China, Human Rights and the Wait for a Duck: Levi Strauss Can Set Example in China," (Letter to LS&Co.'s board of directors), *The Nation,* July 6, 1998.

p. 129 'Even the goodwill of some of its . . .': Helen C. Bulwick, telephone interview, Oakland, December 1998.

p. 130 'On the one hand, it has let it be known . . .': Gare Smith, telephone interview, San Francisco, May 1999.

CHAPTER FIVE

p. 134 'Then the whole system – and the fabric . . .': Faiz H. Shah, "Child Labor In Sialkot," World Federation of Sporting Goods Industry's *Sport Shop/News Bulletin,* August 1997.

Robert A. Senser, "Danger! Children at Work: Child Labor a Global Problem," *Commonweal,* August 19, 1994.

p. 135 'Reebok's kosher soccer ball . . .': Reebok International Ltd., "Reebok International to Label Soccer Balls with 'Made Without Child Labor' Guarantee," press release, November 19, 1996.

p. 136 'It appears that some very sincere people . . .': Sialkot Chamber of Industry, et al., "Project to Eliminate Child Labour from the Soccer Ball Industry (Atlanta Partnership): Status After One Year," Sialkot, Pakistan, February 1998.

Robert A. Senser, ed., "Flaws in a Program that the ILO Deems a Success," Human Rights for Workers (Web site: www.senser.com), August 8, 1999.

Sporting Goods Manufacturers Association, "Industry Partnership with Human Rights Groups Successfully Ending Child Labor in Pakistan's Soccer Ball Industry," press release, February 6, 1998 (Web site: www.no1child.com).

p. 138 'Doug Cahn, a senior Reebok executive . . .': Doug Cahn, personal interview, Boston, November 1998; telephone interview, March 1999.

p. 139 'The Levi's code strictly prohibits . . .': Clarence Grebey, telephone interview, San Francisco, May 1999.

p. 141 'Charles David's marketing director . . .': Rachael Taylor, telephone interview, Culver City, California, April 1999.

p. 145 'So did the cowboy, that mythical incarnation . . .': S. Omar Barker, *Levi's,* (poem), 50-Copy Limited Edition Bound in Levi's denim, (San Francisco: Western Writers of America, 1977).

p. 146 'The company incorporates into its legend . . .': Lynn Downey, et al., *This Is a Pair of Levi's Jeans: the Official History of the Levi's Brand,* (San Francisco: Levi Strauss & Co., 1995).

"Levi Strauss & Co. Named Bernays Award Winner," *Inside PR,*
Editorial Media & Marketing International (Web site: www.prcentral.
com).

p. 148 'Martin Scorsese's *Kundun,* released in 1998 . . .': John Leicester,
"China Protests Walt Disney's Dalai Lama Film," *Associated Press,*
November 26, 1996.

"Disney Supports Dalai Lama Film Despite Beijing's Disapproval,"
Associated Press, November 27, 1996.

Bernardo Bertolucci, et al., Letter to Chinese Ambassador Li Daoyu
(protesting allegations of artistic censorship in China), December 10,
1996, distributed by Human Rights Watch.

Hong Kong Christian Industrial Committee. "Working Conditions
in Chinese Factories Making Disney Products," report, Hong Kong,
February 1999.

p. 151 'A fan identifying herself only as Kathy . . .': Touched by an Angel,
Episode 426, "The Spirit of Liberty Moon," *CBS,* May 17, 1998. (Web
site: ww.touched.com).

CHAPTER SIX

p. 157 'There's a kind of pathos here . . .': Nathan, op. cit.

p. 158 'Walter Abraham Haas Jr., Levi's . . .': Steve Rubenstein, "Blue and Gold
Farewell to Walter Haas," *San Francisco Chronicle,* September 25, 1995.

p. 159 'Levi Strauss, lamentably, made some serious . . .': Nina Monk, "How
Levi's Trashed a Great American Brand: While Bob Haas Pioneered
Benevolent Management, His Company Came Apart At The Seams,"
Fortune, April 12, 1999.

p. 160 'Certainly the company's tradition of ethical . . .': Grebey interview.

p. 162 'As soon as sales showed signs of seriously hemorrhaging . . .': (Financial data in this chapter derives from previously cited news reports,
SEC documents, Levi Strauss & Co. press releases, and company responses to written questions.)

p. 162 'The drastic downsizing followed a failed . . .': Ralph T. King Jr., "Jeans
Therapy: Levi's Factory Workers Are Assigned to Teams, And Morale
Takes a Hit," *Wall Street Journal,* May 20, 1998.

p. 163 'Levi's biggest retail account, J.C. Penney . . .': Monk, op. cit.

Mark Lacter, "Levi's Buyout – It's Official," *San Francisco Chronicle,*
July 16, 1985.

p. 164 'The deal had a peculiar string attached . . .': Confidential interviews
with multiple anonymous sources.

Levi Strauss Associates Inc., SEC filing 10-Q 1996.

Paul B. Carroll, "Levi Will Spend $1.5 Billion to Buy Out Some
Holders, Keep Company Private," *Wall Street Journal,* February 12, 1996.

Peter Sinton, "Levi's Bold Plan For Reorganization," *San Francisco Chronicle,* February 13, 1996.

Obituary, "Rhoda H. Goldman, Civic Benefactor, 71," *New York Times,* February 20, 1996.

p. 166 'The glossy business magazine was unforgiving . . .': Monk, op. cit.

Stratford Sherman, "Levi's: As Ye Sew, so Shall Ye Reap," *Fortune,* May 12, 1997.

p. 167 'Consider the number of news releases posted . . .': (See: Levi Strauss & Co. corporate Web site: www.levistrauss.com).

p. 168 'In a surprising development in September . . .': Leslie Kaufman, "In Effort to Revitalize, Levi Strauss Hires Outsider as Top Executive," *New York Times,* September 8, 1999.

Carol Emert, "Levi Strauss Hires New CEO From Outside Its Gene Pool: Haas picks successor to head S.F. clothing giant," *San Francisco Chronicle,* September 8, 1999.

Bob Haas, "To: All LS&Co. Employees, Subject: Our New President and CEO," internal memorandum, Levi Strauss & Co., undated.

p. 169 'Chew offered a glimpse . . .': Dan Chew, "Transcript: Interview with Philip Marineau," internal document, Levi Strauss & Co., undated.

p. 170 'Before following in the footsteps of his father . . .': Cray, op. cit., pp. 243–5.

Robert Howard, "Values Make the Company: An Interview with Robert Haas," *Harvard Business Review,* Sept-Oct. 1990.

Robert Haas Profile, Levi Strauss & Co. corporate Web site.

p. 172 'There was no one to receive the mantle now . . .': Grebey interview. Confidential interview with former Levi Strauss & Co. executive, May 1999.

p. 173 'The lack of solid information didn't deter . . .': Carol Emert, telephone interview, February 1999.

"The View From the Outside: Levi's Needs More Than a Patch," *New York Times,* February 28, 1999.

p. 174 'In a stinging rebuke, the credit-rating agency . . .': Steve Ginsberg, "Coming Apart at the Seams; Ripped Levi's: Blunders, Bad Luck Take Toll," *San Francisco Business Times,* December 14, 1998.

p. 174 'The company had a rough start in the on-line . . .': Carol Emert, "Levi Strauss Will Halt Sales On Its Web Sites," San Francisco Chronicle, October 29, 1999.

p. 175 'Levi Strauss extended the direct-marketing . . .': Carol Emert, "When a Store is More Than a Store," *San Francisco Chronicle.* August 14, 1999.

Levi Strauss & Co., "Levi's Brand Delivers Global Product Line-Up and Multi-Sensory Shopping Experience At First San Francisco Store," press release, August 16, 1999.

p. 176 'It is a contemporary twist on the naughty . . .': Bulwick interview.

p. 177 'Sales of Levi's traditional clothing . . .': Levi Strauss Associates Inc., Annual Report, op. cit.

Carol Emert, "Levi's to Slash U.S. Plants: Competitors' Foreign-Made Jeans Blamed," *San Francisco Chronicle,* February 23, 1999.

p. 179 'Under the spell of Levi's 1987 "aspiration . . .': Carol Emert, "Levi's President, COO Peter Jacobi Resigns; He Says the Company Needs Fresh Ideas," San Francisco Chronicle, January 12, 1999.

p. 179 'Yet the pundits had Levi Strauss on the defensive . . .': Hal Espen, "Levi's Blues: Today's Teen-agers Are Spurning Their Parents' Jeans," *New York Times* Magazine, March 21, 1999.

Sherman, op. cit.

Howard, op. cit.

p. 181 'By the middle of 1999 indications were . . .': Grebey interview.

Levi Strauss & Co., "Mission, Vision, Aspirations & Values," (Web site: www.levistrauss.com).

p. 182 'It was no coincidence that the policy deliberations . . .': Adams, op. cit.

p. 183 'The relevance of all the high-minded rhetoric . . .': Baron interview.

CHAPTER SEVEN

p. 185 'It was never entirely clear why security agents . . .': Bruce Gilley, "Slippery Slope: Beijing Detains Chinese Manager for Shell," *Far Eastern Economic Review,* March 28, 1996.

P. T. Bangsberg, "Shell Employee Still in Chinese Jail: Authorities Have Been Checking Spying Charges For Six Months, *Journal of Commerce,* July 18, 1996.

Aaron Sheldrick, Chinese Jail Threat To Foreign Businessmen, *Evening Standard* (London), November 11, 1996.

"Chinese Shell Executive Freed From Detention," *United Press International,* March 13, 1997.

p. 186 'For Shell, the case caused some deep trepidation, . . .': Sierra Club, "Boycott Shell Oil, Embargo Nigeria," Fact Sheet, Sierra Club document (Web site: www.sierraclub.org/human-rights/boycott.html).

Shell Petroleum Development Co., "Responsibilities With Regards To Human Rights In Nigeria," cluster documents (Web site: www.shellnigeria.com).

p. 186 'Before all this took place, Shell . . .': David C. Smith, "Multinational Companies and Human Rights in Developing Societies: Interview with Robert Aram," *Ethics in Economics,* (newsletter) 1998 Nos. 1 and 2.

p. 189 'The phenomenon of arbitrary detention . . .': Human Rights Watch/Asia, "China: The Cost of Putting Business First," Vol. 8 No. 7, July 1996.

Robin Munro, personal interview, September 1998.

Lawyer's Committee for Human Rights, "Opening to Reform? An Analysis of China's Revised Criminal Procedure Law," October 1996.

Jonathan Hecht (Harvard law school), telephone interview, May 1998.

p. 190 'If they want to put you in jail, they can do it . . .': Philip Cheng, personal interview, October 1998.

Jessica Carter, "Freed Businessman Vows to Clear Name," *South China Morning Post,* January 9, 1994.

Beverly Chau, "Boss to Sue Over Hunan 'Ordeal,'" *South China Morning Post,* March 25, 1994.

p. 192 'Perhaps the most eloquent advocate of the argument . . .': John Kamm, personal interviews, San Francisco, September 1997 through May 1999.

John Kamm, "Testimony before the Subcommittee on Asia and the Pacific. House Committee on International Relations," April 30, 1998.

John Kamm, "The Role of Business in Promoting Respect for Human Rights," statement delivered to Commission on Security and Cooperation in Europe seminar Implementation of the Helsinki Accords, The OSCE at Twenty: Its Relevance to Other Regions, November 13–14, 1995.

p. 199 'Gare Smith, the State Department human rights official . . .': Smith interview.

p. 200 'Interactive constructive engagement . . .': Abraham Wu, op. cit.

Perkins, op. cit.

p. 205 'The freedom of association dilemma . . .': Jeffrey Ballinger, personal interview, Cambridge, Mass., November 1988.

p. 206 'The company remained essentially in denial . . .': Andrew Young, "Report: The Nike Code of Conduct," Nike Corp., 1997.

p. 207 'Finally, a seemingly born-again Knight . . .': Philip Knight, press statement, National Press Club, Washington, D.C., May 12, 1998.

Maria Eitel and Vada Manager, personal interview, Beaverton, Oregon, Dusty Kidd, telephone interviews, November 1997 through December 1999.

p. 210 'A shoe factory catering to Nike in Dongguan . . .':.Y. Cha and Todd McKean, personal interview, Dongguan, China, January 1999.

Jeff Manning, "Poverty's Legions Flock to Nike: 450,000 Workers Power the Athletic Shoe Maker's Machine, But the Opportunity to Better Themselves Comes At a Cost," *The Oregonian,* November 10, 1997.

p. 211 'Nike's McKean brushes off the allegations . . .': Asia Monitor Resource Center and Hong Kong Christian Industrial Committee, "Working Conditions in Sports Shoe Factories in China Making Shoes for Nike and Reebok," Hong Kong, September 1997.

p. 213 The next battlefront is the electronics . . .': Eli Chan, personal interviews, Hong Kong, October 1998 and January 1999.

'Indeed, the advancement of labor rights was never . . .': Ira Kaye, personal interview, Hong Kong, January 1999.

p. 214 'During the chaos of the massive student protests . . .': Han Dong Fan, personal interviews, Beijing, April 1989, and Hong Kong, January 1999.

p. 216 'Trini Leung, an official at the Hong Kong . . .': Trini Leung, telephone interview, Hong Kong, January 1999.

CHAPTER EIGHT

p. 217 'The Dominican Republic is as good a place . . .': Levi Strauss & Co., Oxfam-Great Britain, et al., "Independent Evaluation of Levi Strauss & Co.'s Code of Conduct Process: A Pilot Study in the Dominican Republic," and "Evaluation of Levi Strauss & Co.'s Terms of Engagement Process," August 1998.

p. 221 'In May 1999 Clarence Grebey, then director . . .': Grebey interview.

Robert Collier, "Levi's Joins War Against Sweatshops," *San Francisco Chronicle,* July 21, 1999.

p. 222 'But there was more at stake for Levi Strauss . . .': Apparel Industry Partnership.

"Fair Labor Association Charter Document: Preliminary Report" Washington D.C.: U.S. Department of Labor, November 2, 1998.

Steven Greenhouse, "Groups Reach Agreement For Curtailing Sweatshops," New York Times, November 5, 1998.

White House press release, "President Clinton Announces Apparel Industry Partnership Agreement," April 14, 1997.

Steven Greenhouse, "Anti-Sweatshop Coalition Finds Itself at Odds on Garment Factory Code," *New York Times,* July 3, 1998.

p. 225 'Jeffery Ballinger, the indefatigable Nike critic . . .': Jeff Ballinger, "Closing Sweatshops," letter to the editor, *New York Times,* November 9, 1998.

p. 227 'Without public pressure on the companies, . . .': Joshua Karliner, telephone interview, San Francisco, May 1999.

p. 228 'The absence of legislative options . . .': Wallance, op. cit.

Gregory J. Wallance, E-mail communication, May 1999.

p. 229 'The Foreign Corrupt Practices Act came into being . . .': Alice Tepper Marlin, telephone interview, New York, May 1999.

p. 230 'George Kell, an economist in the UN secretary . . .': Kell interview.

"The Global Compact," United Nations online document (Web site: www.un.org/partners/business).

p. 232 'Robinson, the human rights high commissioner . . .': Mary Robinson, "Giving a Human Face to the Global Market: the Business Case for Human Rights," speech before the Wintherthur Group Conference, Interlaken, June 10, 1999.

p. 232 'Organized business has been guarded . . .': Maria Livanos Cattaui, "Business Takes Up Kofi Annan's Challenge," *ICC Business World,* online publication, March 15, 1999 (Web site: www.iccwbo.org/ business_world/).

p. 233 'Why can't the WTO get into the act? . . .': United Nations, "Business Leaders Advocate a Stronger United Nations and Take Up Challenge of Secretary-General's Global Compact," UN press release, July 5, 1999 (Web site: www.un.org/partners/business/globcomp.htm).

EPILOGUE

p. 234 'One thing is certain. It's not just the apparel . . .': Miranda Ewell and K. Oanh Ha, "Paid by the Piece" Series, *San Jose Mercury News:* "High Tech's Hidden Labor," June 27, 1999; "Why Piecework Won't Go Away," June 28, 1999.

p. 235 'Said Alice Tepper Marlin of the Council . . .': Tepper Marlin interview.

p. 236 'Global Exchange, the aggressive human rights . . .': Medea Benjamin, telephone interview, San Francisco, May 1999.

Tim Loughran, "U.S. Companies Launch China Workers Rights Effort," *Reuters,* May 26, 1999.

p. 237 'There aren't many candidates out there . . .': Sam Howe Verhovek, "Elder Bill Gates Takes On The Role of Philanthropist," *New York Times,* September 12, 1999.

p. 238 'We are an anomaly, especially in the eyes . . .': Grebey interview.

p. 240 'Smith describes the somewhat cryptic . . .': Smith interview.

REFERENCES

|||

Adams, Justin and David P. Baron. "Levi Strauss & Co. Global Sourcing Guide-lines," case study S-P-12. Graduate School of Business, Stanford University, July 1994.

Alford, William P. "Making a Goddess of Democracy from Loose Sand: Thoughts on Human Rights in the People's Republic of China" in *Human Rights in Cross-Cultural Perspectives: A Quest for Consensus*. Philadelphia: University of Pennsylvania Press, 1992.

Amnesty International USA. *United States of America: Rights for All* (London: AI Publications, 1998).

Annan, Kofi. "Statement to the World Economic Forum in Davos, Switzerland, January 31, 1999." United Nations press release, February 1, 1999.

Apparel Industry Partnership. "Fair Labor Association Charter Document: Preliminary Report" Washington D.C.: U.S. Department of Labor, November 2, 1998.

Ascoli, Nina, ed. "Case File: Levi Strauss & Co." Report presented by Clean Clothes Campaign of the Netherlands to Workers and Consumers Rights in the Garment Industry Conference, Brussels, April 30–May 5, 1998.

Asia Monitor Resource Center and Hong Kong Christian Industrial Committee. "Working Conditions in Sports Shoe Factories in China Making Shoes for Nike and Reebok." Hong Kong, September 1997.

Aung San Suu Kyi. *Freedom from Fear and Other Writings* (London: Penguin Books, 1995).

———. *Letters from Burma* (London: Penguin Books, 1997).

Barker, S. Omar. *Levi's*. Poem: 50-Copy Limited Edition Bound in Levi's denim. (San Francisco: Western Writers of America, 1977).

Baron, David P., et al., "Levi Strauss & Co. Terms of Engagement Audits." Case study S-P-14, Graduate School of Business, Stanford University, July 1994.

———. *Business and its Environment* (Upper Saddle River, New Jersey: Prentice Hall, 1992).

Baum, Richard. *Burying Mao : Chinese Politics in the Age of Deng Xiaoping* (Princeton: Princeton University Press, 1994).

Benjamin, Medea. "A Riveting Announcement," *San Francisco Bay Guardian,* June 10, 1998.

Bertrand, Jacques. "For Independent Monitoring of the Levi Strauss Code of Conduct, Noveca Industries: a Case Study in the Philippines." Montreal: Canadian Catholic Organization for Development and Peace, October 1996.

Business for Social Responsibility. "A Guide to Human Rights and Rule of Law Issues Affecting Business Operations in Burma." San Francisco: Business for Social Responsibility Education Fund's Human Rights Program, January 1997.

Christopher, Warren. *In the Stream of History: Shaping Foreign Policy for a New Era* (Stanford, California: Stanford University Press, 1998).

Committee for the Defense of Human Rights in Honduras and Federation of Independent Workers of Honduras. "Workers in Honduras: An Examination of Working Conditions in Several Plants Producing Goods for Levi Strauss & Co." September-November 1995.

Colvin, Geoffrey. "Levi Strauss's Old-Fashioned Values," *Fortune,* May 5, 1997.

Committee for the Defense of Human Rights in Honduras, et al. "Workers in Honduras: An Examination of Working Conditions in Several Plants Producing Goods for Levi Strauss & Co.," report, Nov. 1995.

Council on Economic Priorities. "International Sourcing Report," March 1, 1998.

Cray, Ed. *Levi's* (Boston: Houghton Mifflin, 1978).

Downey, Lynn, et al. *This Is a Pair of Levi's Jeans: the Official History of the Levi's Brand* (San Francisco: Levi Strauss & Co., 1995).

Emert, Carol. "Levi's to Slash U.S. Plants: Competitors' Foreign-Made Jeans Blamed," *San Francisco Chronicle,* February 23, 1999.

Espen, Hal. "Levi's Blues: Today's Teen-agers Are Spurning Their Parents' Jeans," *New York Times Magazine,* March 21, 1999.

Global Exchange, et al. Letter to Levi Strauss & Co. CEO Robert Haas, June 24, 1998.

Goldhagen, Daniel Jonah. *Hitler's Willing Executioners : Ordinary Germans and the Holocaust* (New York: Alfred E. Knopf, 1996).

Greider, William. *One World, Ready or Not: The Manic Logic of Global Capitalism* (New York: Simon & Schuster, 1997).

Ginsberg, Steve. "Coming Apart at the Seams: Ripped Levi's, Bad Luck Takes Toll," *San Francisco Business Times,* December 14, 1998.

Haas, Robert D. "Risks, Innovation and Responsibility: a Business Model for the New Millennium," speech to Business for Social Responsibility conference, Los Angeles, November 6, 1997.

Hambleton, Ronald. *The Branding of America: From Levi Strauss to Chrysler, From Westinghouse to Gillette, the Forgotten Fathers of America's Best-Known Brand Names* (Dublin, New Hampshire: Yankee Books, 1987).

Hayes, Thomas C. "Hard Decisions Ahead for the New Chief of Levi Strauss," *New York Times,* April 15, 1984.

Heifetz, Ronald A. *Leadership Without Easy Answers* (Cambridge, Massachusetts: Belknap Press, 1994).

Henry, Sondra. *A Biography of Levi Strauss: Everyone Knows His Name* (Minneapolis: Dillon Press, 1990).

Hong Kong Christian Industrial Committee. "Working Conditions in Chinese Factories Making Disney Products," report, Hong Kong, February 1999.

Howard, Robert. Values Make the Company: An Interview with Robert Haas," *Harvard Business Review,* Sept-Oct. 1990.

Human Rights Watch/Asia. "Burma: Entrenchment or Reform?," Vol. 7, No. 10, July 1995.

———. "China: The Cost of Putting Business First," Vol. 8, No. 7, July 1996.

Johnston, David Cay. "At Levi Strauss, A Big Cutback, With Largesse," *New York Times,* Nov. 4, 1997.

Kamm, John. "Testimony before the Subcommittee on Asia and the Pacific. House Committee on International Relations," April 30, 1998.

———. "The Role of Business in Promoting Respect for Human Rights," statement delivered to Commission on Security and Cooperation in Europe seminar Implementation of the Helsinki Accords, The OSCE at Twenty: Its Relevance to Other Regions, November 13–14, 1995.

Katz, Jane Palley and Lynn Sharp Paine. "Levi Strauss & Co.: Global Sourcing (A)." Case study 9–395–127, Harvard Business School, Harvard University, Rev. February 27, 1997.

King, Ralph T. "Jeans Therapy: Levi's Factory Workers Are Assigned to Teams, And Morale Takes a Hit," *Wall Street Journal,* May 20, 1998.

Landler, Mark. "Reversing Course, Levi Strauss Will Expand Its Output in China," *New York Times,* April 8, 1998.

Liebhold, Peter and Harry R. Rubenstein, "Between a Rock and a Hard Place," *Labor's Heritage* (George Meany Memorial Archives), Vol. 9. No. 4, Spring 1998.

Lintner, Bertil. *Outrage: Burma's Struggle for Democracy* (London and Bangkok: White Lotus, 1990).

Levi Strauss Associates Inc. "Annual Report for Fiscal Year Ended November 26, 1995." Form 10-k filing with the U.S. Securities and Exchange Commission.

Levi Strauss & Co. "Global Sourcing & Operating Guidelines: Business Partner Terms of Engagement and Guidelines for Country Selection." Company pamphlet, 1993.

———. "Global Sourcing and Operating Guidelines: Business Partner Terms of Engagement & Country Assessment Guidelines." Company pamphlet, 1996.

————, Oxfam-Great Britain, et al. "Independent Evaluation of Levi Strauss & Co.'s Code of Conduct Process: A Pilot Study in the Dominican Republic," and "Evaluation of Levi Strauss & Co.'s Terms of Engagement Process," August 1998.

Los Angeles Jewish Commission on Sweatshops, report, January 1999.

Mann, James. *About Face: A History of America's Curious Relationship with China from Nixon to Clinton* (New York: Alfred A. Knopf, 1999).

Mao Zedong. *Quotations from Mao Tse-Tung.* (Beijing: Foreign Language Press, 1966).

McCoy, Charles S. *Management of Values: The Ethical Difference in Corporate Policy and Performance* (Boston: Pitman, 1985).

————, et al. "Ethics in the Corporate Policy Process: An Introduction," Center for Ethics and Social Responsibility, Graduate Theological Union, Berkeley, California, 1975.

Miles, James. *The Legacy of Tiananmen: China in Disarray* (Ann Arbor: University of Michigan Press, 1996).

Monk, Nina. "How Levi's Trashed a Great American Brand: While Bob Haas Pioneered Benevolent Management, His Company Came Apart At The Seams," *Fortune,* April 12, 1999.

Nathan, Harriet, et al. *Levi Strauss & Co.: Tailors to the World* (Berkeley: Regional Oral History Office, The Bancroft Library, University of California, 1976).

O'Connor, Rory and Danny Schechter. "Globalization and Human Rights." PBS Documentary. Globalvision Inc., 1998.

Office of Federal Assets Control, U.S. Department of the Treasury. "An Overview of the Burmese Sanctions Regulations." Washington, D.C., May 13, 1998.

Pacific Asia Resource Center. "Nike: Just Don't Do It: Mienai Teikokushugi," PARC Booklet 6, *Gekkan Oruta,* July 10, 1998.

Perkins, Timothy, et al. "Levi Strauss & Co. and China," School of Economics and Business Administration, St. Mary's College of California. Columbus, Ohio: Council for Ethics in Economics, November 1995.

Porges, Jennifer, ed. *At What Price? Workers in China* (Hong Kong: Asia Monitor Resource Center Ltd., 1997).

Rodrik, Dani. *Has Globalization Gone Too Far?* (Washington, D.C.: Institute for International Economics, 1997).

Rosenzweig, Philip M., et al. "International Sourcing in Athletic Footwear: Nike and Reebok" Case study 9–394–189, Harvard Business School, Harvard University, July 14, 1994.

Sandoz, Philip. *Canon: Global Responsibilities and Local Decisions* (London: Penguin Books, 1997).

Schulz, William. "China, Human Rights and the Wait for a Duck: Levi Strauss Can Set an Example in China," *The Nation,* July 6, 1998.

Seekins, Donald M. "One Trip to Myanmar and Everyone Would Love the Country: Japan Incorporated Rolls Out a Big Gun," *Burma Debate,* Vol. V, No. 1, Winter 1998.

Sherman, Stratford. "Levi's: As Ye Sew, so Shall Ye Reap," *Fortune,* May 12, 1997.

Smith, Paul J., ed. *Human Smuggling: Chinese Migrant Trafficking and the Challenge to America's Immigration Tradition* (Washington, D.C.: Center for Strategic & International Studies, 1997).

Spar, Debora L. "The Spotlight and the Bottom Line: How Multinationals Export Human Rights," *Foreign Affairs,* Vol. 77 No. 2, March/April 1998.

Steiner, Henry J. "Securing Human Rights: the First Half-century of the Universal Declaration and Beyond," *Harvard Magazine,* October 1998.

———. *International Human Rights in Context: Law, Politics, Morals* (Oxford: Clarendon Press, 1996).

The United Nations Universal Declaration of Human Rights. Adopted and proclaimed by General Assembly resolution 217 A (III) of December 10, 1948.

Vogel, David. *Lobbying the Corporation: Citizen Challenges to Business Authority* (New York: Basic Books, 1978).

Wallance, Gregory J. "Fallout From Slave-labor Case Is Troubling," *New Jersey Law Journal* (American Lawyer Newspapers Group), December 8, 1997.

Warner, Barbara. "Japan's Growing Nonprofit Sector Responds to Government Shortfalls, *Japan Economic Institute Report,* June 5, 1998.

Wu, Abraham and David P. Baron. "Levi Strauss & Co. in China." Case study S-P-13, Graduate School of Business, Stanford University, July 1994.

Young, Andrew. "Report: The Nike Code of Conduct," Beaverton, Oregon: Nike Corp., 1997.

Zachary, G. Pascal. "Exporting Rights: Levi Tries to Make Sure Plants in Asia Treat Workers Well," *Wall Street Journal,* July 28, 1994.

Zoll, Daniel, "Sweatshop Blues," *San Francisco Bay Guardian,* June 10, 1998.

APPENDIX A

| | |

Levi Strauss & Co. Global Sourcing and Operating Guidelines

Following is the text of Levi Strauss & Co.'s code of conduct, as disseminated by the company in 1999:

GLOBAL SOURCING & OPERATING GUIDELINES

Levi Strauss & Co. seeks to conduct its business in a responsible manner. In 1991, Levi Strauss & Co. was the first multinational company to establish comprehensive Global Sourcing & Operating Guidelines.

BUSINESS PARTNERS

Our Global Sourcing & Operating Guidelines help us to select business partners who follow work place standards and business practices that are consistent with our company's policies. These requirements are applied to every contractor who manufactures or finishes products for Levi Strauss & Co. Trained inspectors closely audit and monitor compliance among approximately 500 cutting, sewing, and finishing contractors in more than 50 countries.

PARTNERSHIPS THAT WORK

For Levi Strauss & Co., implementing our guidelines is a comprehensive and resource-intensive effort. Our goal is to achieve positive results and effect change, not to punish contractors for transgressions. Through our guidelines, we seek long-term solutions that will benefit the individuals who make our products and will improve the quality of life in the communities in which they live.

The Levi Strauss & Co. Sourcing & Operating Guidelines include two parts:

I. The Business Partner Terms of Engagement, which deal with issues that are substantially controllable by Levi Strauss & Co.'s individual business partners.

II. The Country Assessment Guidelines, which address larger, external issues beyond the control of individual business partners (e.g., health and safety issues and political, economic, and social conditions). These help us assess the risk of doing business in a particular country.

These standards are an integral part of our business. Company employees have the authority and the responsibility to take any steps necessary to ensure compliance with all standards and policies. Our employees and our business partners understand that our guidelines are no less important than meeting our quality standards or delivery times.

TERMS OF ENGAGEMENT

1. Ethical Standards
We will seek to identify and utilize business partners who aspire as individuals and in the conduct of all their businesses to a set of ethical standards not incompatible with our own.

2. Legal Requirements
We expect our business partners to be law abiding as individuals and to comply with legal requirements relevant to the conduct of all their businesses.

3. Environmental Requirements
We will only do business with partners who share our commitment to the environment and who conduct their business in a way that is consistent with Levi Strauss & Co.'s Environmental Philosophy and Guiding Principles.

4. Community Involvement
We will favor business partners who share our commitment to contribute to improving community conditions.

5. Employment Standards
We will only do business with partners whose workers are in all cases present voluntarily, not put at risk of physical harm, fairly compensated, allowed the right of free association and not exploited in any way. In addition, the following specific guidelines will be followed:

Wages and Benefits: We will only do business with partners who provide wages and benefits that comply with any applicable law and match the prevailing local manufacturing or finishing industry practices.

Working Hours: While permitting flexibility in scheduling, we will identify prevailing local work hours and seek business partners who do not exceed them except for appropriately compensated overtime. While we favor partners who utilize less than sixty-hour work weeks, we will not use contractors who, on a regular basis, require in excess of a sixty-hour week. Employees should be allowed at least one day off in seven.

Child Labor: Use of child labor is not permissible. Workers can be no less than 14 years of age and not younger than the compulsory age to be in school. We will not utilize partners who use child labor in any of their facilities. We support the development of legitimate workplace apprenticeship programs for the educational benefit of younger people.

Prison Labor/Forced Labor: We will not utilize prison or forced labor in contracting relationships in the manufacture and finishing of our products. We will not utilize or purchase materials from a business partner utilizing prison or forced labor.

Health & Safety: We will only utilize business partners who provide workers with a safe and healthy work environment. Business partners who provide residential facilities for their workers must provide safe and healthy facilities.

Discrimination: While we recognize and respect cultural differences, we believe that workers should be employed on the basis of their ability to do the job, rather than on the basis of personal characteristics or beliefs. We will favor business partners who share this value.

Disciplinary Practices: We will not utilize business partners who use corporal punishment or other forms of mental or physical coercion.

EVALUATION & COMPLIANCE

All new and existing factories involved in the cutting, sewing, or finishing of products for Levi Strauss & Co. must comply with our Terms of Engagement. These facilities are continuously evaluated to ensure compliance. We work on-site with our contractors to develop strong alliances dedicated to responsible business practices and continuous improvement.

If Levi Strauss & Co. determines that a business partner is in violation of our Terms of Engagement, the company may withdraw production from that factory or require that a contractor implement a corrective action plan within a specified time period. If a contractor fails to meet the corrective action plan commitment, Levi Strauss & Co. will terminate the business relationship.

Our Commitment

Levi Strauss & Co. is committed to continuous improvement in the implementation of our Global Sourcing & Operating Guidelines. As these standards are applied throughout the world, we will continue to take into consideration all pertinent information that helps us better address issues of concern, meet new challenges, and improve our guidelines.

| | |

The following text was included in a company publication describing the code in 1996 but was omitted in subsequent editions:

COUNTRY ASSESSMENT GUIDELINES

The diverse social, cultural, political and economic circumstances of the various countries where Levi Strauss & Co. has existing or future business interests raise issues that could subject our corporate reputation and therefore, our business success, to potential harm. The Country Assessment Guidelines are intended to help assess these issues. The Guidelines are tools that assist us in making practical and principled business decisions as we balance the potential risks and opportunities associated with conducting business in a particular country.

In making these decisions, we consider the degree to which our global corporate reputation and commercial success may be exposed to unreasonable risk. Specifically, we assess whether the:

Brand Image would be adversely affected by a country's perception or image among our customers and/or consumers;

Health and Safety of our employees and their families, or our Company representatives would be exposed to unreasonable risk;

Human Rights Environment would prevent us from conducting business activities in a manner that is consistent with the Global Sourcing Guidelines and other Company policies;

Legal System would prevent us from adequately protecting our trademarks, investments or other commercial interests, or from implementing the Global Sourcing Guidelines and other company policies; and

Political, Economic and Social Environment would threaten the Company's reputation and/or commercial interests.

In making these assessments, we take into account the various types of business activities and objectives proposed (e.g., procurement of fabric and sundries, sourcing, licensing, direct investment in subsidiaries) and, thus, the accompanying level of risk involved.

Levi Strauss & Co. is committed to continuous improvement in the implementation of its Global Sourcing & Operations Guidelines. As we apply these standards throughout the world, we will acquire greater experience. As has always been our practice, we will continue to take into consideration all pertinent information that helps us better address issues of concern, meet new challenges and update our Guidelines.

| | |

The following text was published as part of the original Levi Strauss & Co. Global Sourcing Guidelines and was revised in the 1996 version of the code:

GUIDELINES FOR COUNTRY SELECTION

The following country selection criteria address issues which we believe are beyond the ability of the individual business partner to control.

1. Brand Image

We will not initiate or renew contractual relationships in countries where sourcing would have an adverse effect on our global brand image.

2. Health and Safety

We will not initiate or renew contractual relationships in locations where there is evidence that Company employees or representatives would be exposed to unreasonable risk.

3. Human Rights

We should not initiate or renew contractual relationships in countries where there are pervasive violations of basic human rights.

4. Legal Requirements

We will not initiate or renew contractual relationships in countries where the legal environment creates unreasonable risk to our trademark or to other important commercial interests or seriously impedes our ability to implement these guidelines.

5. Political or Social Stability

We will not initiate or renew contractual relationships in countries where political or social turmoil unreasonably threatens our commercial interests.

Appendix B

|||

The United Nations Universal Declaration of Human Rights

Adopted and proclaimed by General Assembly resolution 217 A (III) of December 10, 1948

Preamble

Whereas recognition of the inherent dignity and of the equal and inalienable rights of all members of the human family is the foundation of freedom, justice and peace in the world,

Whereas disregard and contempt for human rights have resulted in barbarous acts which have outraged the conscience of mankind, and the advent of a world in which human beings shall enjoy freedom of speech and belief and freedom from fear and want has been proclaimed as the highest aspiration of the common people,

Whereas it is essential, if man is not to be compelled to have recourse, as a last resort, to rebellion against tyranny and oppression, that human rights should be protected by the rule of law,

Whereas it is essential to promote the development of friendly relations between nations,

Whereas the peoples of the United Nations have in the Charter reaffirmed their faith in fundamental human rights, in the dignity and worth of the human person and in the equal rights of men and women and have determined to promote social progress and better standards of life in larger freedom,

Whereas Member States have pledged themselves to achieve, in cooperation with the United Nations, the promotion of universal respect for and observance of human rights and fundamental freedoms,

Whereas a common understanding of these rights and freedoms is of the greatest importance for the full realization of this pledge,

Now, Therefore the General Assembly proclaims this Universal Declaration of Human Rights as a common standard of achievement for all peoples and all nations, to the end that every individual and every organ of society, keeping this Declaration constantly in mind, shall strive by teaching and education to promote respect for these rights and freedoms and by progressive measures, national and international, to secure their universal and effective recognition and observance, both among the peoples of Member States themselves and among the peoples of territories under their jurisdiction.

ARTICLE 1.

All human beings are born free and equal in dignity and rights. They are endowed with reason and conscience and should act towards one another in a spirit of brotherhood.

ARTICLE 2.

Everyone is entitled to all the rights and freedoms set forth in this Declaration, without distinction of any kind, such as race, colour, sex, language, religion, political or other opinion, national or social origin, property, birth or other status. Furthermore, no distinction shall be made on the basis of the political, jurisdictional or international status of the country or territory to which a person belongs, whether it be independent, trust, non-self-governing or under any other limitation of sovereignty.

ARTICLE 3.

Everyone has the right to life, liberty and security of person.

ARTICLE 4.

No one shall be held in slavery or servitude; slavery and the slave trade shall be prohibited in all their forms.

ARTICLE 5.

No one shall be subjected to torture or to cruel, inhuman or degrading treatment or punishment.

ARTICLE 6.

Everyone has the right to recognition everywhere as a person before the law.

ARTICLE 7.

All are equal before the law and are entitled without any discrimination to equal protection of the law. All are entitled to equal protection against any discrimination in violation of this Declaration and against any incitement to such discrimination.

Article 8.

Everyone has the right to an effective remedy by the competent national tribunals for acts violating the fundamental rights granted him by the constitution or by law.

Article 9.

No one shall be subjected to arbitrary arrest, detention or exile.

Article 10.

Everyone is entitled in full equality to a fair and public hearing by an independent and impartial tribunal, in the determination of his rights and obligations and of any criminal charge against him.

Article 11.

(1) Everyone charged with a penal offence has the right to be presumed innocent until proved guilty according to law in a public trial at which he has had all the guarantees necessary for his defense.

(2) No one shall be held guilty of any penal offence on account of any act or omission which did not constitute a penal offence, under national or international law, at the time when it was committed. Nor shall a heavier penalty be imposed than the one that was applicable at the time the penal offence was committed.

Article 12.

No one shall be subjected to arbitrary interference with his privacy, family, home or correspondence, nor to attacks upon his honour and reputation. Everyone has the right to the protection of the law against such interference or attacks.

Article 13.

(1) Everyone has the right to freedom of movement and residence within the borders of each state.

(2) Everyone has the right to leave any country, including his own, and to return to his country.

ARTICLE 14.

(1) Everyone has the right to seek and to enjoy in other countries asylum from persecution.

(2) This right may not be invoked in the case of prosecutions genuinely arising from non-political crimes or from acts contrary to the purposes and principles of the United Nations.

ARTICLE 15.

(1) Everyone has the right to a nationality.

(2) No one shall be arbitrarily deprived of his nationality nor denied the right to change his nationality.

ARTICLE 16.

(1) Men and women of full age, without any limitation due to race, nationality or religion, have the right to marry and to found a family. They are entitled to equal rights as to marriage, during marriage and at its dissolution.

(2) Marriage shall be entered into only with the free and full consent of the intending spouses.

(3) The family is the natural and fundamental group unit of society and is entitled to protection by society and the State.

ARTICLE 17.

(1) Everyone has the right to own property alone as well as in association with others.

(2) No one shall be arbitrarily deprived of his property.

ARTICLE 18.

Everyone has the right to freedom of thought, conscience and religion; this right includes freedom to change his religion or belief, and freedom, either alone or in community with others and in public or private, to manifest his religion or belief in teaching, practice, worship and observance.

ARTICLE 19.

Everyone has the right to freedom of opinion and expression; this right includes freedom to hold opinions without interference and to seek, receive and impart information and ideas through any media and regardless of frontiers.

ARTICLE 20.

(1) Everyone has the right to freedom of peaceful assembly and association.

(2) No one may be compelled to belong to an association.

ARTICLE 21.

(1) Everyone has the right to take part in the government of his country, directly or through freely chosen representatives.

(2) Everyone has the right of equal access to public service in his country.

(3) The will of the people shall be the basis of the authority of government; this will shall be expressed in periodic and genuine elections which shall be by universal and equal suffrage and shall be held by secret vote or by equivalent free voting procedures.

ARTICLE 22.

Everyone, as a member of society, has the right to social security and is entitled to realization, through national effort and international co-operation and in accordance with the organization and resources of each State, of the economic, social and cultural rights indispensable for his dignity and the free development of his personality.

ARTICLE 23.

(1) Everyone has the right to work, to free choice of employment, to just and favorable conditions of work and to protection against unemployment.

(2) Everyone, without any discrimination, has the right to equal pay for equal work.

(3) Everyone who works has the right to just and favorable remuneration ensuring for himself and his family an existence worthy of human dignity, and supplemented, if necessary, by other means of social protection.

(4) Everyone has the right to form and to join trade unions for the protection of his interests.

ARTICLE 24.

Everyone has the right to rest and leisure, including reasonable limitation of working hours and periodic holidays with pay.

ARTICLE 25.

(1) Everyone has the right to a standard of living adequate for the health and well-being of himself and of his family, including food, clothing, housing

and medical care and necessary social services, and the right to security in the event of unemployment, sickness, disability, widowhood, old age or other lack of livelihood in circumstances beyond his control.

(2) Motherhood and childhood are entitled to special care and assistance. All children, whether born in or out of wedlock, shall enjoy the same social protection.

ARTICLE 26.

(1) Everyone has the right to education. Education shall be free, at least in the elementary and fundamental stages. Elementary education shall be compulsory. Technical and professional education shall be made generally available and higher education shall be equally accessible to all on the basis of merit.

(2) Education shall be directed to the full development of the human personality and to the strengthening of respect for human rights and fundamental freedoms. It shall promote understanding, tolerance and friendship among all nations, racial or religious groups, and shall further the activities of the United Nations for the maintenance of peace.

(3) Parents have a prior right to choose the kind of education that shall be given to their children.

ARTICLE 27.

(1) Everyone has the right freely to participate in the cultural life of the community, to enjoy the arts and to share in scientific advancement and its benefits.

(2) Everyone has the right to the protection of the moral and material interests resulting from any scientific, literary or artistic production of which he is the author.

ARTICLE 28.

Everyone is entitled to a social and international order in which the rights and freedoms set forth in this Declaration can be fully realized.

ARTICLE 29.

(1) Everyone has duties to the community in which alone the free and full development of his personality is possible.

(2) In the exercise of his rights and freedoms, everyone shall be subject only to such limitations as are determined by law solely for the purpose of securing due recognition and respect for the rights and freedoms of others and

of meeting the just requirements of morality, public order and the general welfare in a democratic society.

(3) These rights and freedoms may in no case be exercised contrary to the purposes and principles of the United Nations.

ARTICLE 30.

Nothing in this Declaration may be interpreted as implying for any State, group or person any right to engage in any activity or to perform any act aimed at the destruction of any of the rights and freedoms set forth herein.

INDEX

| | |

ABOUT THE AUTHOR

|||

Karl Schoenberger has written about business and economic development in East Asia throughout his two-decade career in journalism, working as a foreign correspondent for such publications as the *Los Angeles Times,* the *Asian Wall Street Journal,* and *Fortune* magazine. His most recent post was assistant business editor for technology at the *San Jose Mercury News.* A 1995 Nieman Fellow at Harvard University and a graduate of Stanford University in Japanese language and literature, he lives in Albany, California, with his wife, journalist Susan Moffat, and their two young daughters.